YANOWAMO INDIANS
From First Contact to the Present

By
HAP GILLILAND

COUNCIL PUBLICATIONS
1240 Burlington Ave. Billings MT 59102
cie@cie-mt-org   www.cie-mt.org

With appreciation to
Marg Jank
for her hospitality and much information
and to
Sue Clague
and
Rachel Schaffer
for their excellent editorial assistance.

INTRODUCTION

The purpose of this book is to give you, the reader, a clear picture of the lives and culture of the Yanowamo Indians in the South American Rain Forest at the time of their first contact with the outside world, and an idea of the changes brought about by the missionaries, soldiers, and other outsiders in the 44 years since that first contact.

I felt that I could describe the culture most accurately, and most interestingly, not by writing the usual textbook type of anthropological study, but by describing, in detail my own experiences living with the people, becoming a tribal member, and my conclusions resulting from those experiences.

I also feel that you will have a clearer view of the Yanowamo people and the area where they live, if I begin by telling of my experiences and my struggles trying to get into the area at the time the neighboring tribes were first contacted, which led to our first contact with the Yanowamo.

There is one thing that is intentionally inaccurate; the names I have used for individual people. The Yanowamo never tell their names. That is absolutely forbidden. There are also other characters whose names I never learned, or have forgotten. Also, there are times when it is best to change the names because a character may prefer not to be identified. Therefore, many of the names I have used are not the real names of the characters. But that does not change the incidents and activities, which are all described accurately, or as exactly as I can describe them about forty years later!

Most anthropologists write about a culture as if every idea they express is exact, yet two different people may express different ideas about the same things. Also, most have observed the culture and describe it carefully, but have been careful never to adopt any of it for themselves.

However, wherever I go throughout the world, I prefer to live with a family in their home and endeavor to learn the culture by totally living it in every detail. Therefore, people express to me ideas, feelings, and facts they would never reveal to a stranger or to anyone they consider a reporter. I have been adopted, legally or psychologically, into several different families or tribes and feel that I know them better than anyone who remains an outsider.

I decided that instead of just describing the lives and culture of the Yanowamo, you could understand their culture best if I described my experiences living with them, and let you interpret those in your own way.

This book may appear to some of you to be a report on missionary activity and the work of the missionaries. But I have promised to tell you of the changes in the lives of the people, which requires describing the activities of the people who caused those changes.

If I were telling of the lives of the Cheyenne, the Sioux, or the Apache at the time of their first contact, and the changes that came about, I would have to talk much about the army and the changes it forced upon them. But until very recently, the armed forces had absolutely no influence on the Yanowamo. It was the missionaries who made the first contacts, who learned the cultures well, and who brought about the changes, so to give an accurate history of these people, it is necessary to tell much about the influence of the New Tribes Missions.

I had many wonderful experiences with the Yanowamo, and I hope I can help you to understand and enjoy them with me.

So-o-o, come along with me, and away we'll go!

CONTENTS

FORCED CHANGES 2005

___NIYIYOBATERI NOW   2010-2011

DESIRE
1960 & 1963

1.
AN UNKNOWN TRIBE?

"Erma, look! Look at this!" I waved the Gazette in the air. "They've discovered a new Indian tribe in Venezuela. One that's never even been heard of before!"

My wife turned and stared at me. "So what's so exciting about that? You act like you just won a million dollars!"

"Well, it hit me the same way! You know I've always wished I could have been here in Montana two hundred years ago and lived with the Cheyenne and other tribes, and learned about their cultures before there was any influence from the outside."

"Yes, you make comments like that every time you're feeling restless! Or visit with your Cheyenne friends. But you can't turn back the clock. And I've traveled with you enough to be very aware that every group of people you visit, you try to live just like them, like theirs was the most wonderful place in the world. You did it in New Guinea and Mongolia and the Philippines. But this is 1960, and you just accepted a new position at the university. You can't just go traipsing off to South America, trying to turn back the time!"

"Sure, I know. But as the song says, 'You can't stop me from dreaming!' There's a big unexplored area in the Parima Mountains on the border of Venezuela and Brazil. Nobody even knows where the border is because that area has never been explored!"

"So I suppose you want to be the one who explores it!"

"No, I just wish I could be there before someone does."

I kept that news article in my desk, and I did do a lot of day-dreaming and watching the news. Oh, how I wished I could have been with them when two men went upriver from Puerto Ayacucho, the last town on the Orinoco River.

Others had already made contact with the Indians who lived along the rivers, as far as two hundred miles above that last town, but those who had gone farthest had seen no signs of human habitation. So they had assumed the area was uninhabited. That's until two men had gone there looking for wildlife, and had seen a small dugout canoe hidden in the brush along the river. When they started exploring inland, they found two small villages.

They said these Indians, who they called Guaica, were obviously very fierce and unfriendly. They considered themselves very fortunate to have gotten out alive.

But someone would be going there and making friends. Why couldn't it be me? It was three years before I could get my first leave of absence from the university, but all that time I kept my eyes open for any news of that tribe. Only twice in those three years did I hear anything at all, but both of these news items made me more excited about my possibilities.

First, I learned that the Venezuelan government's Indian Commission had stated that they were not going to make any contact with these very warlike people, and no one else should even consider it. That encouraged me. Maybe it would delay anyone else's plans of going there ahead of me.

But I heard later that missionaries from New Tribes Missions had actually made contact with two tribes in that area, the Guaica and the Mikeretari. If missionaries made the contacts, they would try their best to make those contacts friendly contacts. If other, uncontacted villages, heard of these outsiders, what they heard should be good.

My determination to get there did not weaken. It only increased.

As the time for my furlough approached, Erma expressed her doubts about my being able to actually get into Guaica territory. I agreed that it might not be possible, but there were other little-known tribes nearer to Puerto Ayacucho, and even if I only got that far, I could have a very interesting experience, and I could still learn a great deal about their way of life.

The airlines could not sell me a ticket to Puerto Ayacucho as no commercial flights went there. But they said there was a mail plane that flew most days, and it sometimes accepted passengers. So I bought my ticket to Caracas, the capitol.

Knowing that there might be shots I should have, and that I needed to be sure I was in top shape physically, I made an appointment for Dr. Andrews to give me a physical exam before I left.

When I told Dr. Andrews where I was going he asked, excitedly, "Do you know Ken Finney?"

"No. Who is he?"

"He was a missionary down there and made the first contacts with one of the tribes. He just resigned from New Tribes Missions and moved to Billings. You have to talk to him!"

Dr. Andrews turned right around and picked up the phone and called Ken. He told Ken of my plans, then handed me the phone. Ken invited me to come right out to his house.

"You'll love it there," Ken told me. There are now missionaries with two Guaica villages, but they have no regular contact with the outside, and there is no transportation for anyone to get to those villages. But if you don't make it upriver, there are other tribes you can visit!

"There is a family in Puerto Ayacucho that's responsible for trying to get supplies up river to those two missions. They may be able to help you. If not, you can try my system. I found out that all I had to do was sit on the river bank. Anyone, Indian or nonIndian, going by in their dugout canoe was nearly always glad to pick me up and take me as far as they were going. Just be sure you carry a hammock. That's what everyone sleeps in. You can't sleep on the ground like we do in Montana, The ground is crawling with insects, and you don't want to get eaten up. You can buy the kind of hammock you need in Puerto Ayacucho."

"I'll buy one," I said, "Tomorrow."

Ken laughed and said, "Next week maybe, if you're lucky!"

VENEZUELA

COLUMBIA

GUYANA

Caribbean Sea

Amazon River

PERU

B R A Z I L

BOLIVIA

Pacific Ocean

C H I L E

PARAGUAY

A R G E N T I N A

Atlantic Ocean

= YANOWAMO AREA

2
ON MY WAY

My first view of South America was the Caracas Airport. The airstrip ran along the beach, but there was no city in sight, only high, rugged mountains and a line of buildings along the airstrip. As we flew over it, the flight attendant told us the city was about twenty miles up in those mountains, where it was higher and cooler, but there was no level space for an airport near the city.

When we landed, it was not hard to find the small airline that flew the mail to Puerto Ayacucho. When I bought my ticket for the plane leaving at nine the next morning, I asked, "Is there a place I can stay near here?"

"No, you'll have to go all the way to Caracas. It'll cost you sixteen dollars each way for a taxi." I looked at the nice, long leather benches in the lobby. I tied my backpack to my wrist so no one could walk off with it while I was asleep, and laid down on one of those benches.

At six in the morning, a guard woke me and four others who were also sleeping on the benches. I went over to the airline desk and asked, "Can I check my bag now? I'm on that nine o'clock flight to

Puerto Ayacucho."

The clerk told me, "Well, it's a good thing you're here now! The plane's leaving in thirty minutes. They're taking a different plane today, one they don't want to try to land in the dark, so they want to get there and back before dark."

But what about the others that were going on the plane, and don't know it's going early?"

The clerk just shrugged his shoulders as if it didn't matter, and said, "There's always tomorrow."

The small plane circled twice to gain enough altitude to go over the mountains, then headed south. A couple of hours later, we were over the Orinoco river. The Orinoco flows west out of the Parima Mountains, then turns north for a couple hundred miles before it turns east to the Atlantic. We reached it at about the point where it turns east, and we followed it south for a couple more hours.

The always changing landscape and variety of vegetation made the whole trip fascinating.

The pilot pointed ahead. "Do you see all those houses? That's Puerto Ayacucho. And you see these rapids in the river below us? That's called the 'Rapids of Death.' That's why this is the last town on the river. There are sixty miles of those rapids. They may not look big from up here, but that river you are looking down at is a mile wide, so those rapids and falls you see are big enough to keep any boat from going through. That's why not many people can live above here."

After we landed it was not hard for me to get a ride to town. I put my pack on my back and took off down the street. I found a small motel-like place with several small ancient-looking one room houses around it.

I left my pack in my room and set out, determined to get some information. Ken Finny had said there was someone who sent supplies upriver to the missionaries. I found a young boy who spoke a little English. He said he knew a family who spoke English, and he

willingly led me to their home.

Sure enough, this was the family responsible for communication with the missionaries. "Oh yes," Mrs. Baxter said. "We have a boat that goes upriver and takes their mail, along with some food and other supplies, to the missionaries. It goes once every three months. It left last week."

"And that's their only communication with the outside? Once every three months?"

"Why not? Unless someone gets sick, that's all they need."

"Is there anyone else who goes up the river at all?"

"There's a little dirt road goes up about forty miles, to the top of the Rapids of Death. A few fishermen go up there. That's all."

I remembered what Ken Finny had told me, "Sit on the bank. Someone will come by in their canoe."

The Baxters thought I might be able to get a ride up that road, but they weren't encouraging about my getting any farther.

But just getting this far was exciting. After an interesting visit with them, during which they showed me one of the hammocks in their bed room so I'd know what to get, I strolled around town, and thought about all they had told me. I bought myself a light hammock and collected a whole bunch of nuts and other snack food, enough to last me three or four days.

The next morning, I hesitantly checked out of my room and put on my backpack. I decided to stop by the Mission Supply Office again and let the Baxters know I was headed out.

Bill saw me coming and came out the door to meet me. "I'm sure glad you came back, 'cause there's a man here who can give you a lot of information and good advice!" He took me in and introduced me to Commissioner Ramoncito Lujan, who was the head of the Indian Commission for Venezuela.

In spite of his very jumbled English, we had a very enjoyable visit. He told me he had just flown in from Caracas. He had come down to Puerto Ayacucho to check on how things were going for the local Indians.

I asked if he was going on up to the Guaica area and was disappointed when he said emphatically, "Oh no! Our Indian Commission has made no contact with the Guaicas, and we have no intention of ever doing so!"

It was only after an hour of getting better acquainted, visiting, and developing a good feeling of friendship that he started really giving me detailed information about the Piaroa and other local Indian tribes. Then he said, "We do have some contact with the Mikeretari Indians who live a little over two hundred miles up the river. They were discovered only a year or so earlier than the Guaicas, but they are friendly people, and we value our contacts with them. I've been wanting to get back up river to see how things are going with them, but I don't want to make that kind of trip alone, and none of our employees are willing to go that far into the wilderness."

He paused, and looked at me a minute. "And you really want to get upriver! I'll tell you what; If you want to visit the Mikeretari instead of the Guaicas, I'll take you there!"

Boy! Did I jump at that! An hour later, we were headed up the little two track road that followed the shore of the river.

Just above the top of the rapids, the Indian Commission had a couple of small buildings and a whole lot of 50 gallon oil drums full of gasoline. There was an Indian man there who Ramoncito said knew the river. "You don't travel this river without someone who knows it thoroughly, not if you want to come out alive!"

The three of us dragged Ramoncito's canoe out of the shed and down to the river. It was an Indian dugout canoe about fifteen feet long. They had cut a hole in the floor at the back end and put a partition just in front of that, then attached a boat motor to that partition, with the propeller sticking down through the hole in the bottom.

We put two of the big drums of gasoline in the middle of the canoe, then two small ones in front of that, along with our three hammocks and our backpacks.

When they set the motor at full speed, that narrow canoe really moved. The river was a mile wide, and they would follow one shore line for a while, then cross over and follow the other. We were crossing the river for about the fifth time when I looked out to the side and saw a huge whirlpool, more than 50 feet across. I started to ask Ramoncito why they got so near the whirlpool, but then I saw the one on the other side, just as big and spinning in the opposite direction. Then I understood why we needed a guide who knew the river.

A little after noon, we pulled over to the right hand bank and they both jumped out and Ramoncito handed me some nuts he had brought along as a lunch. Then he said, "Now you can honestly say you've been in Columbia. For about a hundred miles here, the Orinoco is the division between Venezuela and Columbia.

We continued on south, up the the river for about an hour before it curved a little more to the east and Ramoncito looked to the west, gave a wave and said, "Goodbye Columbia."

The sun had set and it was nearly dark when we saw the dim light from a kerosene lamp shining out the window of a house, and Ramoncito said, "This is Tamatama."

As we pulled up to the shore, Paul and Dorothy Dye came out of their door and Ramoncito introduced them as missionaries from New Tribes Mission. They welcomed us to their house and invited us to hang our hammocks in their spare room.

Another missionary, Jim Boe, soon came over from his house and joined us. While we filled up on fish and papaya, he explained, "This is a small Mikeretari Indian Village, but it is also a school for missionaries' children. There are missionaries from New Tribes Missions working with several different Venezuelan Indian tribes. We have established this school because some of those missionaries don't feel they can do a good job of teaching their children and still do their mission work, so they send their children here, to our boarding school. Paul and Dorothy are two of the teachers."

I told them about my wanting to live with the Guaica people, and learn their way of life. "But Paul said this was probably as far as I'd get."

"Yes," Dorothy said, "There are only two locations where missionaries are working with the Guaicas. As far as we know, the Guaica people only have two villages on the river. We've been told that they generally prefer locations near small streams that give them a dependable water supply, but quite far from the Orinoco or other rivers that often rise during the rainy season and flood the surrounding forests, so their gardens would be flooded. But there are two villages that are on the rivers. Those Guaicas have learned from the Mikeretari how to make canoes, and live on the rivers. The Dawsons and the Janks have had a mission station at the one on the Padamo river, a branch of the Orinoco, for about two years. And there's another couple at Mavacateri, farther up the Orinoco but there's no way of getting to either of them. You're better off here, with the Mikeretari, anyway. The Mikeretari are friendly people. They have accepted the missionaries from our first arrival, so you'd get acquainted quickly. They are well known for their skill in building dugout canoes, and their ability to manipulate them through the most perilous of rapids is almost inconceivable. But even with a mikeretari, going to either of those Guaica villages could be very dangerous."

I told them, "The Mikeretari sound like great people, and I'd love to spend some time with them, but if you've been here three years, and they willingly accepted you from the beginning, I'd guess they have already adopted a lot of ideas from the outside world. I've lived with the Cheyenne and other Montana tribes and heard from them about their old way of life, but I've always wished I could have lived it. I wanted to experience living the life of a tribe that is still living their original way."

"You mean you would do things their way?"

"Of course! Wherever I travel, I always try to arrange to stay with a family and try to learn their culture by eating their foods and doing everything their way. Most Americans think their culture is the best, and they try to convince other people of that, but how can they know, if they've never really lived the way of others, and tried to understand their feelings, and their likes and dislikes? Too many anthropologists look at a culture, observe their ways, but never become good friends with them or live as one of them, so they may never really understand them."

"But anthropologists tell me that in their training they are told that they should not adopt the ways of the people, only study them."

"I suppose so, but I want to switch over completely while I'm there. And because I feel that way people accept me as one of them. And because I feel that way people accept me as one of them. Because I would live their way, I think I'd be safer with most tribes than most others would be."

"And you really do still want to get up to the Guaicas do you?"

"If I can."

"Well, there might be a way. There's a Mikeretari man who lives about seventy miles upriver from here. He has a motor for his boat. He's a friendly guy, likes to help people. If you could get up there, he'd probably take you anywhere you wanted to go."

Ramoncito spoke up. "Give me a day here with the Mikeretaris, and I'll take you up there, just as long as it's still in Mikeretari territory. There's no way I'm going into Guaica territory!"

Two days later, Ramoncito and I were on our way up river again. Just as the sun was hitting the treetops, we saw two thatched roof huts.

We pulled in to the shore and a woman, wearing only a skirt, stepped out of a hut.

I was surprised that the man who came out and joined us wore our type of shirt and pants, along with a big smile. He greeted is in his own language.

Ramoncito didn't understand it but answered in Spanish, and he

understood a little of it.

We soon got down to business, but it wasn't easy. There was a canoe with a motor there, and I thought he said that canoe was his brother's, but his brother was gone for the day. He was using another canoe with paddles because he had no way of getting gasoline for his canoe with the motor. This man was quite sure his brother would take me anywhere I wanted to go if I had gasoline.

Ramoncito got one of the small drums of gas out of his boat and put it by the canoe that had a motor. Then he explained about my wanting to go to the Guaica village farther up the Orinoco.

The Mikeretari seemed sure his brother would know the village that had a missionary, and would take me there.

When Ramoncito tossed my pack and hammock out of the boat and was ready to start the motor, I suddenly got concerned. "But what if he won't take me? What do I do?"

When Ramoncito translated, the native assured me that if his brother didn't take me upriver, he would loan me his canoe. I could easily paddle it down-river to Tamatama.

Ramoncito was soon out of sight down the river, I hung my hammock between two trees and enjoyed the view of the river and some birds, till I started thinking. The Mikeretari had said his brother would be back that evening. I thought he had said that. Everything had to get translated. The Mikeretari had tried to use the little Spanish he knew to speak and to understand what Ramoncito said. Then Ramoncito tried to understand his broken Spanish and then tell it to me in the little English he knew. Not one of us had ever been sure what anyone else was saying.

The stars came out, but there was no moon, and no brother. This man had said if I needed it, he would loan me a canoe. Why would he actually do that for a stranger? If I took it seventy miles down-river how would he ever get it back? And if he would actually loan it to me, could I handle a dugout canoe, alone, in that kind of rushing river? Could I find my way? I lay there far into the night, worrying. Why hadn't the man come back? What had I gotten myself into?

I could be stranded here forever.

3
ON TO MAVACATERI

Sometime after midnight, I heard drumbeats and chanting. Down the river came a canoe with two men in it. One paddled the canoe while the other beat the drum, and they both chanted. The sound stopped, and I assumed they must have pulled in to the shore not far below me.

There was enough starlight for me to see the man who came to see me a few minutes later. Through motions he told me we would be going up the river. For the rest of the night, I slept.

It was also through his actions that the man let me know that the boy who got in the front of the canoe the next morning was going along to watch for floating logs that could wreck the canoe. We were on our way!

When a cold rain started, although the man had no jacket, he gave me his small piece of canvas to cover my head and shoulders.

The rain quit, but the forest was so dense clear down to the edge of the water that we couldn't have landed anywhere for hours.

Jim Boe had said he thought Mavacateri, the village with the missionary, was three or four hours' journey above the Mikeretaris' home. Could this man running the canoe have gotten the idea that I knew where I was going, and would tell him when we were there? There was no way I could ask.

More hours passed. When darkness arrived, we stayed out in the middle of the river. The dense forest was like two black walls on each side, but the streak of deep blue sky filled with stars told us where to go.

Then, by the starlight, we saw a brown bank with a clearing in the forest above. As soon as the canoe hit the bank, the boy jumped out and went running up the bank.

A minute later the missionary, Charlie Caldwell, was leading us up to a house. His wife, Carol, swung open the door, welcoming us into a room lighted by a kerosene lamp.

The next morning, after my Mikeretari guide and his son left, Charlie and Carol took me to see the village and meet the people. But before we went, Carol warned me, "Don't ever let them hear you call them Guaicas. They'll get angry, and they won't like you!"

"But I thought that was their tribal name."

"Yes, that's what all the outsiders think. The two explorers who discovered the tribe learned that these people will never answer any question you ask about them. But they are glad to tell you anything about their neighboring villages, who are all considered enemies.

"So they asked, 'Who are the people in that next village?' And they answered, 'They are the Guaicas.' When they got to the next village they asked, 'Who are those people who we just left?' 'Oh, they are the Guaicas.' So the explorers assumed that was the tribal name. They never learned that it actually means 'Our inferior neighbors.' The real name of the tribe is Yanomami."

The village was what some people describe as a "roundhouse," a circle of lean-to roofs, all facing the center, so I could stand in the middle and see everyone in their homes. Because Carol and Charlie took me there, the people immediately accepted me as a friend, so much so that the second morning I was there, five men came to the Caldwell's house, bringing their bows and arrows, and an extra set for me. They motioned for me to come with them.

Carol said, "They want you to go hunting with them, but do you think that's wise, with you not knowing any of their language?"

"Sure. You don't have to talk to hunt, and I do know how to use a bow and arrow. I got my deer with one last fall, although I used a three-foot-long Plains Indian type bow, not one of these seven-foot-long ones."

We had a great day, although I didn't have a chance to shoot, and all the game they brought back was one bird and a big snake.

4.
ANOTHER POSSIBILITY

I had a wonderful time with the Yanomami people, but I really wished I could have been with Carol and Charlie when they came there. two years earlier. Although none of the Indians had actually been converted to Christianity they they appeared to be copying the way of life of those missionaries.

The mission supply boat was supposed to come up the river once every three months and I was sure they would give me a ride down river. When I had been there almost a month I asked the Caldwells on what date that boat would be there they burst out laughing. "Well, it should be just about two months from now but it could be as much as a month earlier or a month later."

I had told my wife that I would try to be back in a little over a month. If I was gone four months she would be terrified, and if I was not at the University to teach when the fall semester started, I was really in trouble. I wondered if there was any way I could get an Indian to take me down river. The Caldwells laughed at that too.

Two couples, the Dawsons and the Janks, were missionaries to the one other Yanomami village that had been contacted. That village was on the Padamo river, a branch of the Orinoco. They had been far up the Padamo river, but never up the Orinoco above the junction of the two rivers. They had planned to some day go up the Orinoco and visit the Caldwells and see their village. When Jim Boe, the missionary working with the Mikeretari Indians told them about one of those Indians taking me up the river, and said he knew I had no way to get out and get home, they decided that was reason enough to make the trip.

When I saw their canoe pulling up to the dock, I dashed down to see who it was, and gave all four of them big welcoming hugs.

That evening we were all sitting in the Caldwell's home and I was enthusiastically telling the visitors how much I had learned, but I said I had wished that I could have been there two years earlier,as I had always wanted to live the life of an Indian tribe, as it was before any outside influence. But I probably would never have that opportunity because these people had definitely changed a great deal in the two years the Caldwells had been with them, and I knew of no still uncontacted tribes.

"There may be others," Charlie said. "We're on the west edge of the Parima mountain range which covers the three or four hundred miles east from here, across southern Venezuela, and into Brazil. It's almost completely unexplored, but those who have gone into the edges have all said those mountains are uninhabited."

"Yes, that's what all the geographers say."

"Well, our medicine man was telling us there are two other tribes in there that are related to the Yanomami. He is sure no outsiders have ever seen them. They are the Yanowamo and the Balafili, and they live far back in the Parima Mountains. I'm sure he'd be glad to tell you all about them."

The next morning, we went to see that medicine man. We sat on one of his hammocks and as he talked Charlie translated for me.

"The mountains are very high and very rugged and hard to cross, but somewhere in the center of them is a place called Niyiyobateri. That is where the Yanowamo people, the world's first people, live. It's in a very large savannah, a flat grass covered area between the mountains. In spite of what Carol and Charlie try to tell us about creation, we still believe that savannah is where the first men were created, and all people, everywhere, are descended from those people. Most of us also assume that is where the spirits of the good, generous people go when they die."

"Have any of your people ever gone up there to visit them?"

"We've tried very hard, but it's not possible. At least three times, some of us have gotten part way but were driven out by the fierce residents. Long ago, four friends and I decided we would go east, up over the mountains, to Niyiyobateri. We got to where the mountains were very rugged and very steep, with many high cliffs. We tried to make our way up between those cliffs, but then we were attacked. We were captured and all four of the men with me were killed, but when the men who captured us learned that I was a witch-doctor, and my spirit might be able to call on the evil spirits and do witchcraft against them, they turned me loose."

Wally asked, "Which route do you think would be the easiest, if I wanted to go visit the Yanowamo people? Up the river, or over the mountains?"

"Don't go. Don't even think about it. You'd be killed."

The Dawsons and the Janks took me back with them to their home base, where I had a wonderful week in the the Jank's home before they took me on down the river to Tamatama, where their oldest son and two of the Dawsons' sons were going to the Mission School. It was the end of their school session, and they needed to go there to get their boys anyway, so it was a convenient time to take me there.

When we got to Tamatama, Jim Boe told me they had just finished clearing a narrow airstrip, so a small plane could now land there. A Mission Air Fellowship pilot was coming two days from then to pick up two teachers who wanted to go out to Puerto Ayacucho for their vacation.

When Peter, the pilot, landed the next day, I was there on the airstrip with Jim Boe to meet the plane. After talking with Jim, Peter told me he could take me along with the two teachers to Puerto Ayacucho, but the teachers couldn't leave for two more days, so we would have to hang around that long.

Peter and I spent that evening together, and I told him about the medicine man and what he had told us about the people far up over the mountains. His eyes lit up, and he said, "Paul Dye told me almost the same story about the big savannah a month ago, but everyone at our headquarters says anyone would be a fool to try to get into that

unexplored area."

I said, "Well, I guess I'm a lot like Kit Carson, who did some of the early exploration into Montana. He always said, 'When I look at someone's map and there's a white spot, an area that no one has yet found out what's there, that's where I want to go.' "

"Well, you better look at my map!" Peter led me out to his plane, where he climbed in and pulled out the U.S. Air Force map that he was using to fly with. The top part showed northern Venezuela, with the rivers and towns, and other details. The bottom part was a good map of western Brazil. In between was a big blank space with only two things on it. One was a dotted line, where they thought the mountain divide was that separated Venezuela and Brazil. The other was a note that said "If anyone learns anything about this area, please report it to the U.S. Air Force."

I said, "Someone's got to check that out. Don't you think it ought to be us?"

"You'd really want to take a chance like that?"

"I'm just dying to get there!"

"You might!" he said, and we both laughed, but then he got serious. "They've got plenty of gas here. I'll load up tonight."

The first thing the next morning we were on our way. As we flew east, the first few miles were hills covered with very dense rain forest, but they soon started getting much higher and more rugged. I looked at the dashboard.

Although we were staying about the same distance above the surface, we were rapidly gaining altitude. Those mountains were continually getting higher and steeper, and we flew between them. The sides of some were very high, perpendicular cliffs, but they were flat on top.

Soon there began to be clouds in the sky, and we flew over some of those clouds and under others.

Three places we saw rivers coming off the tops of the mountains. We were sure those waterfalls were more than a thousand feet high

Soon we came to a bank of clouds too high to fly over or under, so we had to fly right through the dense clouds, where we were guided only by the compass. Peter began to look jittery. "If we can't get above this, we'll have to turn back.

"Yes, we -- " I almost screamed when we suddenly came out of the clouds and there, directly in front of us, was a solid wall cliff.

Peter made a quick bank to the left and as the plane tipped up and swerved, the cliffs were much too close to the wheels of the plane.

Soon, the land began to flatten out; then the forests were replaced by grass. The grass-covered area looked to be a couple of miles across,and maybe three times that long.

"This must be the 'Big Savannah' we're looking for!"

"Yes, and that must be Niyiyobateri, the big shavano, the roundhouse, that we heard about." We glided over the top of the shavano. It was definitely larger than either of the ones I had seen before. It was right next to the forest-covered hills on the other side, so I could see that people could go from inside into either the grasslands or the jungle.

As we circled around to go over the big shavano again, I asked Peter if he thought there was a possibility that the land around it was flat enough so that if we wanted to come to that area, he could land the plane on it.

"Not a chance," he said. "We never even consider landing anywhere until someone has checked it out thoroughly on foot. With the tall grass, you can't tell how smooth the ground is. Even where it looks perfectly smooth, there is more than a fifty percent chance that there would be bumps that would wreck a plane. Even down in the flat country at Tamatama, they had to do a lot of smoothing to make that little airstrip we took off from."

I was glad when Peter decided to fly on to see a little more of the area. About five miles from that big shavano, near the other end of the flat area, was another much smaller shavano.

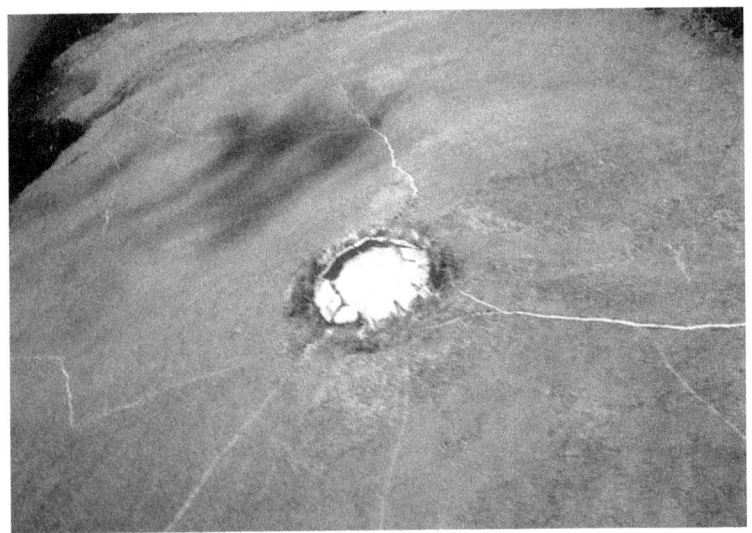

As we flew on east, we saw one village completely surrounded by dense rain forest; then we looked down on one that sat right on the top of a mountain, with steep, grass-covered hillsides dropping away on all sides. "That one's built in a very safe spot," Peter remarked. They could see any raiders long before they got there, and if raiders did try to climb up there and attack, they'd be shooting at them from above. It would be pretty easy to defend themselves."

"Yes," I said. "But if they're like the Yanomami, the women have to go out every day and collect and bring home food and fire wood. How would you like to carry a heavy basket of firewood up that hill every day? How far do you think that village is from the big one on the savannah?"

"I can tell you in a few minutes." He checked his watch, then flew over that village and straight back to the savannah and the big shavano. "It's thirty-five miles by air, but I'd guess it would be fifty if you had to climb up and down, and around the mountains in between."

"I don't plan to do it tomorrow," I said. But I wondered, could I really try to do that some day?

After our plane landed in Tamatama I had one evening with Wally and Marg Jank, the missionaries who worked with the Dawsons, before Peter would be flying me out to Puerto Ayacucho, and I'd be on my way home. I was still so excited about all I had seen that I couldn't resist telling them all the details. I said, "I wish I could climb over those mountains and live with those people. I know it's all wishful thinking. I don't suppose there's any possibility of ever doing that."

Wally gave me a big grin and started to speak, then looked over at Marg. She gave him a smile and a nod, so he went ahead and told me, "Marg and I have done a lot of talking about our plans for the future. The Dawsons were on the Padamo and Orinoco Rivers for a year before we arrived. It's really their mission, and like you, we would have liked to have been there before anyone else. We would still like to go to a tribe where no other 'Nabas' have been. Maybe the Big Savannah is a possibility. Of course I would have to go in first, over those many miles of rugged mountains. But if I could make friends with the people there and find a place to land a plane, I could come back and get a plane to take our family in and start a mission there."

"You are actually thinking of climbing those mountains and going into that territory all by yourself?

"No. Going alone would be foolish. But it would have to be just two people. If there were several in the group, any villages we approached would be sure we were raiders, and we'd be killed. Marg and I were discussing the idea again last night. We were wondering if maybe you would want to be the one who would try to hike in with me. I don't know anyone else who's got the nerve."

"Oh, boy, would I! But wait! No. There's no way I could do it."

"Why not?"

"I've got to start teaching classes at the university again ten days from now. I've got a family to support. There's no way the university will give me another leave of absence till two, or probably three, years from now."

"I wasn't talking about next week. Marg is expecting another baby. I couldn't leave her alone now. And since we are employed by New Tribes Mission, we would have to get their permission. There's lots that needs to be done before we could go. We're talking about at least a couple of years from now. Let's just say three. We have a furlough coming up two years from now, when we go home to Canada to rest up, and visit some of the churches that are sponsoring us. It sounds like our schedules might match perfectly if you could go when we get back here."

"Oh yes! That would be great!" I said. "I just hope no one else, especially no government forces, go in ahead of us."

"It's not likely. If you definitely want to try to do it, let's plan for three years from now. We only get our mail once every three months or so, when the supply boat comes up river, but we'll keep in touch."

"I'll be ready!"

5
FIRST CONTACT

During the next three years I received a note from Wally every three months telling me about their work with at the Dawson's mission, then about their time in Canada, but mainly assuring me that he was still planning to make that climb with me. I kept letting him know that I was still enthused about it and I had not changed my mind.

We kept corresponding and making our plans. But shortly before I was to leave for that exciting but dangerous expedition I received a worrisome message from Wally, saying "All our plans may have to be changed. Cecil Neese and Paul Dye, both of whom have had a lot of time with the Mikeretari Indians, have decided to go in and try to make the first contact with the people of the Big Savannah. But don't let that change your plans. We'll just hope that by the time we get down there, they will be back, and will have made our first contacts for us."

Then came another letter, saying those two explorers were two months overdue, and no one had any news of them.

As I got on my plane to Venezuela I wondered if I should be going! If experienced explorers who knew the area and the other Indian tribes as well as Cecil and Paul did were having trouble, wouldn't it be foolish for us to make the attempt? I wondered, would Wally still consider trying?

When my plane landed on the little Tamatama airstrip I was astonished to see Paul Dye standing there with a grin on his face.

I said excitely, "You're here! Great! I was so worried about you. I thought maybe you had been killed or something!"

"Well, you came close to being right! When we were headed for the Big Savannah, the first village we came to accepted us, but kept insisting we stay. For a while they hid our backpacks so it would very difficult for us to leave. The next village took us captive, but one of the men assigned to guarding and keeping us from escaping became a friend and told us the leaders were planning to kill us to get our baggage. He slipped us out of the village in the middle of the night

40

then guided us as we went on and finally reached Niyiyobateri, the village in the Big Savannah.

"We soon developed friendships there, and we traded knives and matches for food. After we showed them how to use the matches, we told them there were others who wanted to visit them and would bring other useful things, and teach them how to use them. They finally agreed that they would welcome those people.

"We found that there was a smooth, level stretch of ground west of the shavano where we were sure a plane could land safely. Then we finally got Joe Dawson on our radio. He contacted the mission air fellowship and one of their pilots was willing to come and get us.

"When the pilot arrived we were surprised that Wally and Marg Jank and their kids were on the plane!

"It's been a week since we got back, and in that time, the pilot has made two more flights in there with building supplies for the house the Jank family is starting to build. He's planning on making another flight tomorrow, so you should be able to go with him. The Janks are looking forward to your arrival."

The next morning when I went out to the air strip to help the pilot load up, I was pleased to find that it was Peter, the same pilot who had taken me in when we had seen the Big Savannah from the air three years ago, but had found no place to land. He was still using the same small five-passenger plane, so he and I could sit in the front, and use the space behind us, where there would normally be seats, for the Janks' building supplies and my two bags of clothing and trade goods.

We were soon soaring over those high, rugged mountains. I did enjoy looking down at those picturesque mountains and recalling our first exploration trip, but as we flew over the big savannah and circled around for a landing, I was wondering what the people who lived in that big shavano would be like. Would they be friendly? Would they actually welcome another outsider? How long would it take to get acquainted with them?

Peter flew over the shavano, then circled around to come in from the east. The plane rolled to a stop less than a hundred yards from the little shelter the Janks had built to live in while their house was under construction.

Wally and Marg Jank came running out from that shelter. They and their four children were all waving their greetings and heading our way but they were passed by a group of naked warriors, with their red-painted bodies and with bright feathers in their armbands. They came dashing out of the savannah, waving their seven-foot long bows and arrows in the air. Women and children were following the men, and they too were running and shouting. Some of the men slowed down and started doing a strange kind of dance as they approached.

The Janks had obviously informed them that another newcomer was arriving, and they were all out to welcome me, chanting, laughing, dancing around as I climbed down from the plane.

Wally made his way through all those painted bodies and gripped my hand in greeting. Marg and her four children stood aside and waited till they could more easily make their way through the shouting, weaving, laughing crowd. "Welcome to Parima," the Janks' children shouted, obviously imitating the loud, demonstrative ways of the Indians.

Most of the people soon scattered but as I looked at the group who were still gathered around me I was very aware of their size. Most of the Indian men's heads came just about to my shoulders, and the women were even shorter.

Two of the Indian men grabbed my backpacks and my hammock, swung them to their shoulders, and headed for the shelter Wally and Marg were living in.

I tried to give everyone a smile and a wave before the Janks took me over to show me how fast their house construction was coming along.

I asked Marg if they had received that kind of welcome the day they arrived.

"Oh, no! Even though Paul Dye had told the people we were coming, and most of the men of the village consider themselves brave and powerful people who have confidence that they could overcome any enemy, none of them were ready to come out and investigate anything as strange as an airplane, especially when they then saw that we, like Paul and Cecil, were strange-looking people with clothes and white skin. Since we looked so strange, and they had always assumed that any stranger was an enemy, even the warriors hesitated to approach us.

"But then out of the forest came one lone man, who seemed to have no fear at all. We soon learned that he was the medicine man from Hill Top Village, a village about fifty miles east of here. Since that village has no enemies he could safely go anywhere. He happened to be wandering through the area that day and had, of course been very curious when he saw the plane land. So he had come to see what it was.

"When he came bravely out of the forest to meet us the men of the village no longer hesitated. He was partially responsible for our being able to immediately develop a friendly relationship. From what we have heard since then, we think that without him, the local people might have tried to take us captive."

Wally interrupted our conversation to say, "We better get down to the shavano. You need to show the rest of the people you are as interested in meeting them, as a lot of them were in meeting you."

And I had wondered if it would take a long time to get acquainted!

The shavano was one big circle, about two hundred yards across. Around the outside was a solid stockade of perpendicular poles, eight to twelve feet tall. Two sets of poles, running parallel to the ground, were tied to them, holding them all together, forming a powerful barricade which circled the entire village.

That barricade looked strong enough to keep anyone from entering. But with their welcoming attitude, who was it going to keep out? I asked that silly question, and before the afternoon was over four different men had warned me that raiders could attack at any time.

As we stepped through the gateway I saw that in the four-foot space between the stockade and the bottom of the thatched lean-to roofs, were lots of banana peals, chunks of rotted fruit, pieces of animal skins and guts, along with other junk.

As we stepped through the six foot wide entry way between the roofs, a group of men gathered around us.

Those men started shouting to their wives, telling them to bring some food, then they led us under one of the lean-to roofs and motioned to the hammocks we were to sit down on.

We were soon snacking on bananas and several kinds of berries. Marg looked shocked when I tried the roasted caterpillars, but I said, "If it's one of their usual daily foods, it can't be unsafe to eat."

As we snacked, I had time to study the Shavano. I could see that each family had a lean-to roof standing at about a 45 degree angle from where the back edge set on the ground to the top which was about fifteen feet high. Those roofs were all covered with palm leaves, which would make them very waterproof even in times of very heavy rain.

Under each of those roofs the family's living space was about ten feet square.

Each roof had three or four poles holding up the front end and most had a bar across between those poles, about four feet from the ground. That one bar was the only front wall of the house, so you could look across the village and see nearly everyone in their homes, except a few who had palm leaves or other things hung over the bar.

Of course the bottom of the slanted roof was the back wall of each home. The homes were built side by side against each other and there were no side walls so although hammocks were hung between poles that helped hold up the roof, there was nothing else to obstruct anyone from walking all the way around the village, through every home, without ever stepping out into the large open space in the middle

The homes right next to the gate had a lot of bamboo poles leaned against the crossbar in front of each hone so that if raiders got all the way through the gate, the village warriors would have something to get behind to protect themselves, and to shoot from.

Marg remarked that there was no bar across the side of the home, like there was in front. The whole shavano was all one long room, curved enough, and long enough,to make a complete circle. She said she had learned that everyone was always welcome to walk into any home as if they were all one big family.

My reaction was, "Wouldn't it be great if we could be that friendly back home?"

"Wouldn't it though! But you could never do it there!"

There were seven-foot long bows and arrows leaning against the crossbar in the front of every home. And there were fiber carrying bags and gourds of water hanging down. Bunches of bananas and pineapples, and chunks of meat hung from the beams. And scattered over the ground was a litter of fruit skins, twigs, leaves, feathers, and pieces of bone.

Some of the hammocks were well-woven cotton ones, but most were just strips of bark that looked to me as if it would be easy for the children to fall through between the strips.

The lean-to we were in was a typical home. Behind the mother,

between the three hammocks I could see the place for the fire. Beyond the hammocks was the day's firewood. And on the ground was the burden basket she used to carry that wood. I was surprised to see that she already had a big kettle she had gotten in trade, from the Janks.

In the home next to the one we were in, there were more than

three in the family so they needed two fires, as only three hammocks could be hung close enough to get the warmth of the fire and since no one had clothing, or anything to cover themselves on chilly nights,

48

they needed two fires, as they would have to depend on the fires for warmth.

Since Wally and Marg had spent five years with the Yanomami Indians, and their language was very similar to that of the Yanowamo, they were already able to understand most of what the people were saying. I had learned a little of the Yanomami language when I spent a short time with that tribe three years ago, but this was not enough to give me more than few clues as to what our new friends were saying. So when someone talked directly to me, Marg or Wally would usually try to translate for me.

We were soon strolling on around the shavano, and there was always a group of men strolling with us. When we stopped in front of one of the homes, one of the men started pointing at me and telling that family, "He's one of us. Look at his feet. All Nabas have big feet. His are little like ours. And he eats caterpillars. The other nabas will never do that!

When I had climbed from the plane an hour ago I had been a little shocked to see that all the men were naked, but now I realized that was not true at all. They were not naked. Every one of them had a string around his waist, and a little string hanging down from that one held up his penis so it didn't flop around. To them, they were properly dressed.

I took a picture of one one of them who did have a piece of cloth that Wally had given him, and had showed him he could wear it as a loin cloth.

Some of the men had lower lips that stuck out an inch or two inches in front of the rest of their faces. Wally told me they each had a leaf, usually a tobacco leaf, that they rolled up and put in between their lower lip and the teeth behind it. Although they had tobacco, and used it that way, none of them had ever heard of smoking.

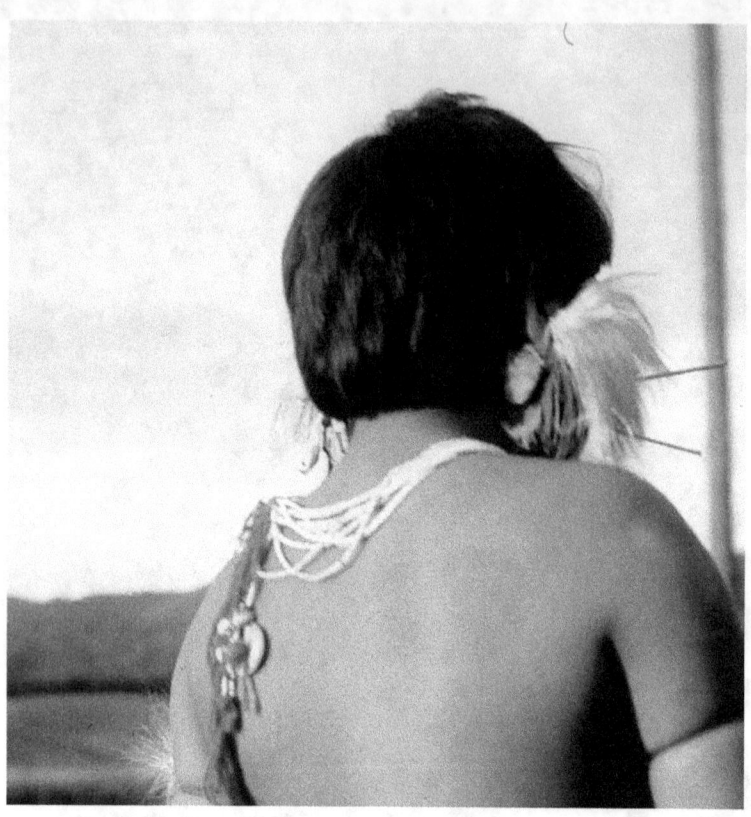

The younger girls are fully dressed with just a string around their waist. I later learned that, in their society, every girl who has reached the age of puberty must wear a fringed skirt until she is married. They said that most of the married women continue to wear their skirt until it is worn out.

But that was not all they wore. Some also had bands around their upper arms, and if they had been out in the jungles gathering food, they might have flowers tucked into those arm bands, and a little bouquet of flowers through their ears in place of their ear plugs. Most had one to three necklaces; strings of red or white seeds, and they had reeds through their noses and lower lips.

The men also wore ear plugs through holes in their ears, and those were usually decorated with feathers.

They could see my interest in learning to do things their way, so they assumed that I would want to be properly dressed. One of the

men came to me with a sharp pointed sliver of wood, and said he was ready to pierce my ears. I quickly told him it wouldn't work because I had to wear my glasses. That gave him an idea and he took out his own ear plugs, split open the bottom side of each one and fitted them over the bows of my glasses. I really appreciated that. It made it possible for me to wear the ear plugs that every Yanowamo wore.

Most of the women painted their faces. Each one was painted differently, and usually different each day. I thought about the women at home, who also paint their faces, but the same every day!

Even the tiniest babies had their ear lobes pierced, and reeds through their ears. The baby's ear plugs were the size of toothpicks. The mothers kept making them larger until the men's were about half an inch thick, and the women's only a little smaller. Nearly all the women's ear plugs were decorated, usually with feathers stuck in the end. But some used a bouquet of flowers instead of an ear plug.

I turned to watch a group of children playing. When Wally saw my interest in the burden basket that one little girl carried on her back he told me that every woman had a burden basket that she carried on her back whenever she left the village for any reason. It was tightly woven from reeds, and could carry a lot of weight. And they started making them for their daughters when the girls were still tiny. The little girls always wanted to wear them because it made them look like their mothers.

The basket was supported by a strap that went over their heads, because a person can carry more than twice as much weight on their heads as in any other way.

I asked Wally if Marg had gotten one of those baskets to use.

He said, "She's been trying to trade for one, but she hasn't yet found a woman with one to spare. You will soon see how essential those burden baskets are. One of the men just told me that since you seem to want to learn how to live their way, his family wants you to go with them when they go into the forest to gather food a couple of days from now."

6
HOME LIFE

Right after breakfast the next morning two men came up to help Wally, and we spent the morning working on the Jank's home, but I was anxious to see as much of the daily lives of the people as I could, so right after lunch, I decided to go down into the shavano by myself to look around, get my own view of life there without the guidance of others, and maybe see how the people reacted to me when the Janks weren't with me.

I looked across at the gate on the other side and wondered if it was really important to have all those bamboo poles leaning against the railing of the homes nearest to the gate, which they had said were there for protection, in case of raiders.

I strolled the length of the shavano, then stepped out of the gate at the other end. There was a whole bunch of people out there so I sat down on the ground to watch and talk with them. I enjoyed the friendly attitude of the people and their willingness to talk, but with my lack of language skills, I was still having difficulty conversing with them. I looked at the forest-covered mountain side above us.

I had been warned not to go into the mountains alone here because of the danger from raiders, but surely there couldn't be any that nearby. I decided to take a short stroll up the mountain to where I could get a good look down at the shavano.

I took the little trail up the mountainside. The forest was very dense on both sides. In nearly every opening there were beautiful flowers. There were a few berries, but I didn't dare eat any because of the possibility they could be poisonous. Then I saw some monkeys. They were eating one kind of berries, so I knew those were safe to eat. I tried them and they were delicious. I picked two handfuls and went on.

The only other wildlife I saw was some butterflies, and too many mosquitos and gnats! Just like back at the house, I was continually busy swatting those gnats.

The crooked trail wound between the big trees of the dense forest. In places only a dim light filtered through to the ground. In one of those dark, dense sections, as I stepped around a sharp bend in the trail, suddenly, close in front of me, was a man. With his bare feet, he had made no sound.

I was shocked! Could that be a raider? In one hand he carried his seven-foot-long bow and arrows, but in the other, and draped over his shoulder was a long black, red, and white snake.

After his first surprised expression, he had a big smile on his face. He laughed at my look of alarm. But then he had his own shocked expression. "You're out here without a weapon? That's insane!"

"But I don't have a weapon."

"You don't!?" He looked at me like he couldn't believe that. But then he grinned at the expression on my face as I studied the eight-foot long snake he was carrying.

"Isn't that a bushmaster? Aren't they dangerous?"

"Yes, but it will sure taste good!" Then he saw the fruit in my left hand. "I see you already know the ukoqui fruit are good. Your friend wouldn't eat any till we told him they were safe."

"I watched the monkeys."

"Well, you already know the system!"

He stepped past me and said, "You better come with me. You'll be safer."

When we got back to the shavano and to his home, his wife pointed to where the sun would be just a little before sundown and through motions let me know I should come back when the sun got to that spot; then she rubbed her tummy to let me know we would be eating.

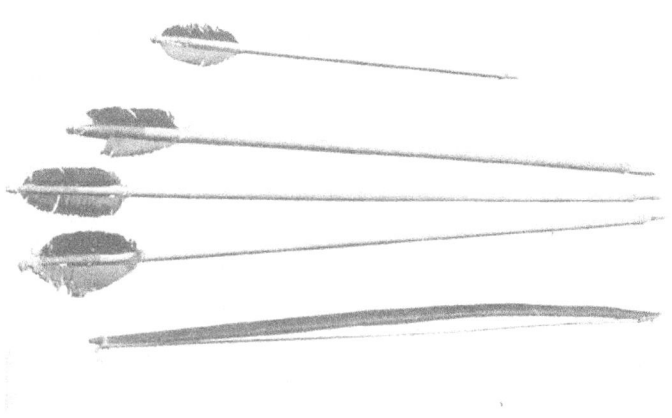

When I got there a couple of hours later, the man and his wife and their young son and daughter were sitting on their hammocks watching the bushmaster roast on the open fire.

In spite of my difficulty with the language, we had a great evening. It didn't require language for him to show me the seven-foot-long arrows and the bow he had just finished making and had not used yet.

He let me look over the old set he was replacing. I agreed they were pretty well battered, like they had been used a lot. "Now that's what you need," he said.

"Yes, especially that short arrow." It was only about four feet long. "That one is only a little longer than the ones I use at home. I got my deer this fall with one about two-thirds that long. I could handle that."

"Oh no! You couldn't use that! That's a child's bow. No one but a small boy, just learning to shoot, would use that one.

He laid three of his old arrows down so he could demonstrate how he attached the ten-inch-long feathers to the seven-foot arrows.

Then we took a better look at the arrow heads. The middle one was a hard wood tip fitted into the end of the reed arrow. The bottom arrow just had a wide bamboo tip. "Those are the hunting arrows," he said

The top one was a poison-tip arrow, which they used for war. The poison tip was a piece of bone, sharpened at both ends, then tied on so one end made a barb that would keep it from coming out of the body it went into. He said if you pulled hard enough the poisoned arrowhead would come off and stay in the body of the victim.

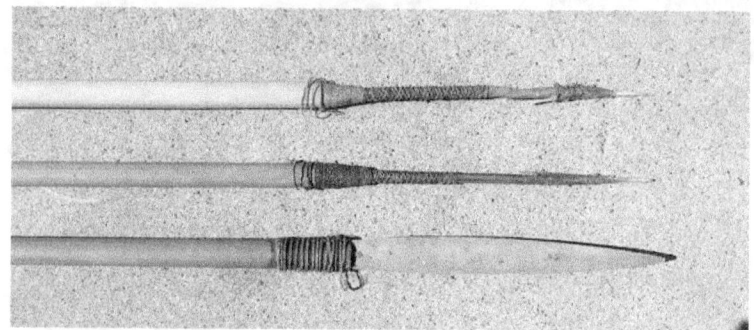

He told me how the poison was made from a root and the bark of a pupugna tree. He said that after they prepared the poison, several men would put their war arrow tips together, take them away from the village, build a fire to cook them, and boil the poison into the arrow head. One of the oldest men would volunteer to keep that fire going all day, and everyone else would stay far enough away to be sure they didn't breathe any of the fumes. The man who did the cooking was always honored for his bravery.

He said, "Every time you leave the shavano, you should be carrying two of the hunting arrows and one war arrow, just in case of raiders. And then if you are going out for a long day of hunting or are

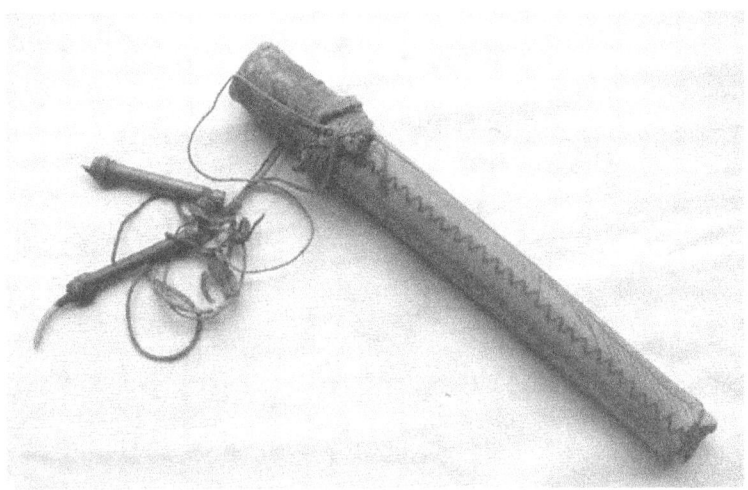

going to be gone a couple of days, hang a case like this on your back with some extra arrow heads in it in case you break an arrow and need to make a new one."

Attached to the arrowhead case by a leather thong was a little stick with the tooth of a rodent inserted in the end of it. I asked, "What is this?"

He explained that it was his knife, the only kind he had ever seen till he saw the ones Wally and I wore on our belts. It was made from the tooth of an agouti and was the only sharp instrument he had.

It was hard to believe that they could make all their bows and other things with a tiny tool like that, with only a sharp tooth for a blade. I could imagine how long it would take to carve a bow with that small tool.

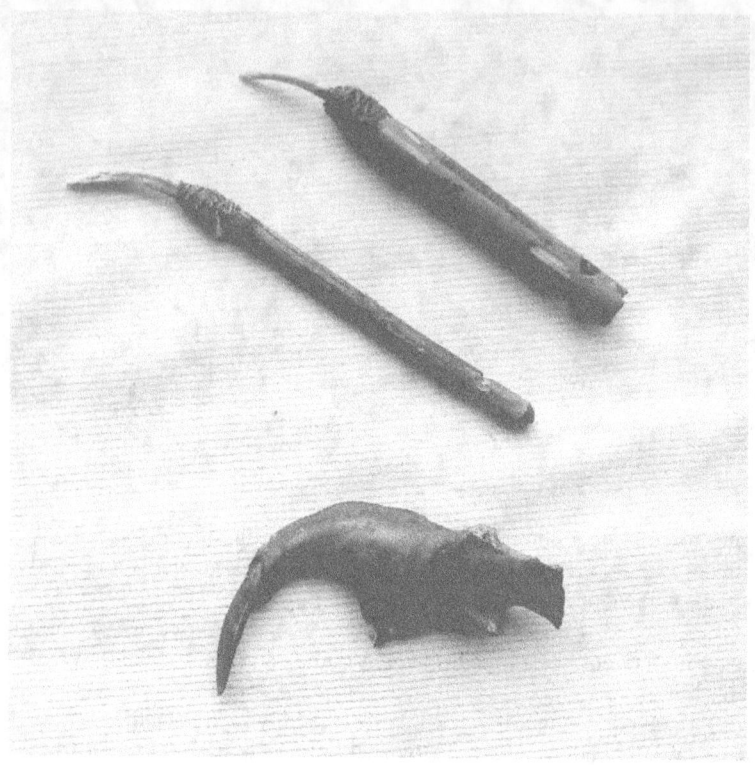

Along with the knives, he showed me the lower jaw of an agouti so I could see where the blades came from.

While he was telling me about all that, his wife was finishing roasting the snake I had admired when he was bringing it home. That and the plantains (bananas that have to be cooked) and some red berries made a very good meal.

His wife then showed me how she was weaving a hammock so their two children wouldn't have to try to sleep in the same one. They had several strips of bark they had gotten from a tree that had very strong bark that was flexible and could be split into strips but wouldn't break. They punched holes in the end of each strip so they could attach several of them together side by side, and they attached other strips across the center to hold those side by side; then they tied a rope to each end and had a good hammock.

When they saw my interest in that, they took me across the shavano to watch another woman who was weaving a hammock, using only string.

She had two bamboo poles which were about eight feet apart, and she had wound the string around and around those two till she had about fifty or sixty strings stretched between those poles, making a layer about a yard wide. She was now weaving other strings across this, but she couldn't just weave in and out. She had to tie that cross string to each of those long fibers.

I asked how long it would take to weave that hammock. She

said, "Remember those little red berries we ate for dinner? I started twisting that string when they were ripe last year. They'll be all gone by the time I finish this."

"Over a year? And you made all that string yourself?"

"Of course. Just like she's doing." She pointed to the lady in the lean-to home next to hers. We stepped over to watch that lady twisting little pieces of cotton together. These she attached to the spindle that lay in her lap. When she got about three feet of this cotton twisted together, she held the end of the string up high with one hand while she spun that little spindle with string on it till that three-foot piece of string was twisted tight. Then she would wind that string on her spindle and start twisting more.

Now I knew why I had been told to bring balls of string for my trade goods. But I still wanted to know, "Where do you get the cotton?"

"From our gardens. There are just two things we and our ancestors have always grown in our gardens -- cotton and bananas. We would be in bad shape if we were without either one of them."

7.
THIS IS FOOD?

The next morning as we ate breakfast, I was telling Marg and Wally about the snake dinner and all the things my hosts had showed me last night. We were just finishing eating when a group of people strolled into the guest room, all chattering and laughing.

I jumped up and headed over toward the low wall that separated the rooms. My host from last night stepped up to the other side of the wall. In each hand he had one of those seven foot long bows and three arrows. He reached out toward me with his right hand and said, "You'll need these today. Never go into the forest without them. There's raiders, you know."

I paused, perplexed. "I won't need them today. I'll be working on the house."

"No. You've got to come with us. If you live here and want to be one of us, you have to know how to get your food."

I turned to see Wally's reaction. He was grinning. He nodded. "I guess he's right!"

I headed for the back room of the house. I opened my pack, and took out a machete from my trade goods. I walked back out and held it out to my last night's host. "And you'll need this!"

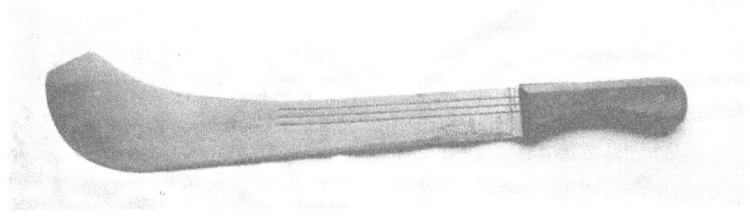

He took it in his hand, turned it over, felt the sharp edge, and said, "I sure will!" Then he looked hesitantly at me and asked, "Can we trade?"

"We'll both try them out today; then we'll decide."

"Do you know how to use that bow and arrow?" Wally asked.

"Yes, I got my deer with a bow and arrows last fall in Montana, but with arrows not a third this long or as big around. These seem

65

awfully clumsy to me. I wonder how accurately they can shoot with them."

There were seven men and six women who started down the trail across the savanna. All of us men carried bows and arrows. I was the only man wearing more than a string around his waist. Five of the six women who accompanied us were wearing the short fringe skirts. One of them had replaced hers with cloth she had gotten from Marg. I was sorry to see the change. I thought the red fringe was much prettier.

All the women had the big burden baskets on their backs, slung from a strap across their foreheads. One of them had something more, a six inch wide band made of bark that went over her right shoulder and down to her left hip, where her baby sat in the bottom of the loop and her hand held it against her side.

What a great way to carry a baby, I thought. I should teach that to my relatives.

We crossed three swampy areas. Since, in those areas, we were wading in water half the time, I was glad I had come in low-top tennis shoes rather than the leather shoes I wore at home. The people I was with all thought wearing any kind of shoes was silly. None of them had ever worn anything on their feet or seen anyone with shoes till the Janks showed up.

From there, we followed the river that separated the savanna from the dense rain forest until we came to the "bridge," a tree that had fallen across the river. It was a log about six inches in diameter.

They pointed to my shoes. They were right. I slipped my shoes off and one of the women took them and my camera. One of the men stepped onto the log and started across, motioning for me to follow.

In my bare feet, I stepped gingerly onto the thin log and followed, holding my long bow and arrows horizontally in front of me. I was glad I had them to use as a balance pole.

Halfway across the river, the man in front of me raised his bow and arrow and shot into the bank of the river about fifteen feet away. I tried to keep my balance as he ran the length of the log, grabbed his arrow, and held up a lizard about six inches long. I no longer wondered if those long arrows could be shot accurately.

When we started into the forest my last night's host led off, and I started to follow, but he turned and said "No!" He and three other men took the lead, then three women followed. They motioned for me to follow them, then came the other women, with three men in the rear. Throughout the day, whenever we were on a trail,we took those same positions. I was always in the middle, between the women.

When we came into an open area, the women set their baskets

down and started looking for berries and edible plants. Several of the women dug up roots they called uhina , which were about the size of a large potato, and which I later learned were used like potatoes and tasted somewhat like them, only I thought these had a better flavor.

When we again entered the forest, we passed through some palm trees. When the men saw three dead palm logs lying on the ground, they immediately chopped into one of the logs to see if it had started to rot. Yes, it was rotten enough so the witchity grubs were starting to eat out the soft rotten center. They immediately started to chop into the log with their stone axes. I took the machete from the man who had invited me and showed him how simple it was with a machete to chop halfway through the log. We made another cut about eight feet away, then split off the top half of the log between the two cuts. The women dug into the rotten pulp in both of the halves, and found a lot of the big white grubs with black heads. I joined them in doing this. We put all the whole ones into their baskets to take home and roast, but whenever we accidentally broke one in two digging it out, we just ate it on the spot.

When we started on, they showed me some wild pineapples. There were quite a few, but only one small one was ripe.

We found two bird nests, one with baby birds in it and one with eggs, which they took along. And we picked another kind of fruit that was similar to guava.

They all stopped, and one of the men started climbing a tall tree. I asked another man what he was after.

"Bees, can't you see them?"

I could see some wasps around us and a wasp nest in one of the low branches, but I couldn't tell the difference because the bees were up at the top of the tree.

One of the men said, "Take those things off your eyes so you can see. Let me look at them."

I handed my glasses to him and he put them on.

"They make everything fuzzy. No wonder you can't see well." He handed them to another man, who reacted the same way. They both thought those ear decorations would be fine at a leajou, but wearing those things that gave me poor vision was foolish. They didn't believe it when I said they made my vision better because they had tried them and saw how bad it made theirs. They just stood there and shook their heads and said it was just one of those foolish things the nabas do.

The man who had climbed the tree started reaching into a hole in the tree trunk, pulling out big pieces of bee comb and tossing them down to the ground. Some of the pieces of comb had honey in them. Some had bee larvae. Some had both. I joined the rest in picking up and eating the comb, regardless of the content. I found that the bee larva, sweetened with honey, was good. But I asked how that man could be up there digging into that bee hive with all the bees swarming around. Why didn't he get stung to death?

My host explained to me that the bees of the rain forest don't have stingers. "Didn't you notice the wasps and the wasp nest? The bees look for a tree where there's a wasp nest. If there's a hole with rotten wood, they clear it out and make that their bee hive. That way, the wasps protect them."

Whenever the trees along our trail were somewhat scattered, so we could get off the trail, we scattered out and looked for berries and edible plants.

I caught a big toad, but the woman I handed it to wouldn't put it in her basket with the rest of the food. She said, "We eat other kinds of toads any time, but this is a uanacoco. At this time of the year, when the mother toad has eggs within her, the blood is deadly poison. One time, one of our children ate one and died, so now we never eat those toads this time of the year. Some villages eat them all year, but they have to cut the meat off and soak and scrub it carefully to be sure there is no blood."

We found some pupugna, a fruit a little bigger than an apple, that they said was one of their main foods. On the ground under the tree was some of the fruit that had fallen and broken open. One of the women explained that some insects they called cupim had eaten part of the pupugna. Those insects, which from their description I thought must be moths, would dig into the soil beneath the tree and lay their eggs. We dug into the ground and found the larvae. The women wrapped them carefully in leaves, to be cooked later.

They said if those larvae were left there till they finished growing, the larva would climb up onto the sides of the trees and spin their cocoons.

As we walked on up the trail through the forest, they stopped and pointed to the trunk of a tree. Moth larvae had covered an area about a foot wide and two feet high with a solid coating, then arranged their cocoons on that. "It looks like a mathematician or an artist did that," I thought, but I didn't know the words to say that in their language.

One of the women said that was the kind of cocoons the larvae we had dug up would spin. She took hold of the edge of that plaque, pulled the whole thing off the tree, and put it in the basket on her back.

Some of the women set their baskets down in a grassy area while they gathered more wood. As we walked through the dense forest, the women had all watched for sticks and branches of dead wood which they could break into pieces one to three feet long, and the men sometimes split dead wood into strips with their stone axes. They told me every woman had to bring home enough wood each day to keep her fire going all night, to stay warm. I realized that was important, since they had no clothing or bedding of any kind.

While they were gathering wood,I killed a lizard about a foot long and gave it to the woman with the baby.

As we started on, we found a termite mound. They chopped it across the bottom so they could pick it up. A man took two banana leaves and, folding up the edges and ends, made two big, flat baskets. They picked up the termite nest, held it over the baskets, and pounded it. Hundreds of termites dropped out into the baskets. The termites, which looked like white ants, started running around the bottoms of the baskets, trying to get out, but they couldn't climb out because of the smooth surface of the banana leaves.

Finally we came to a whole grove of banana trees. The stumps and big logs lying among the banana trees told me this was one of their gardens. They had cut down the other kinds of trees that grew there to make room for their banana trees and cotton plants.

I wondered why they made the garden so far from home, but I later learned that nearly all their gardens were one to five miles away, wherever the soil looked good and the trees could be cleared. Walking distance seemed to mean nothing to these people!

The women gathered some sticks and dry grass for a fire. One

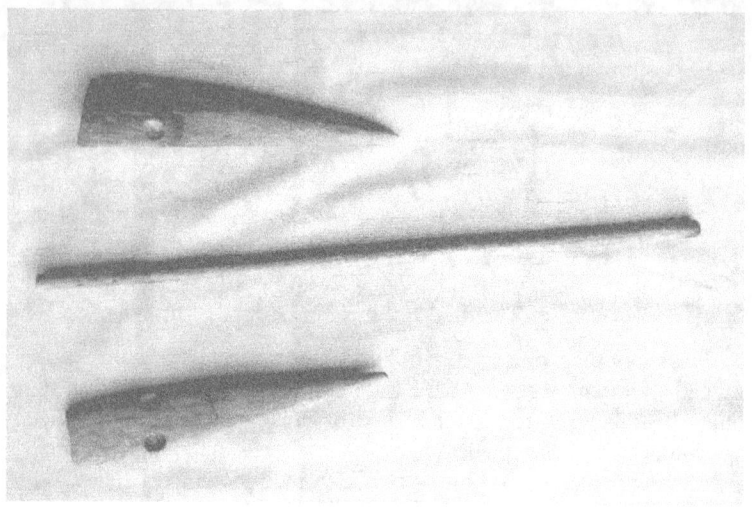

woman pulled two flat pieces of wood and a stick from her basket. Her husband put his bow string around the stick, and one of the flat pieces on the top end and one on the bottom, then pulled his bow back and forth so the bow string made the stick spin. His wife put dry grass next to the bottom to catch on fire when the spinning stick produced enough heat.

I pulled my tiny box of matches from my pocket and lit the fire. Everyone got real excited about that and wanted to see the other matches. I used one more match to show them how it worked. Then they all started reaching out for me to give them my box of matches. I put it back in my pocket and tried to tell them that I had more boxes, and we could do some trading later.

They used one of those banana leaves with the edges turned up for a skillet and cooked some of the termites and witchity grubs, which we all shared for our lunch. I was surprised that the green banana leaf was durable enough to cook on before it dried up and burned. I really enjoyed those witchity grubs.

As soon as they took that off the fire, the woman with the plaque of moth cocoons laid the whole thing on the fire. In a couple of minutes, they were done and we each opened two or three cocoons and ate the moth larvae. They made a point of giving me some extra ones because I was so interested in trying this new kind of food.

When we were ready to start home, the women loaded everything they could into their burden baskets and most had more to carry in their arms.

The woman with the baby had her basket stuffed with wood. She stuffed some roots in between her sticks of fire wood. She still had three lizards and a pineapple to carry. She needed one hand to hold the baby that rode in the sling up against her hip, and she hadn't yet picked up her big stalk of bananas.

When I offered to carry the stalk of bananas for her, she got very angry. She really lost her temper and yelled at me. I was puzzled. All I had done was offer to help! I thought maybe she thought I was implying that she couldn't do her job. But was that enough to cause her to shout in anger?

Then I learned the truth. It was my responsibility to protect her. I should have nothing in my hands but my bow and arrows. I should have them in ready position, so if raiders, a jaguar, a snake, or any other danger should appear, I should be ready to fire instantly. In her interpretation, when I offered to help her, what I was really saying was, "You're not worth protecting!"

I did a lot of thinking about that as we started down the trail. When I was a boy, I had idealized the Indian cultures. I wanted to grow up to be a naturalist, and my parents agreed with me that the Indians were one of my best sources because of their knowledge of all the animals. I had liked their concern for each other and admired other parts of the Plains Indian cultures, but there was one thing I had thought was awful: On the trail, the men always walked ahead of the women. Their wives were expected to walk a few feet behind and carry all the load. That was cruel. It contradicted the other attitudes of their culture. Now I understood. The Plains Indians did it for the same reasons as the Yanowamo. I should have followed what I, myself, had always said, that you should never criticize another person's culture till you knew it well enough to understand it, and the reasons for their actions.

I remembered the time John Woodenlegs, President of the Cheyenne tribe, gave my wife a ride to a meeting. When they got there, he walked several feet ahead of her into the building, then turned to her and said, "Your men think they should let the ladies go first. We want to protect them. We don't shove them in and make them face the danger first."

On our way out, we came to the river in a different spot from where we had crossed before. There was a larger log for a bridge, but the men did not start across. They all laid down their weapons and dived into the water. But I had clothes and didn't want them soaked. The women were still standing by the river talking. I stood there, wondering what to do.

One of the women stepped over, pointed to my pants, then acted as if she were taking hold of a belt and pushing it down to her ankles. Then she pointed to me, then the river. I obeyed, stripped off and dived in.

When we men came out the other side of the river fifteen minutes later, the women had brought our weapons and my clothes across the river, and they were all on the bank waiting for us.

When we got back to the Janks home, two of the women stepped in and gave Marg my share of the food we had gathered.

When the women left, Wally's first question was, "When you entered the forest, where did they put you?"

I described being in the middle, between the women, with three men leading the way, and others following

"Boy, you really do rate. They're really keeping you safe. If there are raiders waiting to attack, they will wait in a well hidden spot along the trail. Before they are seen, they can jump out and kill the first man or two, then take off before the others can shoot.

"Or if one of the raiders is very brave and wants to prove his courage, he will hide and wait as the group goes by, even though he knows that they will all be watching closely and might discover him. That's dangerous for him because they are all such good observers. They wouldn't have even grown up if they didn't see and hear everything. After everyone passes, he will jump out and kill the last man. So they were putting you in the center, the only really safe position."

"So the women and I, in the center were in a really safe position?"

"Well, if you are not scared. But when that raider who waited shoots the last one as he passes, all the rest know someone has been killed, they all whirl around and tear off toward home. They run right past the raider, so he has a chance to shoot one or two more!"

8

PROBLEMS WITH THE LANGUAGE

I've been quoting the people as if I knew for sure what they were saying. It is, of course, my interpretation. Three years before this I had learned a little of the Yanomami language, which was quite similar to Yanowamo. That meant that I knew more than half of the words that were spoken, but with that, along with the sign language people naturally use and their actions, I was usually able to translate most of what they said, although sometimes it might be somewhat inaccurate. Whenever I quote what people are saying, remember that I am trying to quote in English, as accurately as I can, my own understanding of what they said in the Yanowamo language. And what I say to them was, of course, in my broken Yanowamo.

I had another advantage when I started writing this book. On that first trip, and each of my others, I carried a miniature tape recorder attached to my belt. Whenever I talked to the Yanowamo people, I tried to remember to click on that tiny recorder, so I could listen to the conversation again, at a later time. On my third trip there, several years later, I took along my tape recordings from the first two trips. Davy, Wally and Marg's son, who was by then 12 years old, heard me telling Wally that I'd like some help translating those tapes, because I hoped to someday write a book about the tribe. Davy immediately spoke up and said he would be glad to help. Because he had grown up speaking both English and Yanowamo, it was easy for him to do. I got out the tapes and whenever we had some spare time. I would turn on the recorder and as he listened he would would say in English what he heard in Yanowamo, and I would record what he said. I also frequently turned on the recorder when Marg and I were discussing the culture, which has helped me with my me with my very enjoyable memories.

Until a week before our arrival these people had not known there were any people who were different from them. They still didn't understand that there could be a completely different language. When I couldn't understand what they said, they thought my hearing was poor.

When I said, "Immabaloli" ("My hearing doesn't see you"), they would pull my head down so they could talk into my ear. They would talk really loud, or they would repeat the sentence a half dozen times and be completely mystified as to why I couldn't understand it.

I frequently took my little notebook out of my shirt pocket and made a few notes of words I learned and wanted to remember. I was glad I still wore a shirt. None of the other men would have a place for a notebook or a pencil. Sometimes I'd pull out the notebook to find a word I needed.

They saw me doing that, so they thought that somehow that little notebook made me think better. When I couldn't understand what they said, they would point to my shirt pocket, or if I was near enough, they would reach out and pull the little notebook out of my pocket and hand it to me, thinking that if I held onto that notebook it would improve my hearing.

I not only hadn't learned enough words, but the construction of the sentences was very different, and there were many words in each language for which there were no synonyms in the other language.

Wally and Marg were fluent in Yanomami, the down river language, and were quickly learning the words that were different so they already understood nearly everything that people said to them.

One thing that really helped me in learning the language was the hymns the Janks translated. They and the Dawsons had translated several of the well known hymns into the Yanomami language. I quickly learned those songs, and as I sang them to myself, I thought the English words. That really helped me learn more words. That was the system I had used during the Second World War to become fluent in Pompangan, one of the languages of the Philippine Islands.

9

MY REAL NAME

The two women that Marg called Laughing-Lady and Scar-on-the-Shoulder had just left the house. I said, "I notice that you have your own nicknames for everyone, so you can identify individuals without knowing their real names. Is it true here, as it was with the Yanomami, that you can never say an adult's name?"

"Absolutely!" Wally said. "And never ask anyone his name. It would make him angry. It would mean that you want him to do something that could get him killed. You see, if anyone knows your name, he can do witchcraft against you. These people don't know about diseases and germs, so nearly all sickness and death is blamed on witchcraft. If you say any person's name aloud, someone who doesn't like him may hear it, and they believe that person can do witchcraft against him or tell an enemy his name and get him killed. Therefore, according to their beliefs, if you say a person's real name, you may be condemning him to death. So when you talk about a person, you say, 'The man who killed the jaguar' or 'Doko's father.' Or just make up your own nickname for them. That's the way the 'real people,' as they call themselves, identify people. They don't use names."

"But you just used a child's name, 'Doko.' "

"Oh yes. That's all right. Everyone likes children, No one would ever want to harm a child. Not even an enemy's child. So you can freely use any child's name.

"They give every child a name when it is born, just like we do, and they use those names till the child is about ten. Therefore, the adults know the names of all their friends, because they learned them when they were children, but they never say the name aloud."

"But I heard them call you Wally, and I've heard Enrique's name several times."

"Yes, but that's our name for him, not his 'real name.' When we first got here, two weeks ago, the men were very shocked when I came right out and told them my name, and Marg's name. But having learned the custom from the Yanomami, I explained to them that these were naba (outsider) names, not our 'real' names. They couldn't be used for witchcraft. It took a few days and a lot of discussion before they finally accepted the idea that saying naba names could be safe. Then they were all jumping around, shouting our names, celebrating. ,

"Enrique came to us shortly afterward asking us to give him a naba name. This was a new idea, someone having a second name, a naba name that they could freely use. We decided that since he is the medicine man, the main leader, that would be a good place to start. But we will have to only give Spanish names, because the Venezuelan government rules say we can absolutely never teach anyone any English. If we teach anyone a single word in another language besides their own, it has to be Spanish, and only Spanish. Be careful when you talk about any person. If you use a person's name, be sure they understand it is a 'naba name,' not a 'real name' "

It was just a couple of days later that Enrique and five of his friends saw me in the shavano and came marching across the big, open space looking like they really had important business. They came directly to me, then stood together, and Enrique said, loudly, "What is your name? We want to know your name."

I was shocked. I thought that question was still absolutely forbidden, and now they'd asked it right out there where everyone could hear!

I suddenly got a bright idea. I tried to act like them. I stood up, threw my shoulders back, and said proudly, so everyone could hear, "My name is Abufidoblau." I had said the word "Happy" in Yanowamo instead of English.

They were as shocked as I had been at their question. That was a Yanowamo word, a Yanowamo name. They couldn't say that!

They turned and talked together. That had to be my "real" name, my Yanowamo name. But I had said it, and said it loudly. It must also be my naba name. If they could say naba names, could they actually say that one?

Suddenly they were all saying my name, dancing around, laughing. Then they started telling me that I not only had a Yanowamo name, but "Abufidoblau" was one of the best possible names. "Bufi" means heart, soul, spirit: the part of a person that has feeling. You could use it with another word to express every emotion. "His bufi (heart) is low (discouraged); His bufi is red (angry). His bufi is white, black, high, low." "Doblau" means "perfect," so my name, Happy, Abufidoblau, says, "His heart is perfect"

They said it was the right name for me and they were glad it was also a naba name so they could use it. They also started telling me they considered me one of them, not a naba. I ate caterpillars and rats. I

79

helped them dig grubs out of rotten logs and ate them. Things no naba would do! Now they learned I also had a Yanowamo name. This was one more reason they knew that I was really a Yanowamo, one of them, even though I looked like a naba. They thought when they made that statement they were really honoring me, because nabas were ignorant!

I had to agree. When it came to knowledge of how to live here, under their conditions, nabas didn't know much.

These men quickly spread the word. I had a Yanowamo name, but it was one they could say aloud. I was, like they had been saying, both naba and Yanowamo.

As I walked around the shavano later that same day, I several times got cheers and shouts of welcome.

When I walked into the house that afternoon, Wally looked up and said, "Well, hello Abufidoblau!" Then we both burst out laughing. I was surprised that he had already heard about my name.

He remarked, "So that's what your name, 'Hap,' means, Happy."

"Yes, when I was a teenager I had half a dozen nicknames. Every group of people I knew used a different one. Then someone started calling me 'Happy.' Within a month everyone had switched over. For a couple of years that's the only name I heard. Then it got shortened to Hap. It's as legal as any name because my birth and my name were never recorded, and still haven't been. We were on a homestead too far from any town."

"Well, from now on it's Abufidoblau! Since you got them talking about names, four men came in requesting that I give them naba names. I decided to use the North American Indian system and told them we'd do it when they did something important that earned it. One of them was your host, who fed you the bushmaster snake. Do you have a Spanish name for him?"

"Let's call him Carlos."

"And that teenage boy who's always here to help wants a naba name too, and I think he deserves it, but he says he wants you to choose the name."

"Well, I only know one other Spanish name. My favorite uncle was Uncle Rosito. I have no idea why he was given a Spanish name, but I'd like to name that boy after him."

Then I said there was one other who should have a name. That was a young man about the age of Rosito. Like Rosito, he was always trying to help me, but unlike Rosito, who was always quietly helpful, this boy was loud, flamboyant. He loudly stated that I should be one of them, so he wanted me to learn everything that would make me a great warrior. Since he was into everything that went on, I was always wanting to say something about him, and I needed a name to call him by.

Wally laughed and said, "That boy was with those who asked for names, so I've been considering it. Let's call him Jose. We're getting some people together tonight, a group who want to hear more of the good news of the gospel that I'm trying to teach them. I think that's a good time to announce those three names."

10

DAILY LIFE

Much of the grass in the big savanna was cut-grass, a grass that has sharp, spiny blades. It would cut the legs of people like the Yanowamo who have neither shoes nor pants to protect their legs. So the Indians frequently set fire to the grass in those areas so they can cross them safely.

The Janks realized that since there was tall grass covering the ground right up to their house, one of those fires could spread all the way to their home, it could easily set fire to the house they were building. Therefore one of the first things they had the pilot bring in for them was a gasoline-powered lawn mower. Then, right away, they mowed a large space around their house.

The pilot laughed at them for wanting a big fancy lawn around their house that no outsiders would see, but the Indians understood the need. They thought it was a great idea and begged them to let them cut the grass all the way around the shavano.

QuickTime™ and a
decompressor
are needed to see this picture.

It was surprising how rapidly the Jank's house was going up. The walls were a series of bamboo logs set on end, against each other.

They made two layers like that a few inches apart, and packed wet clay in between. The pilot had brought in some corrugated aluminum

The house had four rooms. The main room was for living, dining, cooking, and eating. Two small rooms behind it were for sleeping and storage.

In front of the main room was the visitors room, and those two rooms were separated only by a four foot high wall. They made it that way because of the Yanowamo custom that anyone should be welcome to walk into your home at any time without hesitation and without knocking. The visitors room made that possible. People could walk in to the visitors room any time, and talk with us across that little wall, or we could step through the door and be with the visitors.

The whole house had only a dirt floor.

With the help of several Indian men, who were paid with the trade goods the Janks brought, it was only a little over a week after my arrival until the house was far enough along for them to move in. I hung my hammock in the little storage room.

The Janks were spending a lot of their time building that home, but since they were there to teach the Christian religion, they tried to spend at least half of their time talking with the people. They tried to learn the ways of the people so they could teach them more effectively, and also try to change some of their ideas to the more Christian concepts of right and wrong.

I tried to be a help with their house building, but I was glad I could also spend at least half of my time down in the shavano, just learning the ways of the people.

Wherever I travel, throughout the world, I have always found that if I want to really understand a culture I need to experience it, and only if the people see that I am trying to totally adopt their ways, will they reveal their innermost thoughts and really try to tell me about their private lives and feelings. Therefore, unless something is really against my moral values, I enjoy trying to do everything their way.

I couldn't quite do that here when it came to clothing, because I was not willing to run round the Janks home naked.

One afternoon one of the men came walking into the shavano, carrying an ocelot he had shot. I mentally compared it to a bobcat that I had shot with a bow and arrow back when I was working with the Cheyenne. This ocelot looked much like that bobcat, except it was a little larger and had a long tail.

In the few clothes I had brought down here with me were two pairs of brief underpants. One was spotted. I realized how much the spotted underpants looked like the spots of the ocelot so I decided now I had appropriate clothes to wear. From then on, much of the time, if I was going out with the men, away from the house, I wore only those brief underpants.

Twice I heard one of the women, who had not been real close to me, say that I must really be a good hunter if I had killed an ocelot.

Of course, much of the time I had to also wear my shirt to protect me from the gnats or the burning sun. That shirt was the only item of clothing that any of the men thought made sense because it was protection from the gnats. So Wally had used shirts as the pay for two of the men who had been helping him in building his house.

I was impressed by the physical condition of almost every Yanowamo. With an average height of four and a half to five feet, you wouldn't expect their strength. But they were strong for their size, had had a natural gracefulness, strong muscular arms and shoulders, and a remarkable muscular coordination. And they had excellent teeth. There was not the great variety in shape, build, and condition that we find in our society.

I usually spent the morning helping Wally so I didn't get down to the shavano till late morning or afternoon, but I wanted to see their whole way of life, so one morning I got up and went down to the shavano at dawn.

Just as the sun was coming up, one of the men did a sort of swaying dance in front of his lean-to and began chanting. Everyone stopped their activities to listen to the chant.

I listened carefully, but I hardly understood a word.

When it was over, I went to the home of Enrique and asked about it. He said that was the Yumo, the news chant, done every morning at sunrise.

"Is it always by the same man?" I asked.

"No, there are five or six men who take turns doing it, but they are the only ones who can do it well. It is a very difficult chant to do. They have to keep the rhythm, and the person who does it almost has to know a different language. The words are spoken differently, and doing it takes a special ability that some of the men try to develop, but not all of them can learn how. Most of the people understand it, so it keeps the leaders informed, but no visitors can understand it and take the secrets of the village back to their homes."

I adopted their habit of saying the opposite of what you mean and answered, "Oh, I understand every word!"

Enrique laughed hard, slapped me on the back, and said, "Of course you do. You're one of us."

I wondered, since they had a different dialect that they used for the news chant, why hadn't they immediately understood my speaking a totally different language?

As I wandered around the shavano, I got acquainted with a family who had a pair of pet marmoset monkeys, what they call elos. Those monkeys had a baby and the owners told me that the father monkey did all the taking care of that baby, carrying it with him all day, only bringing it back to the mother when it was feeding time.

I did my best to learn the kind of actions that would keep my relationships with both men and women proper. Many rules of conduct are reversed from the customs of our society.

I learned that I should never touch a woman under any circumstances. But I could laugh and joke with a woman. That is perfectly all right, no one will misunderstand. This is not considered flirting. But if I looked like I was going to hit her, that would be considered flirting and then her husband would get jealous.

In our society, a man doesn't often put his arms around another man. It is not very appropriate. But with the Yanowamo a man will very often walk up to another man and put both arms around him and give him a big hug.

There are two common ways of communication with another man besides just visiting with him. One is hug him; the other is threaten him. If you pick up a stick and act like you are going to hit him over the head with it, or just act like you are going to punch him in the chest with your fist, that is considered a friendly greeting.

I enjoyed the Yanowamo people's generosity and their willingness to share their food, so one evening I decided that I, too, could be generous and share with my friends. I dug a can of ham out of the supplies I had brought with me, then wandered around the shavano stopping to visit with several families. When I got to Tookaloma's home, they invited me to come in and sit down.

I said, "Opie," which means "I'm hungry."

They quickly got out some corn and bananas, but I took my hunting knife and opened the can of ham and started cutting it up. I handed a little piece to each of them.

They each took a taste, but then Tookaloma's father made a face and took the bite out of his mouth and said, "Salt!"

His wife then boiled all of my ham, then poured out the water she had cooked it in, to get rid of the salt. Then she added a vegetable I had never seen and we all enjoyed eating it.

The next time I was down in the shavano, that same family invited me to join them in a dinner of ants and ant eggs. They apologized for not having more variety, but said they had just finished eating up all their crabs and shrimp.

We all laughed about it.

I frequently saw people coming into the shavano with the animals they had shot, and the other foods they had collected. Then I observed the ways the women prepared them to eat. They often left the skin on the meat so they could cook it directly on the coals of the fire, or sometimes they would wrap both the meat and vegetables in banana leaves, and cook them together.

At other times, I watched them cooking vultures, boa constrictors, coral snakes, grasshoppers, butterflies, spiders, tree frogs, fish, and various kinds of birds. The white larvae of the ants were an important part of their diet, and so was a red fruit which they called temare.

Because of my obvious interest and the generous nature of the people, when I took an interest in what someone was cooking, they nearly always insisted that they wanted to share it with me. I thoroughly enjoyed trying all those different foods, but I realized that they then had to eat lightly because they usually brought back from the forest only enough for their own dinner and breakfast.

In pioneer days in the Western U.S. when you found the remains of a campfire, you could tell who had camped there. If there were sticks that had been laid across the fire and burned in he middle, it was a white man's fire. The Indians always put only the tips of the sticks in the fire. It was the same here. The fire was always kept small, and the sticks of fuel were laid around it like the spokes of a wheel so you could keep pushing them in and keep the fire going. Most of them kept it going day and night, and never let it go out. That provided heat in the night and drove away many of the biting insects.

Only the men build new fires with their spinning-stick fire starting tools, but every woman must go out into the forest and bring in enough firewood to keep her fire going.

They often had earthenware pots of food setting in the edge of the fire to slowly roast, but only gourds were used for eating and for storing their foods.

One day, when Marg was there with me, and someone shared some caterpillars with us, Marg told me she couldn't stand the idea of eating those or some of their other foods. But I told her, "If it is part of the usual diet of the people, it can't be harmful, so why not enjoy it!"

Laughing Lady saw Marg turn down the caterpillars and said, "Can't you see that Abufidoblau enjoys them? He's one of us. You don't like tadpoles either, do you?

Marg said to me, in English, "Could you eat those slimy, wiggling black masses of tadpoles that they collect in their baskets?"

I laughed, and she couldn't help but laugh with me, and cheerfully confessed her strong dislike of tadpoles.

Laughing Lady went on, saying to Marg, "And you don't carry a basket on your back like we do, do you! And you're always wearing clothes! And you can't talk straight either. That's why we can't do it."

"Can't do what?" Marg asked.

Laughing Lady hesitated. She appeared embarrassed, like she wished she hadn't said anything. But finally she explained, "We think if we accept the gospel, we might end up like you!"

That, obviously, would have been a terrible fate.

There was a long pause of total silence before Marg spoke up. "White people are not all the same. There are many other cultures. Some of them are very different from either of ours. We can't imitate each other, and we shouldn't. But there are Christians in all those areas. You don't have to act like me to be a Christian."

There were sudden looks of pleasant surprise, so Marg went on: "I know that God likes the Yanowamo. The gospel is as much for you as it is for us foreigners. Eating tadpoles isn't sin. Neither is our eating sandwiches. God doesn't mind whether or not you carry baskets on your backs or wear reeds in your ears. It isn't your hair style or your diet that God wants to change. It's your doblou (your hearts). Your hearts are frightened and worried. You're frightened by the spirits of your enemies, because you don't know God."

Laughing Lady agreed. She jumped up and broke the seriousness of the conversation by laughing, and exclaiming, "Well, I sure don't want to talk like you, or like the Guaicas down river, either." She swung her basket to her shoulder, and said, "I'm going after some crabs. Can we still go on catching crabs when we're Christians?"

She didn't wait for an answer.

As she walked away, I stood there and tried to summarize in my own mind what it really means to be a Yanowamo: Fierce but gentle, proud, tender, trusting but suspicious, quick to laugh but also quick to take offense. You must be very loyal to your friends, but deadly to your enemies.

11
BECOMING ONE OF THEM

The door opened and Carlos stepped through. "Bring your matches and my machete."

"All right, if you'll bring my bow and arrows."

We both laughed, knowing that was the way each of us was saying we wanted to share and might even be willing to trade.

I got out one of the three machetes I had brought with me and handed one to Carlos. He motioned for me to follow him.

Wally objected. "No. He's going to help..."

But Carlos whirled around with an angry look and almost shouted, "He's got to come with us! He needs to learn!"

I waited for Wally's reaction. He shrugged his shoulders and spread his hands. What else could he do?

When we joined the four men and three teenage boys who were waiting outside, Rosito offered to carry my machete for me. The men shoved me into the line, up front, behind the leader, and we headed up a trail leading into the dense forest. I saw that, along with their bows, all the men were carrying stone axes or other chopping instruments. Maybe I should have hung on to my machete.

I wished I knew where we were going, and why.

More than a mile up that trail, we came out into an opening where all the trees had been cut down except four that were too large for the men to cut down with their stone axes. But they had cut the bark all the way around those so that the trees had died.

Obviously all the other trees had been lying there drying out quite a while. As some of the men broke some limbs to see how dry and brittle they were, Carlos told me this was to be a garden where they would grow their two crops, bananas and cotton. They had been waiting till there were several days without rain so it would be dry enough to burn. He gathered some dry grass and twigs and pointed to my pocket. I reached in and pulled out my matches and said, "Need these?"

We lit his tinder then stuck it under some of the dry dead limbs, then we walked to three other places around the edge of the clearing and started three more fires. The men didn't run away from those spreading fires immediately. They grabbed some burning sticks and started throwing them at each other, laughing and yelling, pretending to threaten each other. Their play started more fires and we turned and ran the best we could across the log-strewn area and hurried into the forest

away from the tremendous heat of the fires as they spread across the clearing.

I didn't feel really safe. What if the fire spread into the forest? But none of the men were concerned about that. Even though there had been a few dry days, which they needed, to have the timber in the clearing burn well, the forest was always much too damp to burn.

We didn't start for home, as I expected. We headed in the opposite direction and soon came to another garden spot they had just started to clear. Two of the men started chopping away at a tree that was still standing. I was surprised that they would attempt to cut down that large a tree with their stone axes.

I took my machete back from Rosito started chping. Everyone seemed pleased to see how much faster we could cut a tree down with a machete than with their stone axes. I didn't want to look lazy, so I kept chopping till a little after noon before I took time out to examine all the tools the other men were using.

Four of the men were using axes. Two of them had stone ax heads. They were made like the ones I had seen in museums, that the Plains Indians had used, with a wooden handle, split at the top, and the stone ax head tied in between the two halves. Another man had a similar ax with a bone ax head.

I was surprised at the fourth ax. The head was a long piece of metal, obviously the blade of a machete with the handle broken off. It was put together like the stone axes, with the blade through the handle so you could chop with the end, just like with a stone ax. As I examined it, the owner said it was the only metal they had ever seen before we arrived, but they had gotten it in trade with another village

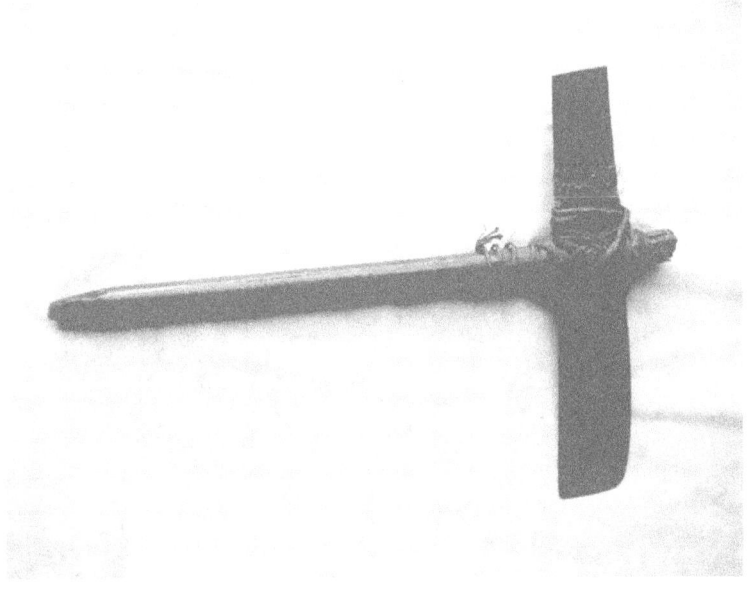

many years ago and had no idea of what the original was like.

I wondered how many hands, how many villages, it had passed through and how many years it took for it to be transported those hundreds of miles.

I held out my machete and said, "Want to trade?"

Carlos looked shocked, and the owner of the ax stood grinning at me, assuming I was just teasing, joking as they did so often. Carlos thought since half the time I didn't know what they were saying, maybe I didn't know what I was saying either. They couldn't believe it when I actually traded. They, of course, didn't realize that when I went home to Montana, I wouldn't have much use for a machete, or I could get a new one if I needed it, but that ax would be a valuable artifact and a great souvenir.

Throughout the day, even though the men were hard at work, they were continually laughing and joking, teasing each other. I wished I could understand more of what they were saying.

When a bird flew across in front of me, I realized that all day long I had seen almost no birds. But then, when it was near sunset, there seemed to be birds of all descriptions everywhere. The hummingbirds were the most common. Wherever we went, the hummingbirds were always darting around ahead of us. There were many different kinds, with many bright colors.

On the way home, we stopped at another garden and picked some bananas, and I got to see what the two gardens we had worked on

would look like next year.

On the way back we stopped to pick the fruit of a Yagua palm. The man who picked it did not climb the palm, but climbed a tree near it, then got a hold of the tips of two of the palm leaves and pulled the top of the palm tree over far enough to pick the big heavy clusters of fruit.

When we got back to the Jank's home, Carlos told Wally he was sorry I couldn't stay home to help him that day, but it was important that I go with him.

Wally laughed. "Yes, I know. Because of his matches."

"No. Because he's one of us now, and he needs to learn. We like him. He's smart. He might even become a medicine man. But the people of his tribe didn't teach him much. He must have had a very poor mother because she didn't even teach him how to talk."

"But he knows another language."

Someone must have told him that the English word "language" that Wally used meant "words" because he answered, "Oh, yes, he knows quite a few 'languages.' About as many as he should have known when he started to walk."

It was only seven days later that we went back to the burned garden, with women going along, and carrying roots of banana trees.

As we were getting ready to go, I heard some talk about raiders and saw some fearful looks on the faces of the women, but no one said anything to me about it. When we got to the gardens we had cleared, I saw that the fire had burned the limbs of the trees, leaving only the trunks. It had also killed all the insects and the weeds so the garden was ready for planting. To cross the area, we had to walk the tops of the logs, rather than try to step over them. Those logs were the permanent trails the people would use to cross their gardens.

There were already a lot of plants starting to come up between those logs. It didn't take long for them to plant all the banana roots the women had brought in their burden baskets.

They had also brought along some cotton seed. They used a sharpened stick to punch holes in the ground, then dropped two seeds in each hole.

When we left there, I didn't stay between the women, where they had put me before. I wanted to be with the leaders, where I would see more of the wildlife. I kept my eyes moving, looking for anything moving, but then I noticed the men frequently watching the trees straight above us. One of them pointed out a monkey high in the top of the trees and he told me, "That's where you'll also see the silky anteaters and the kinkajous and rats. The sloths will not be so high up. You'll see them hanging upside-down beneath the limbs. They live their whole lives upside-down."

I learned that the anteaters were also on the ground, because when we were where the trees were not quite so thick and we could see ahead, we sighted one down on the ground. We stopped and watched it as it stuck its long, pointed nose into a termite nest.

One of the men slipped slowly and quietly forward, to where he could get a shot at it.

After he killed it, and I was looking it over, he put his fist under its nose, pulled out it's thin, foot long tongue and told me, "that's how it was catching those termites."

We headed on down the trail until one of the men stopped to climb the up a tree to get a lot of caterpillars. They said those caterpillars were mature enough so some of them might have already made their cocoons, so they dug into the ground below and, sure enough, they also got a bunch of cocoons.

A little farther on, they found another bunch of the same kind of caterpillars, but they said those were still too small. They would come back and eat them when they had grown larger.

A little later, the women all set their baskets down, and one of the men started twirling an arrow against a stick. I pulled out my matches and started the fire for him.

The women put all the termites and caterpillars on banana leaves, which they put on the fire to roast them. That, with some berries they had picked, was our lunch. They took the anteater and sloth one of the men had had killed home to eat later.

12
CAPTURE THAT GIRL

One day, I was strolling around the shavano, not expecting any excitement, but with these folks you never know. As I walked by Rosito's home, he motioned for me to come in. He was sitting in his hammock making arrow heads. His mother was fixing up the fire to cook a bird and some platnos, and his little sister was playing with the parrot. His teen-age sister was stringing some red and white seeds to make a necklace. This girl was a beautiful young lady, and today she was also decorated up. The red feathers in her ear plugs matched the red scrolling design painted on her cheeks and her red fringe skirt. All of that was improved by the big smile on her face.

When she got up to help her mother, I mentioned to Rosito how nice she looked. He said, "I think she painted her face 'cause she thinks her husband might show up today."

"Her husband? She's married?"

"Of course. Any girl this tall," he motioned to the middle of his chest, "is pretty sure to be married."

I was surprised, and wanted to ask more, but just then a nice looking man, probably in his early twenties, walked in, carrying a stork, another bird, a bunch of roots, and a chunk of honeycomb. He and the girl greeted each other with big smiles, but here was no hug. I assumed that wouldn't be proper. From what I had seen, men never hugged the women, at least not in public.

I got up and left, to let the family enjoy their get-together, so I didn't learn any more. But I was curious. If that was the girl's husband, why was he never around? He must live in another village, but he brought her food, and they enjoyed each other, so why weren't they living together?

During the next couple of weeks I kept my eyes open, but the young man was never there. When I asked Rosito about him, he just said, "Oh, he'll be back."

One day, about two weeks later, I was sitting on a hammock visiting with some other friends, when there was suddenly a lot of screaming and yelling at the other end of the shavano. We, and nearly everyone else, jumped up and ran out to to see what was going on. That young man and two others had a hold of Rosito's sister and were doing their best to pull her toward the gateway of the shavano. Instead of going along happily, she was was really fighting them. Her mother, father, and Rosito came running and grabbed hold of her and fought the men, trying their best to help her escape from them. I thought it must be very painful for the girl being yanked in two directions at once.

Her little sister was weeping loudly and pounding on the naked rear of one of the men.

All the men and women of the village were watching, and yelling and screaming their encouragement, but I couldn't tell for whom they were cheering. I was alarmed, but also puzzled. I wanted to run and help the girl, who was obviously being kidnapped. but a lot of other men were watching, and not interfering, so there must be a reason,

That young man had seemed like such a nice fellow, and had brought nice gifts of food to them last time he came. And Rosito had said he was her husband! Why, when she was really fighting to keep from going with him, would he drag her off forcibly? What kind of treatment would he give her when he got her away from the protection of her family? He must be a cruel man.

But why didn't the whole village try to protect her?

The husband and his friends got the girl out the gate and they were dragging her up the trail that crossed a ridge that came down from the mountain. But they were moving slowly because the family was still trying to drag her back.

I ran out the other gate of the shavano and headed for a bare spot, a view point, a little way up that mountain. Just as I got to where I could look down and see what was going on, the family gave up and let go of the girl, but she kept on struggling. She struggled hardest just as they went over the ridge. But then, as soon as they were out of sight of the village, she suddenly straightened up and appeared to be walking willingly with them. I even saw the four of them laughing together as they went out of my sight.

I hurried back to the shavano and asked my friends what was happening, and why others didn't try to help the girl.

"It was none of our business. We shouldn't interfere."

"But what was happening? Why were those men kidnaping the girl?"

"Oh that was a girl-pulling, a young man coming to get his wife."

"But why, if it was his wife, wouldn't the family let her go, and why was she trying to fight him off."

"Well, if her parents didn't try to keep her here, it would look as if they didn't love her, and if she went willingly it would look like she didn't love her family. The family did really hate to see her go. They know it will be a long time before they see her again, maybe forever, because her husband is from Balafili, the village of our worst enemies!"

It was that afternoon that Rosito explained to me that this was a normal procedure. He too, like nearly every young man of marriageable age, would soon be looking for a wife, but not from his own village. Like in our society, and almost all others, you can't marry a relative, and in the Yanowamo society everyone in your own village is considered family. Therefore, it is not proper to marry within your own village. This means, a young man must either find a girl in a friendly village, or capture one from an enemy village. So there is almost never what we would consider a romance.

The first choice, of course, is to find a future mate in a friendly village, so a young man, about 16 or 18 will go to one of the friendly villages. But he can visit almost any village safely because he will always be welcome as long as he comes alone or with one companion. If there is more than two they would be identified as raiders.

The only trouble is, there are probably no single girls his own age. Since many older men want a second wife, if there are any teen age girls who have not been spoken for by men from elsewhere the older men will have taken them, so the teen-age girls are already married. Therefore, the young man looks for a ten or twelve year old girl who appeals to him. If he learns that she is still single, he sticks around long enough to prove to her parents that he will be a loyal family member, and a good provider.

He and the girl are officially married at that time, but they cannot live together yet, so he probably spends most of his time in his own village. But he has a wife to support, so he must do a lot of hunting and picking fruit and he visits his wife's village frequently, bringing food for his wife and her parents.

Several years later, when the girl is fully grown, probably about 18, he wants to bring her home, but her parents love her and want her near. They can't just let her leave. So this results in a "girl-pulling." We would consider this the real marriage. It is a time of great excitement, observed by many friends, and a time when the family expresses their love for their daughter.

And it is a sad time for her parents. They will miss their daughter very much. And they will also miss the support her husband has been giving them. He has been feeding them for several years.

Every family needs a son and a daughter because, in different ways, both will support them in their old age.

But unlike our weddings, the Yanowamo man might not get the girl he has married and has supported for several years. The parents don't know when the husband is coming to get his bride, and when he surprises them, they just cant stand the thought of their daughter suddenly leaving, and maybe will not be back for months or maybe for years. So sometimes they really do fight the men off and won't let them take the girl. When the men come back two or three weeks later, the family is ready, and the girl-pulling is much easier. It's only a small showoff, not a real fight.

That's unless they have decided this man was not a good enough provider, or for other reasons is not a good husband for their daughter. In that case they will really fight him off a second time, and won't let him take the girl. Of course they wouldn't tell him earlier -- why would they cut off a good source of food and other gifts?

If the man comes back as many as three times and doesn't get the girl, he knows he no longer has a wife. Now, he has two choices: he can start over, and spend three or four more years earning another girl, but he probably doesn't want to do that. So, instead, he goes to steal a girl from an enemy village.

Of course he never shows himself. He hides in the jungle and watches the girls as they go out to gather wild roots or fruits, or go to their gardens. He choses the girl he wants and learns what routes she usually takes. Then he goes back and gets two or three friends to help him, and when the girl is out on the trail they capture her, and possibly one or two of her friends, and take them home.

That evening, I was telling Marg and Wally what Rosito had taught me, but then I said, "I keep wondering about the girls who get captured, are they usually satisfied? Do they always have to accept the man who has captured them for a husband?"

Just as I asked, some women came walking in the door. As usual, they had stopped by to visit with Marg, and to talk about the excitement of the day.

Marg translated my question and one of the women said in Yanowamo, "When I was captured I was glad to be married to a man who is brave, and who was willing to risk his life to get me. But if a girl is already married, and is living with a husband she really likes, either her husband will go on a return raid, and recapture her, or she will try to escape and go back home."

Another woman spoke up. "I was captured by a man who was cruel. Because of the long crooked route through the forest that the men took, getting me to their village, I didn't know the way home, but I was determined to escape.

"I waited a long time, till no one thought I was still going to try to get away, then I slipped out in the middle of the night, but I had no idea which way to go. I just wandered through the forest, and kept on wandering. I had never learned the technique of getting a fire started by rubbing sticks together, so I slept on the cold ground with no fire, and ate all the food I could find raw. Twice, I saw other people but they were strangers so I feared that I would be captured and didn't show myself. Twice the season of the flowers and the mosquitoes came before I finally found my way home."

One of the other women commented that almost no girl leaves her own family willingly. In her own village she has many privileges, she is esteemed, she is loved, she is cared for, and all her friends are there. She doesn't want to go to a strange village, an enemy village, where her family cannot visit her. She doesn't have friends there and her husband will not give her the attention that she gets from her own family.

I kept thinking about how long the men had to work to earn their wives, and how awful things could work out. Finally I asked, "Do you think there is any other society where a man has to work five or six years to earn his wife?"

Marg laughed. "Don't you remember the story in the Genesis chapter of the Bible? Jacob wants to marry Rachel, but her father, Laban, says that in their society the oldest girl must be married first, so Jacob would have to marry Rachel's sister, Leah. Then he would have to work for Laban for seven years to earn the right to mary Rachel, which he did."

The next day Marg took me to visit a man they had named Jacob because he had two wives. He said that after he had supported his wife's family for several years,and had brought her home, she was very lonesome for her best friend who was a little younger and was still single. He had gone back to that village and married that girl. It was only a couple of years till she was old enough for him to have a girl pulling and bring her home. They were a very happy family, with the two girls living together as his wives. Marg said if they asked for naba names she was going to call them Leah and Rachel.

It was only about a week later that a man in Niyiyobateri died, and left a widow. I was surprised that all the women were trying to talk their husbands into taking that woman as a second wife. They really wanted there to be two of them. That second wife would be their constant companion, and would share the work of cooking, gathering food, and raising a garden. But most of the men refused. It would mean twice as much hunting, to get meat, and twice as many children to protect and provide for.

Most of the women really did want their husbands to get a second wife, but there was one exception. While a group of us were walking around the shavano one evening we stopped to say "Hello" to a friend's parents, then went on by. A few minutes later, we heard a lot of noise and children running over to Marista's home. The rest went on, but Wally and I went back to see what had happened. Marista's mother and father were having a fight and he was beating on her with his hands. He got her down and was trying to drag her toward the fire. Then he stomped her on the tummy a couple of times. She got away, but she didn't run away. When he turned away from her, she grabbed a stick of fire wood and started to beat him with it.

After watching a little more, Wally said, "Let's go, before we get involved," so we left.

The next morning, when Marista came to the house, Marg asked her what had happened. Her husband had been to another village visiting for several days. When he returned, he brought another wife with him. It was the widow of a man who had been killed in a raid. He assumed his wife would be very pleased. But she objected.

All day, she had kept nagging him about it. Finally, in the evening, the3 had started to fight about it. She kept at him all evening.

Shortly before Marista came to the house the next morning, he agreed to take the woman back and give her up. He and the second wife had just left for her village.

I already knew about one of the other men in the village who had two wives. One is about his age and the second wife is younger, as they nearly always are. The first one he got when she was small, and raised her. But later he met the other girl and fell in love with her, so he married her, too.

Marg asked one of his friends if he liked his second wife better, and do the wives get along well. He said he didn't know. This husband had never talked about which wife he liked better because it wasn't important. When he got food he gave it to both of them. He divided it equally, and there was no jealousy among them. There was no reason to feel that he liked one better than the other. Neither wife was concerned whether he liked one better than the other. They both enjoyed their companionship and their opportunities to do things together.

Of course there are always exceptions to the usual ways of doing things. A young man they called Olaluca had wandered into Niyiyobateri one day and made himself at home. He may have just been wanting to get away from his home village, or other reasons, but he might also have been looking for a wife.

He was not very welcome at first because Olaluca, his home, was another group of "Guaica people," considered by these people to be even more warlike than the Yanowamo or the Yanomami.

Of course they could not ask a man his name, and he wouldn't answer if they did, so they just called him Olaluca, the name of his village. They couldn't ask him to leave because a man alone is always supposed to be welcome, and they assumed he would leave soon but he didn't. He liked it here, so he stayed. He turned out to be a good leader for hunting trips, was always cheerful, and always willing to help when he was needed. Therefore he soon became well liked by both the Indians and the missionaries.

There was one nearly grown up girl in the village whose parents had rejected anyone who had asked to marry her, so she was still single -- very unusual for a young lady her age!

She and Olaluca started paying a lot of attention to each other, and were soon doing many things together. They were obviously falling in love. Then they asked to marry each other. This was unheard of; a couple marrying because they were both in love and chose each other? Her parents strenuously objected because of his tribal origin, but the two kept insisting.

Then Olaluca was able to shoot a jaguar that had been on the prowl around this village for quite a while. This endeared him to the girl's parents, and every one else was thankful to him. Everyone agreed the marriage would be a good idea.

After their marriage it was noticeable that they were in love. When he was visiting with me or others, she would stand behind him with her arms around him -- something no other woman would do.

Others commented that they were obviously in love, and had actually chosen each other because of that, instead of her parents making the choice. When I commented that I hoped others would learn from their example, everyone laughed at me. It couldn't happen twice!

13

THERE COULD BE WAR

Three of our friends dropped in one evening for a visit. They said they thought they ought to let us know that some of the men of the village might be going on a raid, and that could endanger our lives, if there was a return raid. Wally asked why in the world would they be going on a raid? That was completely against all the principles he had been teaching them.

They said that they realized that, and that's why they thought they should warn us. They reminded us of a woman who had died a few days earlier. She had not been sick long, and after she died Wally had not identified a cause of her death. They said that nearly everyone in the village believed that she must have been killed by witchcraft. And since the Balafili were our worst enemies, they must have been the ones who did it. They said that several of the men were seriously talking of raiding Balafili.

Wally asked who those men were. They tried to say they didn't know, but after much discussion, it turned out that one of them was our good friend Jose, but since Jose knew the Jank's objection to killing, he had asked everyone to keep it a secret from us.

I asked a lot of questions that led to a discussion of the way the villages were continually getting into war.

It was part of a never-ending cycle. Someone is killed, or a death is blamed on someone from another village, and that death must be revenged. Then that village must go and revenge that death. There is no way to end the cycle.

As I asked questions and as we talked, some of the people admitted that these wars in which the Niyiyobateri people had always been involved, were really a detriment to the tribe. Hulacobateri, the neighboring village which has been at peace for a long time has very large gardens. And they have plenty of food for their people. They are quite well off that way. But the people here in Niyiyobateri, who are nearly always at war have only about half as many canugos (gardens), although the village is three times as large. Therefore, they have a shortage of food and even when food is available in their gardens they may be afraid to go out and work in their canugos for fear they will be ambushed on the way.

The most common way of attack is for the raiders to ambush the people on the way to the canugo, because this is the one place the enemies can count on finding people. Therefore, when the people are expecting a raid they do not dare go to their canugos at all.

Wally said they could handle this situation by a whole group going to the canugo together and having guards from several families go with the women, and then have that family help guard others when they went. Then there would always be a large group going together, and raiders would not dare attack. But this is not the usual Yanowamo way. Instead, each family prefers to work only in their own canugo, so when raiders come they are in danger of being killed.

Usually the raiders hide beside the trail, in a spot where they can ambush those who come down the trail. If the raiders think the group looks prepared to fight, they may shoot the first person in line, then take off, and only one person is killed. And the raiders get away because those who are attacked will usually turn and run back the direction they came from.

But a more common practice is to wait until nearly all the people have passed, then they shoot the last one in line. If the one shot is still able to scream, the first thing that happens is that all the people will come dashing back the way they came from and run right across in front of the raiders who can then easily shoot more of them as they come running by.

Usually, the best way of escape would be to run in the direction they were already going. But when a person is terribly frightened he can't take time to think about that.

Of course, as soon as a person is killed, his friends and relatives have to revenge his death. So they head out for a return raid on the village they are pretty sure is the one that raided them.

They usually look for a certain person in the village, the one they think has raided them, and try to kill that person that they know is their enemy. If they know where those particular individuals have their gardens, they can hide along the trails to those gardens. But if they can't get that person, they can shoot any person from that village and this will revenge the death.

Then, of course, that village comes back to revenge this one. And so it continues.

Wally tried his best to discourage this possible raid, saying it would just result in more killing and more danger for all of us. Some of the men reacted strongly, resenting his interference, saying that the Janks should not try to stop them from fighting back. Others were bitter, saying that if Wally was really a friend he would stop objecting and use his gun to help them.

But after much talk about the harm of continuing the war, and Wally's talking about Jesus statement that "You should love your neighbor as yourself," the men who and been meeting with Wally, and listening to his teachings all agreed that a retaliation raid would appose that principle,and would be no help in the long run.

We hoped that all of them had given up the idea of a raid, until Jose and three of his friends took off "on an overnight hunting trip." When they had been gone three nights, we suspected they were doing more than hunt for game. Their wives were obviously becoming tense and jittery.

Wally took one of the children aside and asked if the men were on a raid. The girl gave him a frightened look and nodded. But then she changed her mind and said they were just on a long hunting trip.

Finally the hunters returned. Silently, they all walked down the airstrip, in the gate of the shavano, and to their houses. As they passed, I got a good look at one of them. His face and his chest were painted black. I then had no doubt about the purpose of their "hunting trip."

I followed them into the shavano. I asked a woman if the men had shot someone. She shouted angrily, "I told you, they just went hunting.

I said, "But hunters come back loaded with meat. Hunters don't paint their faces black. People don't act frightened when they return."

Finally she calmed down and said, "They might have shot some of Wally's friends."

"Wally's friends?"

"Well, they must be his friends. He told us not to shoot them. And he wouldn't help us fight them."

All the people gathered in small groups, talking in whispers. Wally moved from one group to another, asking questions, but as he approached each group they suddenly quit talking. They assured him that they certainly wouldn't kill anyone.

One of the men admitted that they had been on a raid, but assured him that they had killed no one.

He asked Jose what had happened, but Jose insisted that he was not one of the raiders.

The next day one of the women came in alone and told Marg that she was worried about us and thought we should be moving inside the shavano where we would have some protection because there was sure to be a return attack because when they raided the enemy village, Jose had killed two men, and if the enemy village knew who the raiders were, there was sure to be an attack.

We, of course, were very concerned, but there was nothing we could do but wait.

14
PEACEFUL LEADER

I looked up as a man and two women who I had not seen before walked into the visitor's room of the Jank's home. Both Marg and Wally seemed overjoyed to see this man.

Four men from the shavano came pushing through the door a minute later. They had seen him arrive, and they also gave him a hearty greeting.

There was nothing noticeably different about this man, except for his jaguar-fur headband, and the eagle feathers in his arm bands. But they were all so happy to see him that I was anxious to get acquainted with him.

When they introduced me to him, they called him "Hekura ." I quickly learned that he was the leader of Hill Top Village, the village on the mountain top that Peter, the pilot, and I had seen and wondered about.

He was the brave man Marg had told me about. The one who had been in the area the day they had arrived, and had been very curious when he saw the plane land. He had come to see what it was, and his action had convinced the local men that it was safe for them to do the same.

The planes that had come since that first one, and brought all the supplies for the Janks and the Hadleys, had not flown over his village so Hekura had not known about them when they came. But when Peter brought me, he flew over Hill Top Village. When Hekura saw our plane he wondered about it and decided to come and see if it had brought more people.

I was surprised that he had a name everyone could say aloud, but Wally explained that it was not actually his name. The word "Hekura" meant "Shaman, and leader of his people." It was the name of his position, so Wally and Marg had made that their nickname for him, and the local people had done the same.

The two women who had come with him set their burden baskets on the floor and uncovered them so we could see that the baskets were completely filled with papayas. On an earlier trip Hekura had brought them a ball of string the Janks had given to him, so they asked if we had any string to trade. The Janks shook their heads sadly. They loved papayas, which did not grow near Niyiyobateri, but they had used all their string to pay those who were helping them build their house.

I was glad the folks in Puerto Ayacucho had told me the three things I should take were machetes, matches, and string. I went in and got two of the balls of string and handed one to each of the ladies. They both looked very happy as they dumped all their papayas out, then they headed out to the shavano.

I was amazed that any woman would carry a heavy load over forty or fifty miles of mountain trails for one ball of string then I remembered the lady who had spent a year making enough string for her hammock and understood.

I was also surprised that this one man and two women would walk alone that far, after all I had been hearing about enemies, especially now, when we were hearing many reports of raiders near by.

Then Wally explained to me what he had learned when Hekura was here before: our village, Niyiyobateri, was at war with five other villages, and the men here did not dare go over a mountain pass in any direction, into someone else's territory, or they would be killed, but Hekura's village was at peace with all the villages.

Apparently Hekura was such a good leader that his people all followed his leadership, and never did anything that would make additional enemies. Besides having Hekura's leadership, Hill Top Village was considered a powerful village, so all the other villages knew that if they harmed Hekura they would face serious consequences.

"I guess that makes him a very powerful chief," I said.

"There are no chiefs," Wally said. "I think Yanowamo land is the only place in the world where no man has authority over anyone else, 'except a man over his wife,' they will tell you. But, just like everywhere else, that doesn't always apply.

"If a man is a good leader, others will follow, but only if they want to. When a man wants to organize a hunting party, or a raiding party, he'll pick the men he wants. If those men think he's a good enough leader, and can be successful, they'll join him. Those who don't want to go, will stay at home. Or if people are in the middle of a project, and they don't like what's happening, they simply walk off. No one has the authority to tell anyone what they should do.

"But Hekura is such a good leader that his people take his advise, and they follow because they want to, not because they have to."

Hekura and I quickly became good friends. That afternoon, as we were visiting, we went into the back room and I showed him the other trade goods I had brought. I also showed him my arrows. I had brought a half dozen of my good arrows that I used for hunting in Montana, thinking that I could shoot much more accurately with them than with the seven-foot arrows I had seen the Yanomami use. I had three with just pointed steel tips, which we called "bird arrows" and three with the wider spreading razor sharp steel tips for big game.

Hekura suggested we take them out back of the house and try them out. After practicing a while with both his and my kind of arrows, I decided since I was using the six-foot-long bows I could shoot almost as accurately with the very long arrows as I could my short ones. I told him I thought I ought to just use the long ones, since I was trying to fit into the local culture in every way I could. He agreed with me.

Three of the men from the village saw us practicing and came out to watch us. They really liked my arrows and said they would gladly trade anything they owned for those three razor-sharp ones. They didn't want to use them as they were. They would cut them in two and insert the front part as the tip of their long arrows, just like they did the hardwood points that they carved themselves.

When the men said that my arrow tips would make great war arrows, I realized that if someone from another village was shot with one of those arrows, there would be no doubt in the minds of the people of his village as to whose arrow it was. Their revenge would be directed toward me, or Wally, as individuals.

When I said that, Hekura agreed with me. We took those arrows in the house, wrapped them up, and hid them away securely, where we were sure no one could see them until I took them back to Montana with me.

15
SHOULD WE HIDE?

It was later in the afternoon of that same day that a commotion in front of the house drew my attention. Three men came dashing in to warn us that two groups of men had been spotted out in the forest. Neither of the groups had come out into the open so they must be raiders.

One of the men from our village had just returned from Balafili, where he had gone to visit his wife's family. He could do this safely because he went alone and was considered related to them. While there, he had heard them talking of a return raid.

Now the people here had actually seen these two groups of men who they assumed were raiders. And there were rumors that two other villages were joining forces with the Balafili to come here on a raid

Wally asked this man if the people of the Balifili village knew about them, the missionaries. He hesitated to answer, but Wally insisted. "If they knew, then what did they say?"

"They said you should be killed because you will try to protect us with your rifle."

These men suggested that we all take our hammocks and move down into the shavano for our own safety, but Wally said, "No. We are trying to let everyone know that we are friends of everyone. We do not take sides. Besides, if we were out of our house, anyone could come in and steal everything we have. We'll just trust in the Lord."

After some more discussion, the men decided that if we had that much faith in our God, there was nothing they could do about it. They'd just hope we were right.

It was the next morning that Rosito came in and showed us the remains of an ashoa. The ashoa was a big fruit about three inches across, and nearly a foot long, but it had the consistency of a raspberry, with no skin over it. He said the big fruit stayed together till it ripened on the tree, but if you picked it and tried to carry it, it just fell apart. All you got home with was pieces like he was showing to us. So when the ashoas were ripe those who wanted to eat them went and camped under the trees and ate nothing but ashoa for several days.

"You do this every year?" I asked. "Every time the ashoa ripen?"

"Oh yes, and several times in between. We have to go much farther other times, to go hunting. That's why we move the whole village every few years. When we first came here, there was was lots of wild life, plenty of meat. But the longer we stay, the less game there is. But we have to have meat. We can't live without it. So we make a couple of long trips to get lots of game and bring back a lot of dried meat. There are some villages that don't make big gardens, and they keep traveling, moving real often. They have several shavanos, but they're not good ones like ours. Ours is the biggest shavano, so sometimes, when we are hunting, only part of us go."

"How long are you usually gone when you go hunting? How many days?"

"Sometimes this many." He held up one hand, five fingers. "Sometimes this many." Held up both hands three times.

Wally looked a little surprised, and said, "Thirty days? A month ?"

Rosito said that this time they were only going to pick ashoa and the entire village was going, They would just be gone as long as the ashoa berries lasted. They thought all of us should go with them. To me, it sounded like fun, but Wally and Marg didn't think they should go and leave their home and possessions.

As the men talked about leaving, they gave Marg and Wally a lot of advice.

"Don't hang your clothes on the line. The raiders will steal them. Don't go to the the river for water, you'll get shot. If you see any men with black on their faces, they are raiders. Shoot them with your gun, because if you don't, they'll shoot you with their bows and arrows, then they will take your wife and run away with her. But don't be afraid if you stay inside your home. All the Guaicas usually have someone in particular they are planning to kill. If they can't get him, they'll try for someone from his village. They will know you are not from our village, not one of us. It's us they will want to kill. But hang on to your clothes and your things. They'll steal everything they can get their hands on."

Marg said their statements about who the raiders might be trying to kill were some relief, but she thought all those warnings about their stealing things might be a way of getting raiders blamed if they, themselves, stole something.

She told me about the time her swimming suit disappeared and the people all blamed it on visitors who had been there the day before. But then Wally walked into the shavano when he wasn't expected, and one of the men was dancing around, showing off in that swim suit.

Hekura said if the people were going to go and pick ashoa he'd like to go along, and he'd like for me to go too. He told Wally he would protect me, if I'd go with him.

Wally and Marg hesitantly approved the idea as long as I'd be with Hekura

I had brought a pocket size tape recorder with me when I came here, and I had been using it to tape some notes, records of my experiences here. I also taped some conversation to help me improve my language skills. So I stuck my little pocket tape recorder into my backpack to take with me, along with my my hammock and rain jacket.

Wally came in with a big grin, almost laughing, and spoke quietly to me so no one else would hear, "I don't think their main purpose in going out there is to eat ashoa."

"Why do you say that?"

"You know that no man can ever show fear. If he does, they have no respect for him. That's why they respect you and consider you one of them, because unlike other Nabas, you do every thing they do without showing any fear. Anyway, you can be sure that they would never say they were leaving the village because of the threat of an attack by raiders. No man would even consider saying that, because it would look like he was a coward. But isn't this a really convenient time to find that the ashoa are ripe!"

The whole village took off, walking in single file across the savanna and into the hills. There actually were three groups. At the head of each group were six or seven men, then a dozen or more women, with their children, followed by another group of men.

I noticed that four men were carrying bundles of something and at times were quite a ways behind. I asked Hekura what they were doing. He said that wherever there was dust or mud, so we left tracks, those men were scattering old dry leaves on the trail. "If you were back there, looking for tracks, you would find no evidence that we had come on this route."

The whole village took off, walking in single file across the savanna and into the hills.

Part of our route was through snake infested swamps to avoid main trails.

We walked all day, but it was a leisurely day. The Yanowamo were never in a hurry. There was always time for a lot of talk and laughter along the way.

I noticed that four men were carrying bundles of something and at times were quite a ways behind. I asked Hekura what they were doing. He said that wherever there was dust or mud, so we left tracks, those men were scattering old dry leaves on the trail. "If you were back there, looking for tracks, you would find no evidence that we had come on this route."

We crossed the river on a fallen log and from there on our route was mostly between the river and the mountain side, so it was winding trail. The men said it would have been closer if we had stayed on the savannah side of the river, but there was too much cut-grass there, and their bare legs and bare feet would have gotten all cut up.

Hekura and I were walking with the leaders when the trail wound along the mountain side for a ways. It gave us a great view of the savanna, the mountains on the other side, and the river below. As we came around a bend, Enrique stopped suddenly and pointed down. A jaguar was creeping along the other side of the river, as if ready to attack something. Suddenly it leaped into the water. I couldn't see what it dragged out into the brush on our side of the river.

I was surprised that none of the men went after the jaguar, but at the moment they were more concerned about the safety of their children. They made sure they were all in between the adults, and no one was scattered out.

Soon after that we were again down near the river where the trail wound through the flat swampy areas. It took several arrows for the men to kill a boa constrictor that crossed the trail.

A higher, more direct route would have been much easier, but the people took this route through the snake infested swamps to avoid the main trail where others might travel. I was glad they did.

It was late in the afternoon when we came to two trees with the fruit they called ashoa. It looked like hugh raspberries, the size of cantaloups without any skin over them, so when we picked them the juice just dripped from them.

Men climbed up two of the trees and started chopping off the branches that were too weak to climb out onto to get the fruit, so that we could pick that fruit too. When they hit the limbs the ashoas were on, the juice from them came raining down on us. As they picked them they got that bright red juice all over their hands and arms. I jumped out from under the tree real fast, wondering if all those splotches of red paint would wash out of my shirt. No one else cared how much dripped on them. They liked to paint themselves red, why not let the fruit do it?

I would have preferred to be without my shirt, or even my pants, but I brought them along because without them the gnats and mosquitoes would have driven me crazy, and I would have gotten badly sunburned.

They had laughed at my shirt when I first arrived, but since then, three of the men had actually traded with Wally for shirts to wear on the days when the gnats were the worst.

Those huge berries were so soft and drippy we couldn't carry them with us so we all ate till we were full. The fruit was delicious. It had little black seeds that were also edible but they said to fill up on fruit but save the seeds. They could take the seeds along and they would have them available any time in the future when they were hungry. I did eat a few and found that they were good, too.

About an hour later we came to another grove of ashoa trees. and some palm trees that we could camp under. They told me that when they traveled they normally built a tapiri (a temporary shelter) every night, but since it didn't look like it would rain tonight, they wouldn't build any here. If they did, and their enemies came through here in the near future, the tapiri would tell those enemies that we had come this way, and they would keep looking for us.

We were already full of ashoa, so we just hung up our hammocks and laid down. I kept my eyes open long enough to enjoy the birds, but fell asleep when the gaily colored parrots and toucans were replaced by the bats.

The next morning, we traveled faster because we were now far enough into the wilderness so we didn't need to worry about staying out of sight, or hiding our tracks.

It was only a little after noon that we found the large grove of ashoa trees that was our destination. These trees were scattered and there were enough other trees for everyone to hang their hammocks.

Everyone scattered and went into the surrounding forest. In a short time each family had gathered enough big branches and large leaves to build a tapiri.

For each of those shelters, they got three poles and put the lower ends in a triangle pattern and leaned the poles toward each other and tied the upper tips together. Then next, with strips of bark from nearby trees, they tied other pieces of wood on, and covered one side with big palm leaves for shelter, but left the other sides open.

Hekura and I built our tapiri right next to Rosito's family's. Rosito's mother came over and made sure we had enough palm leaves to shelter us

Just as in the shavano, each family had a spot for a fire and enough space to hang three hammocks around it so they could keep warm during the night.

At each spot where they would build their fire, they placed some dry leaves and little sticks, then they placed four long sticks with the tips in the fire, so about three times each night, when the fire died down, they could just push the sticks in toward the center, then blow on the coals to get a flame, then go back to sleep. Rosito's mother helped set up the fire place for Hekura and me and I used my matches to start both their fire and ours.

I intended to offer to start other fires with my matches, but most of the families already had their fires going. Some of them had actually carried firebrands all that distance. They had one kind of wood that if you lit one end of the stick you didn't have to have flame to keep it burning. The ember on the end would continue to smolder as you carried it, and you could put dry leaves on it, blow, and get a flame.

I stopped to watch one man who was in the middle of starting his own fire by spinning a fire stick he had brought with him against a notch in a larger stick with leaves around it. He didn't use his bow to spin it like the Cheyenne had taught me to do. He just spun it between his two hands for more than five minutes before he got a flame. I'd have had blisters by that time. I wondered whether he enjoyed starting a fire that way, or just liked to prove his independence.

About three times during the night, we had to wake up and lean out of out hammocks and blow on the embers of the fire, then push the long sticks in, so they would continue to burn and keep us warm.

In the middle of the night, I was leaning out of my hammock blowing on the coals, trying to get the fire going again, and I fell out of my hammock. I didn't know anyone saw me do that till the next day when Rosito's mother came to me and handed me a fan that she had woven for me so I could blow on my fire more easily.

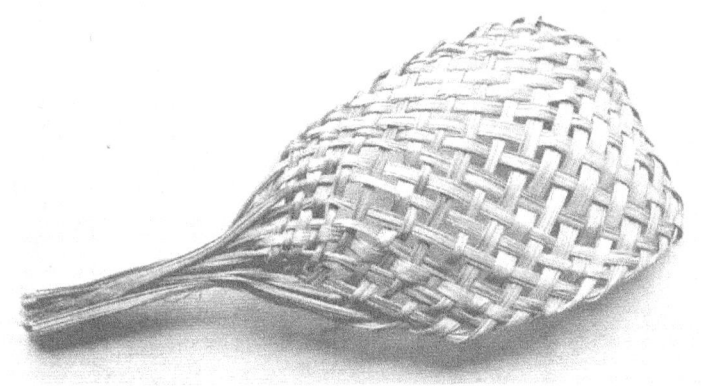

16
LIFE IN CAMP

For the next few days we mostly sat around talking, joking, and eating ashoa. Some of the women did go out and dig some roots and found some grubs and caterpillars to add to our ashoa diet. Each night the children were told they could not play or do anything noisy because if there were raiders nearby it would tell them where we were.

After a day or two everyone seemed to feel much more sure that the raiders would not find them here, so they did not stick as close to camp.

Although the original intention was that most of our food for our days in camp would be the ashoa fruit, there was no reason for not making use of our time gathering other available foods. The whole village had been very short of food the last few weeks because of the danger of going into the forest, but out here they felt there was less danger from raiders so they might as well gather all the available food and really fill their stomachs, and even take some back to the shavano.

Scar Shoulder went out and killed a basho monkey then found her baby. He carefully carried it back to camp. His wife tenderly cuddled it, then put it in the hammock with her own baby, saying, "Our baby can spare a little of my milk for a moon or two, and this will grow into a great playmate for our girl. Their other girl, who looked about four years old, seemed overjoyed.

Scar Shoulder dressed out the insides of the monkey he had killed, but he didn't skin it. His wife put it on a spit and put it over her fire so the flames would burn the hair off as it roasted, then she put it in a big earthenware pot and boiled it, with the skin still on.

They added some roots the women dug, called uhina that looked a lot like potatoes, and they drank the broth before they ate. We each cut off a chunk of meat, pulled the skin and hair off, then ate the meat and roots, along with some fruit from the buariti palm.

Hekura and Rosito and I were wandering around a little ways from camp when Hekura pointed to a big hole in the ground. He seemed real excited. Rosito said some of the men had brought some tools along and took off for camp.

With Hekura's motions and descriptions I finally understood that this was an armadillo's hole. He said the hole should go down about three feet then run parallel to the surface, and there would usually be two other entrance, so that if anyone or anything tried to dig it out, the armadillo could get out and get away. We did find the two other entrances. Both were well hidden in the brush.

Rosito was soon back with two digging sticks and a small spade that someone had gotten in trade from the Hadleys, and since it was new, they had brought it along, so they could try it out. We took turns digging with it.

I was getting thirsty from all that work digging, but of course no one had a canteen. I asked, "How far is it to a stream where I can get a drink?"

Hekura said, "There are plenty of water vines. I'll get one. He stepped into the jungle and in less than a minute he was back with a piece of vine about three feet long. He motioned for me put my lips to the end of it and suck. I did and it was just like drinking a glass of water with a straw. That three foot piece of vine gave me all the water I could drink.

I looked the vine over and said, "I'll have to remember this."

Hekura said, "Yes, but be sure you get the right vine. There are two other similar ones that also contain water, but that water is poison." I was soon hard at work digging while the other two were closely

watching the other holes, when two armadillos tried to escape and Rosito and Hekura whacked both of them with their digging sticks. We had to hit them on their heads because of the bony coat of
armor that takes the place of fur on their backs. We proudly took them back to camp to share with four other families for that night's dinner. Armadillo meat is particularly prized by the Indians.

The women wrapped the heart and liver in leaves to cook them. They roasted the body on the fire without skinning it.

Along with the armadillo and the ashoa we had some other fruits the women had gathered. One of them was a bristling red berry which was full of bright red seeds. It not only tasted good, but they told me it was what the women used to make the bright red dye with which they dyed their little red fringed skirts, and they strung the seeds to make their white necklaces.

Others had brought back a crocodile some shrimp and several birds. I was surprised to see the little knives with which they were cutting up the birds. They told me the knives had been made from parts of a turtle shell.

It was a great feast and I enjoyed trying all those foods, and also the *mana* which were the larva of butterflies, which they wrapped in leaves and roasted. The only trouble was that some of the food had been cooked with the mud and blood still on it, and sometimes when the cooks were ready to cook a meal, there was still grease from the last meal on their hands.

17

HUNTING TAPIR

I thought this was the day we were heading back to the Niyiyobateri shavano, but when I woke up, Rosito was shouting, "Come on! get out of those hammocks and grab your bows. We're hunting tapir today and the guys are ready to go!" He swung his arm and spun around to point in the opposite direction from home.

"You know where to find tapir?"

"Yes. One of the men saw one last night, just before dark. It should still be near there. We can't miss this chance. One tapir could feed the whole village! We could have a feast tonight."

Both Hekura and I grabbed our bows and arrows and followed him to where the men were gathering at the edge of the camp.

As we started out across the savannah I wondered why such a large group would hunt together. One or two, or a small group can go more quietly and will see more game. But then, a half hour later, we all sat down and Enrique explained his the plans. He pointed out the direction and described the location where the tapir had been seen. Then he said, "We will go in groups of one or two and make a huge circle around that spot. Then, at noon, when the sun is straight up we'll all start toward that spot. If the tapir sees one of us and runs, and we

.
    don't get a shot at it, it will be running toward someone else who should be able to shoot it. And some of us might get other game on

the way. If you get a shot at the tapir, don't use your poison arrow. That takes too long to kill it and it could get away and never be found. If you use your wide pointed hunting arrows, or even throw your machete, there will be much blood and we can follow the trail.

I took off with Hekura and Rosito. As we walked, I told them about a time when I was six years old. The coyotes, which previously had controlled the population of rabbits, had mostly been killed off. Therefore, the jackrabbits were getting so thick that they were eating up all the crops. So all the homesteaders got together, like we did today, and we circled around a space one mile across, and all of us started toward the center. When any rabbits tried to run between us, the men shot them with their shotguns or sling shots. When we got to the center the rabbits were practically piled up, but we were too close together for the men to shoot their guns, so we little kids got to go in and kill the last of the rabbits with sticks. We did that same kind of hunt three different times.

Rosito said, "I hope it works that well for us."

The three of us came to a creek that led toward the assigned meeting place.

We paused when we heard a grunting sound. Rosito stepped back and whispered to me, "Wild boar."

We moved slowly in that direction, going quietly and carefully, but then we heard the roar of the stampeding herd. We realized they had been downwind from us. Rosito said, "They are much more afraid of our scent than they are of us if they see us."

Hekura pointed out some spots along the banks of the creek where he could see that a tapir had come down and eaten dirt along the river to get salt or some other kind of mineral. As we followed the shore we saw several places where something had obviously slid down the bank into the water. Rosito said tapirs like to sit on a high bank and slide down into the water as if they are on a toboggan.

Hekura told me that if I saw a tapir I should be sure to shoot it right behind the ear. That was the only place an arrow could pierce it's skull, and the only way we could do more than just wound it.

When we came to a high waterfall, we stopped to take a quick quick dip in the pool below the falls.

We climbed up past the falls and again followed the stream. Just before noon we found some caterpillars, and stopped to eat a few for our lunch.

I was surprised when we came to a spot where the men had built a platform up in the trees above a trail, so they could sit and watch for the game to come by under them. I had hunted deer with a man ins

Massachusetts who had such a platform, but I sure didn't expect to see one down here in the rain forest.

When I pointed to a bird they called an "ala" in a tree, I expected Rosito to shoot it but both he and Hekura told me it was my game. I should shoot it. I was glad, because it gave me a chance to prove to myself that I could actually get some game with my longbow.

When we got to the spot where the tapir was supposed to have been, we still had not seen a tapir, so we headed back to camp. The only meat we had to contribute to the feast we were supposed to have that night was my ala.

The other groups were getting back about the same time. One group had a big white stork, but that was all.

However, we didn't need to worry about having enough food for a feast. The children had never left the camp area, but they had enough meat for everyone. They had been catching frogs, and I mean big frogs. Skinning one was like skinning a cotton tail rabbit.

We had all the meat we could eat that night, but it was the children who furnished most of it.

18
BATS AND LEGENDS

That night after dark, we could hear birds singing. It was a beautiful song and my friends told me that kind of bird sang only at night. They loved to hear it because it was beautiful and relaxing. I agreed with them. They said it also made them feel secure, because if those birds detected movement near them they would stop singing.

Then we heard another kind of song, and I started to say, "Well, there are two kinds of birds that sing at night!" But then I saw the shocked look on my friend's faces. When that bird sang, they were obviously shocked and fearful. I wondered why that birds song seemed frightening to them. Then Rosito said, "That's not a bird. It's a *teseoruma*, a spirit, something our enemies try to send to us, to harm us." I laid in my hammock wondering if there could actually be a kind of bird they had never seen! That seemed quite possible because if they heard the bird and believed that was an evil spirit that would harm them, they certainly wouldn't go out there looking for it to see if it could actually be a bird.

After the bird songs ended, and we relaxed in our hammocks the elders started telling some of the old legends of the tribe. It reminded me of a time when I was in a camp in Montana with some of the Cheyenne elders and they, too, were telling their legends.

I couldn't tell at the time how similar the legends were, as I was having difficulty translating. So I turned on my little pocket tape recorder. That would let me get some help in translating these legends later.

After about the third legend, I asked the question I have asked in many places around the world and usually get a "yes" answer. I said, "Do you know the story of the great flood?"

"Of course we do," one of the story tellers said. There was a long pause for thought before he began: "When a girl first reaches puberty and is ready to take her place as a woman in the village, a small shelter is built for her, just large enough for her hammock. It is covered on all sides with palm leaves so that no one can see in. For three days she must stay in that shelter, and cannot see out, and she is not allowed to speak to anyone, neither can anyone speak to her. Her food is handed to her through the leaves, in the form of soup in a gourd container.

"From that time on, she must wear a skirt, so during the three days she is confined in that hut, her mother must make that skirt, and the other things she needs, the very best costume she can make. So her mother gathers cotton, twists it into strings, weaves it into a fringe skirt, and gathers red berries from which she makes a dye to color it red. Then she decorates reeds for her daughter's ears and strings seeds for a beaded necklace. She also makes new reed plugs for the girl's nose and her lips. When the girl comes from her seclusion, she is beautiful in her red fringe skirt, feathered ear plugs, and her red and white beads. Her body and face are painted with red and black designs, and her black hair is decorated with tufts of white down from the stork.

"But there once was a Yanowamo mother who was *waika*. She was lazy and thought only of herself.

"She would not build the palm leaf house for her daughter, so the daughter had to build it for herself. While the girl was in the hut, her mother did not make a beautiful new costume for her. She laid around, waiting for the three days to be over, so the girl could again gather their food and do all the mother's work for her. The only thing this mother did for her daughter was to take one small bowl of soup to her each day. Since the girl was not allowed to speak during those three days, she could not complain.

"The Chief Spirit saw that the girl was hungry and that her mother was not making the proper preparations to welcome her back to village life. On the last day of her confinement, he made it rain so hard that the rain washed the leaves from the girl's shelter. Still the mother was not concerned. She thought only of her own comfort, while the girl shivered through the rest of the day and night in the rain.

"All day and all night the men of the village sang the rain chant and danced the rain dance, but they could not make that heavy rain go away. It continued day after day. 'Rain, why are you so mean to me,' they chanted. 'Rain why don't you go away? Rain, why are you so obstinate?' The thud of their heels pounding the ground in the rain dance echoed through the village, but still it continued to rain.

"First, the trails were covered with deep water so the people could not get to their gardens to gather bananas. Then the gardens were under water and finally the village itself.

"Before the water covered the last ridge leading from the village, the people gathered the food they had left and began climbing into the mountains. Higher and higher they climbed as the water rose, until finally they were gathered on the top of the highest peak. All the rest of the world was covered with water. At the top of the mountain was a high cliff. The people stood at the top looking down into the water and out across the water which covered the land they had known, and still the rain continued.

"The selfish mother looked at her daughter and her friends who were now without food and were about to be drowned by the rising tide. 'It is not right,' she said, 'that all these should suffer because of me. Perhaps if I were gone the Chief Spirit would not punish them anymore for my selfishness. Perhaps it is not too late for me to do something for my daughter. I am no longer important, but somehow I must save my daughter and my people.' As she said this, she leaped over the cliff into the waters below.

"The Chief Spirit saw that at last she was more concerned for others than for herself, as everyone should be. As her body floated away, across the waves, the rain stopped, and the waters began to recede."

When I woke up the next morning I laid in my hammock, thinking about that flood legend, and how similar the reason for the flood was to the legends of the flood throughout the world.

. Then I happened to look down at my feet and saw blood trickling down from my toes onto my foot. I sat up and looked carefully at my foot. I could see two tiny puncture wounds, but I could feel no pain. Hekura looked over there and saw me staring at my feet, and said, "Looks like the bats have been here."

"Bats!? Would that be vampire bats?" I had heard stories of them but thought they were just fiction.

Of course Hekura didn't know that name, but a little discussion verified that that's what had bit me.

"You haven't been bitten before?"

"No. Maybe that's because the Janks have mosquito nets, and they hung one over my hammock. Maybe their use of the nets is partly because of the bats, not just the mosquitoes."

Hekura told me the bats come around at night and suck out some of your blood, but not enough to do you any harm. He said I shouldn't worry about them.

Rosito's mother heard us talking, and came over and handed me a piece of canvas about two feet square, obviously something they had gotten from the Janks. She said. "Put that over your feet when you sleep."

I wondered if she had brought it along to protect her own family, but I didn't ask. I guess I really didn't want to know.

Later, after we got back home, Wally told me, "Those bats might not be as harmless as Hekura thought because they can carry some kind of disease."

"But how could a bat bite me and I didn't even feel it?" I asked.

Wally explained that too. He said that biologists think the bats have something in their saliva that dulls the pain, and also thins the blood so it will come out of that tiny hole, and they can lap it up."

A day later, when we all packed up to go home, I was sorry to have to bid Hekura goodbye. He said it was time for him to get back to his Hilltop Village, and it was in the opposite direction.

I asked about the two women who had come with him, and brought all the papayas. "Won't they be waiting to go back with you?"

"Oh, no. They just came to trade for string. They were going back the next day, regardless of when I went back. They know I always like to be free to travel."

"Like my wife," I said. "I think sometimes she wonders why I feel compelled to make my way to all these out of the way places."

"Mine too!"

When we finally got back to the shavano, the Janks and the Hadleys were anxiously waiting. Wally and Marg told me they had expected the people to come back thin and maybe needing medical attention. But they were glad to see that, instead, most of their friends looked like they were in better condition than when they left.

19

RAIDERS

When we returned from our trip where we had gone to eat ashoa we found plenty of evidence that we had actually achieved our real purpose, avoiding a conflict with raiders. Three families found that things were missing from their homes. But their only real valuables were their hammocks and their bows and arrows, and they had taken those things along to the camp.

The men also found two campsites nearby where the raiders had camped. Apparently they had decided it was best not to attack the Janks in their home, and of course they did not show themselves, so the Janks had been unaware that they had actually gotten into the village.

Obviously we had avoided a war, at least temporarily, but what reason could we find to think those raiders or others would not be back? The peace we had gained was probably not a lasting peace.

It was just a couple of days before visitors from a friendly village arrived. That village had friends in Balafili, our most feared enemy villages, and those friends had told them that the Balafili were still planing a big raid on ours in reprisal for the killing of two of their men.

Although Jose had denied it at the time, we knew that he had led the raid on Balafili shortly before we went to pick ashoa. So one afternoon when Jose walked in and leaned over the partition that separated the guest room from the kitchen and began talking and laughing with Wally, Wally remarked that if the raiders did come again, Jose would be the one most in danger, because they would want to kill the person who who conducted the raid on their village.

Jose laughed and laughed at that statement. He reminded Wally that he was rarely sick, so no one could kill him with witchcraft. He was a powerful fighter, with a strong, muscular body, and many battle scars. No enemy was powerful enough to kill anyone like him. After a short visit he went on his way, still laughing at our concern.

However, the women were still concerned about the danger for all of them, and all of us. They talked about it frequently. They kept telling Marg, "Since there are raiders all around, don't dare to even go to the stream for water by yourself. If you have to leave your house, keep out in the open where you can see anyone coming near."

Since no man can show fear, the men all claimed that they were not at all frightened, but we were able to see that they were not going hunting. The gardens were unattended, and when the women finally had to go to the gardens for roots and bananas to keep from starving, they went in groups, with more men than women.

When I walked through the Savannah I saw new long green arrows leaning against the railings across the front of the homes. And the men were making more of the long very sharp bone arrowheads they used for war.

Then two teenagers who had gone just a short way into the woods to gather firewood came back screaming that they had been shot, one in the leg and the other in his shoulder. They had dragged one of the arrows with them thinking their fathers could look at the arrows and identify the village it came from. Fortunately neither of their wounds was serious, but before bandaging them, Wally and Marg cleaned them thoroughly in case they had been made with a poison arrow.

Jose was one of the loudest in his threats against the raiders. He jumped and shouted, and asked that others join him in going out to search for the raiders, and kill them or drive them away before others from our village would be killed or injured. There was no calming him.

All that night the yelling and chanting from the village made sleep difficult.

The next morning, when the men asked Wally if he would use his gun to defend them in the case that the raiders attacked the village, Wally said, "That gun is strictly to get food. We did not come to kill people. We came to teach another way of life where people do not want to harm each other, and where people do not have to fear death."

"And you think that will make the enemy raiders throw away their bows and arrows?"

It was a few days later that Big Ears and several of his friends came to the house to ask about some bible verses that Wally had discussed with them the day before.

Wally quoted the verses again, and the discussion had just begun, when we heard a lot of yelling and screaming. We ran to the door to see what ws going on. Heading toward the house and shavano were a man and a boy, both on a dead run. The man was waving both arms in the air. In one hand he had his long bow, and in the other were three of those seven foot arrows. His chest and face from his eyes down were painted totally black.

I was alarmed, and felt like adding to the screams I heard coming from the Shavano. This had to be a raider. Only raiders painted their faces that way, and he was heading straight for us, but then I recognized him as a good friend. It was Fast Man!

He began yelling at the top of his voice, "Hide yourselves. Get out of sight. Get your gun ready. The raiders are on the way."

The boy who also came running, following fast man, was apparently the one who had been out in the forest and had seen the raiders. He was weeping as he came running past me, then he hid himself behind Wally.

Fast Man motioned for us to get back in the house, then he took off running back to the east, the direction he had come from. Other men came running out of the shavano, trying to catch up and go with him. Big Ears joined them as they all dashed down the trail in the direction the boy was pointing.

The four who had come to the house with Big Ears to talk with Wally ran into the shavano to check on their families, and to prepare to protect the village.

Obviously we didn't do much all that day except to talk about the possibilities, and what we could do, and the problems we might face. I don't mind saying I was very concerned. If the raiders were here for revenge upon the village because someone from their village had been killed, would they consider us a part of the village? Could they decide we were an easier target, living separately, than someone inside the shavano, who had a hundred others to back them up?

It was late in the afternoon that we heard the loud wailing coming from the forest. A crowd gathered in front of the house and we all wondered what had taken place. I was too naive to realize they were all delaying a death announcement as long as possible. Then Isabelle, Jose's wife, came slowly walking out of the forest, her baby held tightly in her arms, crying her heart out. She said nothing as she passed us weeping and wailing.

I asked some of the women which way they thought they would bring the victim home. "Right here,to your house because that's where the medicine is."

I hoped that meant we might be able to keep him alive.

Before long we could see the slow moving procession coming toward us. It looked pretty grim. Women and men were crying. As they approached us it looked less likely that we were going to see the victim alive.

One of the old men came slowly walking down the trail obviously carrying a heavy load on his back. As he approached it was easy to see that it was his son, Jose, who he was carrying. He slowed down as he neared us. Wally started walking toward him, thinking maybe Jose was still alive and they wanted medicine.

Quickly the old man turned away and walked toward the gate of the shavano. In time of death, words are used very sparingly around here. No one spoke. Wally and I followed along behind the procession as it entered and crossed the shavano, gradually catching up with the old man so the we could get a better look at Jose, in case he might still be living. His legs had been bent at the knees and tied up to prevent them dragging. His head bounced against his father's shoulder at every step. A deep red hole in his side showed where the arrow had sunk into his body. He was covered with blood and for some reason someone, perhaps a member of his family, had drawn zigzag lines on his back with his blood.

The expression on his father's face told of the anguish he felt. The raiders had finally gotten the revenge they had been seeking so long.

Jose was dropped in his hammock in the center of the family's lean-to. There he stayed for a day and a half, lying in his blood in the tropical heat.

Jose had a been one of those who so openly had welcomed me when I had arrived there, dancing around me, laughing, chanting as I climbed down from the plane. He had also been one of those who was most anxious to go out and attack and drive off or kill the raiders. Now he was quiet, permanently quiet.

Grief stricken, the family could do nothing but lie in their hammocks and cry.

20
DRINK THE BONES

Immobilized by shock it wasn't until the afternoon of the next day that anyone began to prepare for the "reaho," the bone drinking ceremony that is their funeral. During all this time of weeping and wailing, by relatives and friends, no one left the shavano. They must all stay together.

When I stepped into the shavano, one of the women came and said to me, "Come and weep with us. Someday we too will die. If we do not weep now, no one will weep for us when we die."

Finally the men went and dug out armadillos for a memorial feast, then began gathering wood for a funeral pyre, which they built in front of Jose's lean-to home.

The chanting and the tears continued throughout the night.

The second morning, when they had a pile of wood about seven feet long and four feet high, they laid Jose's body on the top. Jose's mother and sister painted his face red, then using the tips of pieces of vine as brushes, they painted intricate designs on all of his face and his neck and his body. They put white feathers in his hair, and bright colored feathers in his nose and his ears.

His face looked so beautiful I wanted to step forward and take a picture, but I didn't dare. I was sure they would think that was disrespectful. After his family and friends had an opportunity for one more look, and again began weeping, the men set the whole thing on fire. The wailing continued the whole the time the fire was burning.

While there was still smoke coming from the ashes and some hot red coals still in sight, Jose's family began laying banana leaves on the ashes so they could squat on them and begin gathering all the charred bones. Men brought out their flat grinding stones and began grinding those bones into a fine powder which they put into gourd containers.

Everyone who had plantains (cooking bananas) on hand began cooking them and putting them into a small canoe which they hung on the front of Jose's home. They appreciated Marg's contributing a big kettle of hot water to help make the banana soup.

After the banana soup was ready, they poured one of the gourds full of powdered bones into that and stirred it thoroughly. Everyone was chanting as Fast Man dipped a small gourd cup into the banana

Gathering the bones from the still hot ashes.

soup, stepped over and handed it to me. He said, you must drink it. If you do not drink the bones you will not see Jose in the future life, in the land of the thunder."

s

Note the soup filled canoe above Fast man's head.

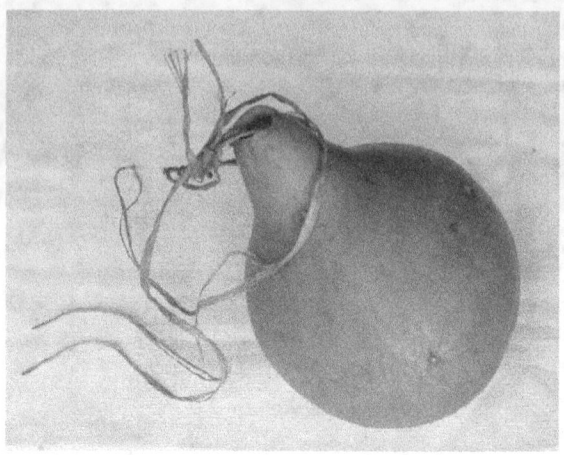

I said, "I am from another place. I will be going back there soon. I will not see your people."

"But you are now one of us."I thought he was going to urge me again, but he only gave me a sad look and passed the gourd to another man.

Every member of the community came and drank a portion of the banana soup. One of the gourds containing the bones was saved, so that if any relatives or good friends of Jose's came from another village, later, they too could drink the bones.`

That afternoon they built another fire and broke both of Jose's bows and all his arrows in two and put them on the fire, then they added all his other possessions. As they burned, Enrique reminded all the people that Jose was gone, he was no more. It must be as if he had never lived. After that day his name could never again be said, and he could never be talked about again.

Later, as a group of men were cleaning up the ashes, I asked one of them, "What happens to you when you die?"

"Well, you go down this trail through the forest. At the place where the trail divides there is a little old man sitting on a stump. When you get there he asks, 'Were you generous?'

"If your answer is 'Yes,' he sends you on the trail to the high place on the mountain where there is lots of wild life of all kinds, lots of fruit and good food plants, and of course all the friendly, generous people who have died before, and you are surrounded by beautiful flowers and beautiful mountains.

"But if your answer is 'No,' you have to go down into the hot swampy valley where all the land is covered with cut grass that makes every step painful, you have to hunt all day to find a bite of food, and no one will share any thing they find."

I had been very aware that sharing and helping each other was a very important part of their way of life, but I was surprised that it was considered so important that it was the "only question."

One of the men who was standing, listening intently to this conversation was Big Knees. He had been mostly standing around, not helping. He was one I had heard criticized because when he went hunting and came back with game, he never shared it like others did. And instead of making a garden, he depended on the generosity of others. I turned and looked at Big Knees, and asked, "What will happen to you?"

He didn't hesitate, "Oh I'm a very good liar."

The system of raiding in the Yanowamo way of life results in a very high death rate. Usually only one person is killed in a raid. But there are enough raids so that more than five percent of the people are killed by raiders. In Niyiyobateri it is much higher than that.

In our society, even with two world wars, and the frequent smaller wars, less than two percent have been killed in wars. But five percent is not considered high by the Yanowamo people.

21

SPLITS THE ROCK

I didn't know it was going to lead to something extra special when, one beautiful sunny morning, Rosito and his friends asked me to go with them and their parents to pick berries. A dozen of us followed a stream two or three miles north, picking berries as we went.

The weather was what I had learned to expect. There was a bright blue sky with three or four big black clouds drifting across it, from west to east. When one of the clouds drifted over us, the rain began to pour. The people stopped under some trees and waited. Some of the women picked big leaves to hold over their heads for the duration of the rain, which they knew would be short.

The cloud had passed and it was getting really hot and the women's baskets were getting full. When the group started to turn back. Rosito said to me, "Don't go with them. We boys brought you along because we want to take you to our favorite place to swim."

I agreed, "It's a great day for that!"

We followed the stream we were on to where it came down the mountain on the west side of the savanna. There, it came over a waterfall which tumbled into a deep-water hole.

Just then an iguana, a huge dragon-like reptile dropped from a tree limb high over the water and made a huge splash.

The other four boys ignored it and dived in, but Rosito waited while I stripped. He looked at my pile of clothes and shook his head like he thought they were foolish.

We swam the length of the pool, till we were very close to the falls, which tumbled into a deep hole. "No rocks," Rosito said, and motioned to the bottom of the falls. Then he dived under the falls and came up behind them. I went to the side of the falls, to where I could see where he had come up. I was surprised at the amount of space back there, behind the falls.

Rosito came out from behind the falls, then motioned for me to follow him.

He and I and the other boys were sprayed by the water as we climbed carefully up the slick wet rocks beside the falls. We climbed to the top of the falls and kept on climbing till we were about two hundred yards above them. We sat down beside the narrow but deep stream that tore down the mountain side.

"No rocks." Rosito said again, motioning to the stream.
I agreed that there were none sticking up out of the water, but plenty along each side.

I wondered why they he had twice mentioned the lack of rocks blocking the stream, till one of the boys stepped over and sat down in the rushing water. Suddenly only his head was in sight as he stretched out and floated, feet first, in the rushing stream as it tore down the mountainside. He stuck his arms up out of the water and shouted excitedly, as his body disappeared over the crest of the falls. A few seconds later, he gave another joyful shout from the pool below the falls.

"Are you ready?" Rosito asked.

"No."

We watched as the other two boys jumped in the water and whizzed down over the falls.

"Your turn!"   It was said emphatically.   "Get a big breath. You'll need it."

I very hesitantly sat down on the smooth rock beside the stream, then it took all my nerve to get a big breath and slide down into the water. I was suddenly swept down the mountain side. I grabbed another big breath as I went over the brink. I needed it as I was instantly deep under the water, swimming hard to get out from under the falls before I ran out of air.

Rosito was not far behind. We were all laughing and shouting.

"Are you ready to go again?"

"Sure am!"

Our second and third times over the falls were just as exciting, but more fun because for me they weren't quite as frightening.

As we started up the mountainside the fourth time, I was again being very careful of those slippery wet rocks, but not careful enough! My feet flew out behind me and I landed in the crevasse between two large rocks. It made bruises and gashes on both sides of my forehead, and my foot went under a rock and cut it also, but I followed the Yanowamo way of jumping up and laughing.

The boys all whirled and looked at me with great concern. "Are you all right."

"Yes."

144

"Are you sure?"

"Yes, I'm fine."

"Yes, but look what you did to the rock! You split it wide open!"

We all looked at the crevasse between the rocks where I had landed, and laughed.

I felt a trickle of blood coming down my cheek, so we went to the stream and cleaned it off but there was nothing more we could do.

The boys offered to head for home immediately, but I said no, I didn't want to spoil the fun.

Rosito and I stayed in the deep pool while the other boys made a couple more dives over the water fall.

When we got home, there was a group of Indians sitting with Wally, outside his house. The Jank's children came running to meet me, so I then ran with them to the group by the house.

The men saw the blood and skinned places on my head and wanted to know what had happened. I couldn't understand their questions and couldn't explain very well in their language, so I decided to do the Yanowamo way and make a joke of it, acting it out like someone had been hitting me in the head with their fist. They knew it was a joke so we were all laughing.

Wally then added his story of me being in one of the chest pounding duels with my head thrown back, and someone had come up behind me and hit me with clubs.

They, of course, knew that was a joke too, and all laughed about it. So then Rosito explained exactly what had really happened.

When we went on into the shavano, the women saw my skinned head and were very concerned. I told them it had quit hurting and the boys assured them I was fine.

The women looked at me and shook their heads. "All that happened and he's still Abufidoblau (Happy)?"

It was about a week later that Enrique, the village leader announced that the whole village should have a picnic dinner and a ceremony, but didn't explain why.

The women happily spent the afternoon preparing all the food. Besides the usual foods they had been feeding me we had tadpoles, roasted anteater, bee larva, and monkey meat. It was a good party, with everyone conversing and laughing, and gladly sharing everything they had.

After we finished eating, Enrique had them all sit together in the middle of the shavano and he started talking. He told them that Then Enrique continued. "You all know that we sometimes give our warriors or others a new name to honor them. Tonight we are giving Abufidoblau a new name, which will be his Real name, his Yanowamo name. Therefore it can never be spoken aloud after tonight."

although my name, Abufidoblau, was a Yanowamo name, and they had all accepted me as one of them, I was not actually a member of the tribe. The only way I could be a real member was for me to be a relative. Therefore he was officially adopting me as his older brother.

His children and his nephews all gathered around me to welcome me as a new member of the the family.

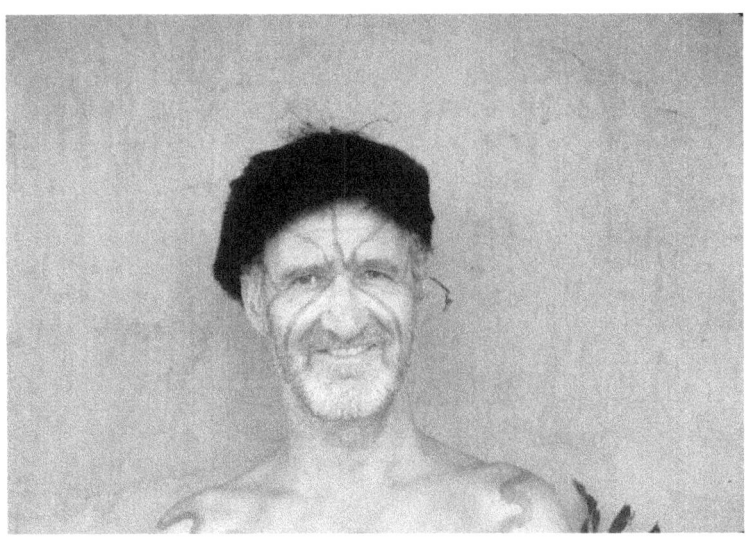

He came over and put a black fur headband around my head, which made me look a little more like a Yanowamo, with their black hair, then he went on: "His new name, his Real Name, his Yanowamo name, is Ya-fi-di-oh-lay-wa (Splits the rock with his head)."

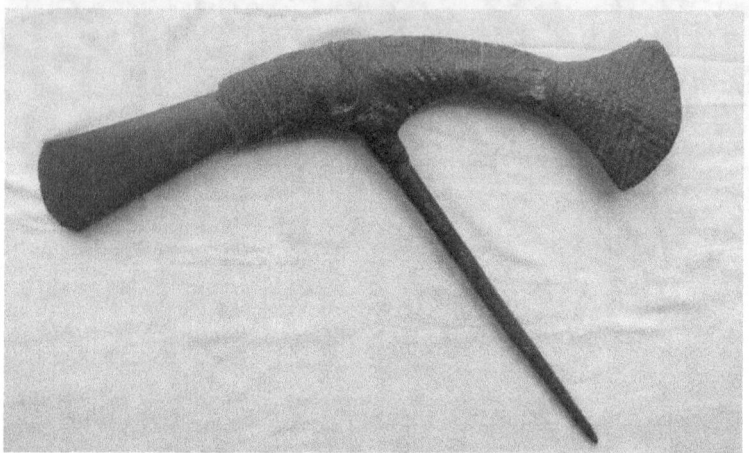

He then presented me with a war ax and told me I should carry it on my shoulder in future ceremonies, to show that I was a warrior and a leader.

Everyone made a point of talking to me and calling me by my new name at least two or three times that evening, while they were still permitted to say it aloud. And Enrique kept calling me "Older Brother." Of course I never heard my new name again, except three different special occasions when someone whispered it to me.

I wondered why Enrique specified *older* brother till Marg told me that in the Yanowamo language there were two words for "brother." It was either "older brother" or "younger brother." There was no word that just meant brother.

After I returned to Montana, at my next get together with John Woodenlegs, president of the Northern Cheyenne tribe, I showed him my war ax and how it was carried. And I told him about that special night, and my new name "Splits the Rock With His Head."

He said, "For more than two years, the Cheyenne Tribal Council has been wanting to honor you with a new tribal name, but we haven't been able to come up with a name, appropriate to all the things you do. You have been getting these government grants for us and thinking of ways for us to get around all these tough government regulations. That's difficult 'cause some of those rules are hard as rocks. 'Splits the Rock With His Head' is the right name for you."

A month later the Tribal Council had a special ceremony to give me my new name, which of course soon got shortened to "Splits-the-Rock."\

22

STEAL YOUR SPIRIT

One morning Wally and I decided to go and visit the village of Hulacobateri, which was about five miles away, across a swamp. It was a long and difficult walk, but finally arrived at the stockade that surrounded the village. We walked part way around, till we came to the gate. That gate had a bar across the top, then several poles leaned against that bar closed the entrance. We had to move the poles aside to get in.

Wally went in first, because they knew him and would recognize us as friends. As soon as he stepped through the gate, the people started shouting "Ooh, aah." Then when we walked to the center of the shavano and did the visitor's pose, it changed to "Aah, Aah," their word for welcome.

I found out that Wally had adopted their kind of humor when, right after that, he said, "I want some bananas," and they said they didn't have any. He said, "I bet you do." and went running around,

past the barrier that is in front of each home, quickly looking into each of the lean-to sections. Everyone sat there laughing at him.

They love jokes, especially if there is a lot of action.

They had seen Wally's photos so they knew what a camera did. It made something that looked exactly like them. They knew there couldn't be two people that looked exactly the same, so they were sure that camera must be stealing their spirit.

The men couldn't object having their pictures taken because a man can never show fear. But about half of the women wouldn't let us take any pictures of them, and no one would let us take a picture of any baby or small child.

As we walked around the inside, I was surprised at the number of pets they had: dogs, monkeys, parrots, and several other kinds of birds. We started giving the people pieces of hard candy, which encouraged most of them to let us take a lot of pictures, but some of them still refused.

I just took pictures of the animals. There was no objection at all to that, and it was a good way to get acquainted with the owners, who were all proud of their pets.

23
CHEST POUNDING

Three women who came in to visit Marg were talking excitedly. "Visitors are coming! Visitors are coming. They're our enemies, but they're our friends!"

That didn't make sense to me, so I headed out to the shavano to see what all the excitement was about. Rosito was anxious to tell me. "Yes, Edwardo has been telling us about the long trip he and his wife just returned from. They were visiting his wife's relatives in their village three days south of here. She was captured from that village when they were deadly enemies. But it has been years since anyone except Edwardo has seen any of them. He says all the men who were our enemies have died of old age. So Edwardo convinced them that since Wally came here, he has taught us that we should all be friends, even with former enemies. That we will all, some day, be rewarded for developing a love for all people."

"You mean some of your people are really listening, and are convinced they should make changes because of his teaching?"

"Yes, Edwardo is. He says he told his relatives that they should pay us a visit, so we can now become friends, and they can learn some of the new ways that Wally is teaching us. They are on their way -- five men and their wives and children. Edwardo came ahead of the others to tell us, so we will not consider them enemies, and go out and attack them before they get here. They will be here day after tomorrow, so we have tomorrow to get ready."

That evening, and all the next day, Edwardo his family and friends were preparing for their guests. The men went out and killed an anteater for a feast.

Most of the other people in the village were doubtful. They were surprised that Edwardo actually believed that if you followed the teachings of the God that Wally talked about, your enemies could become your friends, and they were even more surprised that Edwardo could convince their enemies.

I heard two men talking, asking, "If this is to be our way of life, if we can't go on raids, and kill our enemies, how can we prove our manhood?"

153

As Edwardo's relatives approached the gate, Fast Man, Scar Shoulder, and two other men walked over to greet them. "That's the welcome committee," Rosito said. "They're going to challenge the men to a chest pounding duel. It's a game. An exciting way to make friends!" We headed over to a spot near the entrance, where we could get a good view of the action. So did a lot of others.

When the visitors were about twenty feet away the four men from our village each tightly clinched their right fist and raised that hand high above their head.

The visiting men all looked hesitatingly at each other, as if this was not what they expected. This was the old way. But then four of them did raise their clinched fists and stepped forward.

Scar Shoulder stepped ahead of the other three, looked at one of the men in the other group, then again raised his clinched fist and stood with his bare chest puffed out.

The man who he had challenged stepped forward, and with his fist, and all his strength, struck Scar Shoulder in the middle of his chest. Scar Shoulder staggered backward, took a moment to recover, then with his fist, and all his strength, struck that man and knocked him to the ground.

Andres, a man from our village, challenged another of the visitors. As before, Andres, the challenger, had to let the other man hit him first, but in this case, after he was struck, Andres was unable to stand up and strike his opponent.

Then it was one of the visitors who challenged the third man from our village. Our warrior struck him, but he did not fall. Then that man struck the one from our village, who also stayed on his feet. They each struck the other with a second blow. For a moment, both of them looked very disappointed that he could not knock the other out, then the visitor stepped forward with both arms out and both men gripped the others shoulders, apparently congratulating the other on his strength.

I was shocked to see Fast Man step forward and challenge the fourth man. His opponent was several inches taller than Fast Man, and looked much heaver and stronger. I knew Fast Man could travel twice as far in a day as anyone else in our village, and could almost run up a bee-tree that no one else could climb, but for him to challenge an athlete twice his size, looked absolutely foolish.

But Fast Man stepped up to his large opponent with his fist up and his chest out. The big man hit him and Fast Man was sailing through the air. He landed flat on his back about six feet from where he had stood when he was struck.

For a moment I thought he was out, then he flipped over, crouched, took two quick steps forward and leaped. With the strength of his leap and his strong fist, he struck his big opponent in the chest and knocked him out cold.

I thought the "game", if you could call it that, was over. The only action left was the man who had fought Andres, who was dancing around, showing off, thinking he was the only real winner of the day. But Fast Man stepped over toward him, with a rock in his hand, held it up in his closed fist and did the challenge pose. That man took the rock, held it in his hand to give his fist more weight and power, and hit Fast Man, who again was sent sailing through the air. Again, he jumped up. This time, he stepped over and took the rock, and with it in his fist, struck his opponent in the chest and knocked him down. He wasn't out, but it took two men to help him to his feet.

The game was over, and the hosts considered themselves the winners.

Much later in the day, when we were visiting with the guests, I saw Fast Man twice go off to the side of the shavano and cough up blood, but he continued to pretend that he felt no effects of the chest pounding.

It seemed rather strange to me that the best way to seal a friendship was hit each other as hard as they could hit, and it was obviously painful, but I decided that maybe this greeting did fit into their culture and way of life.

It was the next afternoon when I saw Scar Shoulder coming across the savannah. I wanted to congratulate him on his success yesterday, but didn't know what I should say. Then, just before we met, he raised his closed fist in the obvious chest pounding challenge.

I was shocked! Would he actually challenge me to a chest pounding? Maybe I could just look away, and pretend I didn't see him. But I wasn't about to back off. I took one step forward. Then he burst out in laughter. We both stepped forward slapped each other's shoulder, and laughed our heads off.

That became our habit, our friendship pattern. Every couple of days, when we happened to meet, we would both raise our clenched fist in the chest pounding challenge.

Someone would see us, get excited, and start yelling for everyone to come, there was going to be a chest pounding dual. But we would both burst into laughter, and go on our way.

The other man who had participated in the chest pounding saw us do this so he wanted to get a reaction from me too. He stood beside Scar Shoulder and pointed at me and said "Basho Kawi."

I knew that basho was their name for one of the little monkeys, a kind that some had for pets. But I had to ask the meaning of kawi.

Scar Shoulder stroked his chin, then pointed to mine. I hadn't shaved since I got there. It was too difficult with a safety razor and cold water, when I was accustomed to an electric razor.

Who was he, to be calling me "Monkey Beard" when he was the only man in the village with whiskers. Like all Indians, the Yanowamo had no whiskers, only this man had a little tuft of black hair on the bottom of his chin. I knew there was another kind of monkey that was called "elo," so I pointed to him and said "Elo Kawi." We all burst into laughter.

From then on, he and I had names for each other, "Basho Kawi" and "Elo Kawi" and we always made a point of using them every time we saw each other. Now he, too, had a Naba name that could be spoken aloud. We were the only men in the village with beards. "Only monkeys should have them"

A couple of weeks later, when a group returned from visiting another village, the men were nursing sore chests from the chest pounding fights they had participated in. Two young men were particularly sore, but they were proud of having participated. Other young men began planning a mock fight among themselves, so they could have their chests toughened up, ready for the real thing -- like football players back at home, I thought.

I was told that sometimes, instead of pounding each others chests, they hit each other on the the head with sticks or clubs. That's why most of the men had scars showing on their shaved heads.

Now it was more obvious to me why the men all shaved the tops of their heads; so people could see their scars.

I was told that a chest pounding can sometimes be held when, after a death, friends of the deceased are invited and come to drink the bones. These may be traditional enemies, but in their mourning together and the chest pounding, they have beaten each other, and they have both shed blood. Now they respect each other so they can be united as friends.

24
PUNISH THAT GIRL

I ran down past the shavano because all the yelling and screaming seemed to be coming from the swamp area below it. I was sure this must be another girl-pulling, a husband after his bride.

When I got in sight of the action, sure enough, three men were pulling a young woman, but not toward a trail. They were dragging her right out into the deep mud of the swamp She was screaming for help and so were the members of her family, who were on the shore.

More men and women were coming running out of the shavano to see what was happening, just as I was, but they were soon into the action.

The men dragged that girl out to where they were more than knee deep in soft gooey black mud and water; then they pushed her, face-first, down into the water, apparently trying to drown her.

Six women rushed out to save the girl. Three of them wrestled with the men, trying to pull them away from their victim, while the others helped the girl get up onto her feet and start toward the shore.

Then other men ran in to help the men, and more women got into the fray, trying to help the girl, and were, themselves, pushed into the mud.

Soon the whole village was into the action, either joining the struggle or jumping up and down screaming their encouragement.

Almost all the women were running into the water, grabbing big chunks of black gooey mud, then running out and throwing it into the face of any man who wasn't involved.

A teen age girl was a few feet in front of me. Two men grabbed her. One got her hands and the other her feet and they carried her, face up, to the edge of the water then swung her back and forth a couple of times and tossed her in the air. She landed on her back about fifteen feet out into the goo. She flipped over, grabbed a big ball of mud, and went after one of the men.

I saw half a dozen others tossed the same way.

Soon, every person, man or woman, was totally covered with that sticky,gooey black mud. Even their faces were covered so I couldn't recognize anyone.

I was the only man not covered and two different women came running out of the swamp with their big gobs of mud, heading for me, I was certain that I, and my clothes, were going to be as black as everyone else, but both times the woman turned and threw her gob of mud on a man near me.

I got the impression from some of the yells that the girl who was first dragged into the swamp was being punished for something, and tried to keep track of her. Three times she was pushed into the mud, and three times she was rescued by the women. But the women didn't accompany her clear out to the shore, and protect or sympathize with her. As soon as the men decided to ignore her she was left alone to stagger to the shore, where she laid flat on the ground, recovering.

The battle went on for more than a half hour, and it became obvious that everyone was so enjoying the excitement that it became more of a party than a battle.

When things finally calmed down I recognized Rosito and asked him what the score was, why this was happening

He explained that the girl who was being punished had been out with some friends to their garden, getting their day's bananas. She needed bananas too, but her garden was a couple of miles in the opposite direction, so she got lazy and just picked a stalk of bananas from someone else's tree.

In our society she could have been arrested for stealing, and then tried and punished. But in the Yanowamo culture there is no one responsible for protecting other people or their property. There are no

stablished laws, no standard punishment. If someone commits a crime against someone else, it is strictly up to the victim to punish them. This was the way the family who owned the banana tree had decided to punish her.

When the big mud fight was over, the first activity for everyone had to be a bath. The whole village went down to the river and bathed and swam. Women went back to their homes long enough to get some food, which everyone shared, and the whole rest of the day was just a big picnic and party, which everyone enjoyed.

To me, the most surprising part of the whole event was what happened the next morning. A group stopped by the house on their way out to the jungles to gather food. The group consisted of the girl who had stolen the bananas and the family who had punished her.

The family had no reason to still be angry with her. Sure she had stolen from them, but they had had the satisfaction of punishing her, so they could no longer be angry. They had given her a very bad time, but she had no reason to be angry with them because she had deserved it. They had really become better acquainted, so they were happily going off to enjoy a day together.

Where else in the world could people be that sensible and that forgiving?

25

ARMY ANTS

We were just finishing breakfast when a plane circled once before landing. Marg jumped up and said, "That's the Wilcoxins. They are one of the families who really support our missions. They radioed and said they were coming to visit our mission, but just for one day. The pilot's staying to fly them out tonight."

"What do they want to do while they're here?" I asked.

"Just look around, meet some of the people, see what life here is like. They wanted to bring some gifts for the people, to help them get acquainted. I said machetes and string would be good if they wanted to trade for baskets or other things the people made, but to keep those things concealed in bags. If they were in sight, the people would get too excited and things could go wild. They said they'd bring some of candy too, just to pass out. I told them to make sure it was the kind of candy that each piece was wrapped, or the humidity and heat would melt it all away."

"Yes! I had some candy in my bag when I came, and I had an awful time washing all that sticky goo out of the clothes around it."

As the plane rolled to a stop the people came streaming out of the shavano, all anxious to see who was arriving.

As the pilot opened the door and let down the steps for his passengers to exit I saw the expressions on the faces of the two women. Even thought they had been warned, they still looked a little shocked at the sight of all those "naked savages" dashing toward them. However, the man confidently stepped out, and down to the ground, then turned to help the two women. Each of the women had a paper bag in one hand. Before she even stepped down, the second lady reached into her bag, and held up a handful of that hard candy.

Suddenly there was a stamped. Everyone was yelling as they ran forward with their hands out. Since everyone was trying to get to those paper bags first, the ones in the back were pushing the ones in front of them, and those were pushed against the two women with the candy. Those visitors were pushed and shoved uncontrollably. The one who was still trying to get down the steps fell. Luckily she fell on top of people, not all the way to the ground. The visitors, and even those around them were getting banged and bruised. The women tried to hold the bags above their heads out of the reach of the people in front of them, who were all shorter, but the people were jumping. Both bags of candy were ripped apart and the candy they contained was flying in all directions, scattering over the people.

Then the people realized what a terrible welcome they had given their guests, even bruising them and they backed off, saying, "Now those guests will hate us. They'll consider us their enemies!"

All day, as we took the visitors around the shavano, people would back off thinking the visitors were probably still angry with them. We did convince some of them that the visitors understood, and were taking the blame on themselves. The visitors did enjoy asking many questions as Marg and Wally translated for them.

However, when it was nearly to the time when the pilot had said they must leave, I was walking with Mrs. Wilcoxin toward the gate of the shavano. She said, "I'm sure from your actions, and the expressions on your face, that you enjoy your time with these people, but how can you put up with the stink? I can smell this home we're passing by, clear out here in front of it! Why is the whole shavano so filthy?"

I asked, "Don't you have garbage scattered around your house? If not, why not?"

We keep the house cleaned up. We put the trash and the garbage in the garbage bin."

"Did you see a garbage bin here? If you had no laws, no public employees, no one responsible for, or with authority over anyone else, what would you do with your garbage?"

"We'd haul it off."

"And if no one owned a car, how far would you have to carry that garbage in your hands, or on your backs before you came to a place where you could put it without putting it in front of someone else's house?"

"But there must be somewhere they could dump it."

"Yes. Right there." We were just going out the gate of the shavano, and I pointed to the space, three or four feet wide, between the stockade and the back of the lean-to house. It was a space wide enough to walk in, and you should be able to walk all the way around the village, but it was filled with too much junk. Then I pointed to the outhouse behind the Janks house, "You notice the Janks don't have a bathroom, they have an outhouse."

"Yes. I used it."

Well, the Yanowamo have their own kind of outhouse. It's two or three acres of flat land southeast of the shavano. You just walk carefully out there and squat. But a child who's only two or three years old may not like to go that far alone. He may just slip around the corner of his lean-to roof."

"But I still wouldn't like living in a place with a bad smell all the time."

"I like that perfume you are wearing. It's charming, but you aren't aware of it all the time, are you."

"I forgot I had it on."

"Well, you never notice any smell that's around you all the time. I'd forgotten to notice the smell of the shavano till you reminded me."

"Well, we'll be getting in the plane in a few minutes. I'll have a lot of good memories, of the hospitality of the people, their continual laughter, their beautifully woven baskets, their interest in learning the things Wally and Marg are teaching. There are so many good things to remember that I'll probably not even think of the bruises I got this morning, or the gnats and mosquitoes, or the smell!"

The next Sunday morning I woke up at dawn, and laid there wondering what the Wilcoxins would be telling their friends at church this morning. Then suddenly there was a loud roaring sound, as if it was the middle of a very heavy rain storm. But it was light enough to see out the window, and it was not raining.

Then I looked down and saw that the house had been invaded. It wasn't raiders, but it was just as frightening. I gave a yell of warning to Wally and Marg. Maybe it was more like a scream. Wally called back, "Don't be frightened, Hap. Just stay in your hammock, and be on your guard."

Big black army ants were pouring into my room from all sides, through every crack and crevice. It seemed like a real army. I looked for a way of escape. I didn't see any. I put my foot down from my hammock and tramped on some of them. It didn't frighten the others at all. They just kept on coming. I ran to the window and looked out. A strip of ground about ten feet wide was totally black and moving, all flowing toward me. There was no escape.

164

I took Wally's advice. I ran back to my hammock and raised my feet, and brushed the ants off. I watched as some of the ants came streaming down the ropes supporting my hammock. They came to the metal rings that held each end of my hammock together. They apparently didn't like the smooth metal, and turned back, or dropped to the floor. Two of them got across the metal ring but I swatted them.

There were always insects in my room but I hadn't known how many till the ants drove them out of the cracks and crevices. I could see a beetle and some cockroaches on the wall, crickets and spiders and other little bugs came running out. The ants caught and killed every one of them, and carried them across the floor and out through the crevices on the other side.

Those ants were several times as big as any ant I had ever seen, and they were strong. They found no insects too heavy to pick up and carry. I wondered if there would have been anything left of my body if I had been on the floor and I had not been able to get up.

I laid there and watched those ants all morning, till suddenly they were all gone. There were none left. No stragglers.

Flying above those ants was a pair of small birds, which I later learned were called ant birds. I thought they were occasionally diving down and eating an ant, but as I watched more carefully I saw that they were only picking off the insects or other small creatures that the ants drove out of hiding and carried away.

As Marg fixed lunch she said, "That was the best, most thorough house cleaning I ever had, but I'm sure glad we had most of our food in tightly sealed cans they couldn't get into."

That afternoon I took a walk down through the shavano, and was surprised at the fresh clean smell. I wished Mrs. Wilcoxin could see it now.

People were going out to their gardens to replace the food that was missing, but they were laughing, looking more cheerful than usual. I thought they must be very thankful for those army ants that had done a job no one else would do.

I mentioned the difference it had made to Rosito. He said, "Your people talk about the creator. Maybe he created those ants for a purpose."

WILDERNESS

26
LEAJOU

"It's a leajou at Mountain Top Village, Hekura's village," Enrique said. "It will be a great get-together, a time when people from several Yanowamo villages enjoy getting together. There will be a feast, dancing, and everyone will have a great time together. Everyone acting as if they are all good friends!"

"Oh! A powwow!" I said. I love powwows. They're the big events in the lives of all the Montana Indians. I try to get to all the ones on the Cheyenne and Crow reservations."

"We don't call it that here," Wally said. "The Yanowamo call it a leajou."

"Well, to me it's a powwow! Is it like a powwow, where everyone is welcome?"

"Yes. The leaders of all the surrounding villages will be invited," Enrique said. "It's a time for settling old problems, and reestablishing old friendships with those who have become enemies. Not only friends, like us, but also former enemies are invited. Hekura is the one leader who everyone trusts, but he will invite friends from villages who are enemies of other guests, with the possibility of their reestablishing former friendships. Hekura sent two men all the way over here to invite me and said I should bring a few others from our village. Those two got here last night. But I can't go! Two of my family are sick. I can't leave them."

I'm sure he saw the disappointment on my face, because in the Yanowamo way he laughed loudly and said, "Don't bawl your eyes out! I'm sure Hekura will be glad to have you go in my place and represent Niyiyobateri."

"Me? Represent Niyiyobateri?" I said doubtfully.

"Why not? You're one of us now. You're my older brother! I'll send several others along. We need to be well represented, but you're the leader, taking my place. Rosito knows the way. He can be your guide."

166

I could hardly wait. At last I was actually going into completely unknown, uncontacted territory.

When the day arrived and we were ready to leave, Enrique gave me a Jaguar skin headband to wear in place of the black fur one they had given to me before. I was proud to wear it for this occasion. It, and the arrows he handed me, made me look more like the leader I was supposed to be, but I knew I wouldn't wear that headband after I returned here because it would be telling people what was untrue. Wearing that headband said that I had killed a jaguar with my bow and arrows. There was no way I could actually go out and do that!

It made me glad that Rosito was anxious to carry my backpack with my hammock and my mosquito net, and a few small trade items that I took along, just in case. That distance of nearly fifty miles was going to be a very long day's walk.

As we walked the length of the Big Savannah, and passed the village of Hulacobateri, three more people joined our group.

We were soon into the mountains, climbing up and down on a narrow trail that was sometimes below very high cliffs, or at times on narrow ledges along the tops of them but we were nearly always climbing, either up or down.

When we crossed the top of this mountain ridge, Rosito informed me that no other outsider had ever been beyond that point. It was exciting to me to know that from there on we were in what was to the outside world, totally unexplored territory.

It was a very long, arduous day, but a pleasant one, as no one was concerned about speed. Whenever we came near bushes that ha berries we took time out to climb up to them and eat a few. When animal tracks crossed our trail, Rosito stopped to point them out and identify them for me.

After about twelve hours of climbing I was really dragging, so I was glad when they finally stopped and started hanging their hammocks in the trees.

The next morning we had been climbing less than an hour when we reached the top of a mountain where we could look across a deep valley at Mountain Top Village.

While the mountain we were on was covered with forest, the mountain the village was on was grass from bottom to top. The trails that led to it showed plainly.

This was the village Peter and I had seen when we had flown over this unexplored area long ago, and we knew it was the home of the brave leader we called Hekura.

We climbed down and were crossing through the forest at the foot of the mountain when everyone stopped and put down their

packs. "This is where we get fixed up, ready to go in their village, Rosito explained.

As everyone started digging into their packs, getting out their paints and feathers, people from several other villages joined us.

One woman was carrying several burden baskets, her gourd water jug, the palm leaves for her roof and all the cords and reed strips she would need to tie that roof up. She had brought her whole home

and all her possessions with her. Obviously, she was planning
on staying longer than the rest of us.

Everyone started getting painted up for the ceremonies to take
place in the village on the mountain top. I knew they expected that to
take a while because some of them even hung up their hammocks so
they could relax. Many of them painted their whole bodies with a red
oily dye, then they began painting black designs on each other's faces,
and their whole bodies.

This woman painted her husband, then he painted her.

Soon, someone came over and painted my face for me.

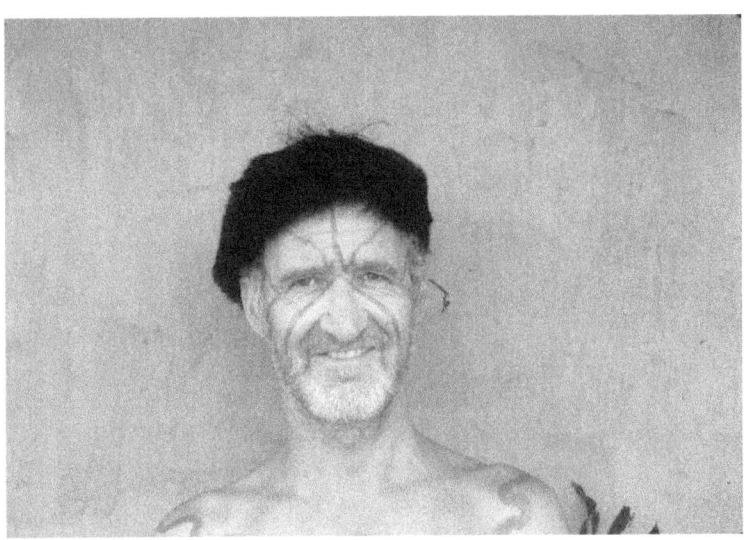

Then others painted the rest of me.

One of the girls came over and taught me the dance I would need

to do as I entered the village. She demonstrated the dance, then had me practice so I could be sure I was doing it right.

Soon everyone was painted, had their bead necklaces on and the reeds through their ears, noses, and lips.

Even the small children were painted and decorated.

Finally we were ready to make the long climb to the village on the top of the mountain.

When we got to the top it was interesting to see a little old lady standing just outside the stockade that surrounded the village, closely observing everyone who entered.

We were told that we must enter only two at a time. Two of us would step through the gate, then one of us would turn to the right and the other to the left and go all the way around the shavano, doing our dance. Then those two would step aside, and two more could enter.

All the residents of the shavano stood in front of their homes, each holding their best weapons, but also stepping, swaying, keeping

time with the beating of the drums. Even the children took part.

Rosito and I stepped through the gate then turned in opposite directions. We each danced forward, using the steps the girl had taught to me.   With an arrow in each hand, held high over our heads, we danced forward till we were directly in front of one family, then we dropped our weapons and danced back to the previous home, then

danced forward, picked them up and danced forward to the next home.

Rosito and I met at the other end, passed each other and continued on around the village. When we reached the gate, two more visitors came through the gate and did the same.

Instead of weapons, two of the guests were carrying shredded palm leaves, saying clearly that instead of raids and war, they wanted peace with their hosts. I was surprised to learn that even here, palm leaves had the same meaning they had in biblical times.

I was also surprised to see one man with his entire face and his chest completely painted black, a symbol that all the raiders used. He was clearly saying that although he came to this celebration of friendship, he was still an enemy, and should be considered one.

It took well over two hours for all the guests to enter, and during the entire time, this girl stood and danced with her arrow over her head. She never lowered it once!

As soon as all the guests had entered, the feast began. There was plenty of armadillo, fish, and all kinds of vegetables. I was surprised to see the women who had come with us unloading fruits and roots from their baskets.

I hadn't known that the baskets they carried over those many miles of mountain trails included food to share.

I felt honored that I was allowed to help cut up and distribute the meat of a tapir.

As we began eating that meat, some of the men began chanting. Their chants actually had a rhythm that made them sound like poetry, but they did not rhyme.

After that, the women began to sing; then later, the men began singing. The men had their chants and their own songs, and the women had their songs, which were different, but they never sang together.

27

INTO THE UNKNOWN

The leajou (what I called a powwow) was pretty much over and some people were leaving. I saw two men doing a dance in front of Hekura. He saw me watching and motioned for me to come and join him. When I stepped over to see what was going on, Hekura motioned toward the dancers and told me the dance they were doing was their way of inviting him to come to their village. He said they had seen me with him and saw that we were good friends, so they wanted me to come with him.

It sounded like a great opportunity, but I hesitated. I had heard too much about the tricks people pulled, sometimes inviting others to their village so they could be killed. I said, "Are you sure it is safe?"

"You are one of us now. Don't talk about safety!" He waited to see my hesitant reaction before he burst into a good laugh and said, "Yes, they are good friends of mine -- and you'll be with me." He promised that after we visited them, and others, he would accompany me all the way back to the big Savannah.

I camped that night with my friends, down in the forest below Hilltop Village. The next morning when I told my friends I was staying here so I could see other villages with Hekura they thought I was being was absolutely foolish. But they said the decision was up to me so they shouldn't try to change my mind. They said they would inform Wally and Marg, then they gave me a fond farewell, as if they thought they might never see me again.

When they left I moved my hammock up to the home of Hekura and his wife. The people in the homes next to them made me feel as if they were glad I had stayed.

It was only a couple of days before Hekura and I headed for the village that had invited us. They had said it was "near by" but I had learned from experience that long walks meant nothing to these people. "near by" probably just mean nearer than Niyiyobateri, where I had come from.

We started out early in the morning and were still walking steadily late in the afternoon. I wasn't alert to much but trying to keep up with Hekura. As he lead the way down a winding trail into a dense forest, he stopped suddenly and I almost ran into him. I looked over his shoulder and watched a huge jaguar step into the center of the trail and crouch, as if ready to spring.

I expected Hekura to either leap behind the nearest tree, or quickly raise his bow and arrow in position to shoot, but he did neither. He slowly moved his right hand over and took one long arrow from the three he kept with the bow in his left hand. Holding the middle of that arrow, with the back end of it touching the ground, he took one step forward, then crouched, with the back end of the arrow against the ground next to his foot.

The jaguar leaped, one big leap, and came down right on top of him. I was too busy getting out of the way to see exactly what happened, but when I whirled around, the jaguar was stretched out on the ground with the last third of that arrow sticking out of it's chest, and Hekura was shooting another arrow into the back of it's head. When the jaguar had come down on top of that long arrow the tip of the arrow was in the right place to enter the front of it's chest. With the back end of the arrow against the ground, the speed of the jaguar's leap, and it's weight, sent the arrow straight through most of the length of the jaguar's body. Then, when Hekura shot another arrow into the back of it's brain, the jaguar didn't struggle long.

Hekura said, "This will be a good gift for the friends we are going to visit." He used my hunting knife to cut the jaguar's body in two, just in front of the hips, and to clean out the insides. When we started on, I had that rear section on my shoulders, with a leg over each shoulder and the tail against the back of my head.

Twice in the next hour I asked for a rest stop, and I was glad when we saw the roofs of a shavano ahead.

When we walked to the center of the shavano and dropped the jaguar then did the visitor's pose, the men of the village all loudly joined in the welcome chant.

The women stayed back in the space below their lean-to roofs, but the men all headed out to the the center to welcome us. I saw one man start to raise his fist in the chest pounding challenge, but I was glad to see the others quickly step in front of him and group themselves around us. Those people were friends of Hekura's so they welcomed us with open arms. One of the men said to me, do not be afraid. These arrows that we carry are hunting arrows, for shooting birds, not people.

Hekura and one of his friends dragged the jaguar over to that man's home, and he showed us where we should hang our hammocks.

Several of the women came over to meet us, and to look at the jaguar but they were soon back to tending their fires, peeling their fruits, and weaving their baskets, and the children were running around, chasing their puppies and their monkeys.

Although I was now very familiar with the custom, it still seemed strange to be introduced to so many people, and never once have anyone mention anybody's name.

That family were good friends of Hekura's so they made us feel very welcome. They fed us well, but I wished the roasted meat they gave us didn't have burned hair on it.

It was a little after noon the next day that two men from the other side of the shavano came over and asked Hekura and me if we would like to go with them to gather epina plants. They said one of the men was very ill. He had bad stomach pains and kept throwing up. They said that since all illness was caused by witchcraft, they knew someone in one of the enemy villages had done witchcraft against him. They needed the epina to invoke the hekura spirits to try to counteract the witchcraft.

One of the men looked at me and said that I was fortunate that I came with Hekura. If I had come alone and the man got sick right after my arrival, they would have thought maybe I was the one who did the witchcraft. All they would have to do was kill me. But they trusted Hekura. As long as I was with him, I was safe.

As they started back across the shavano I looked at Hekura to be sure what he thought we should do. I wondered if it could be dangerous for me to go with them.

Hekura said quietly, "We better go. If we don't go and help gather epina, they may think we are opposed to their using it tonight, and might be the ones who did the witchcraft."

It took us about an hour to get to where the epina was growing. It was a small plant with one bunch of leaves spread around the stem, so that when I looked at it from above, the plants reminded me of tiny umbrellas.

Twice before, when I was out on a trail with someone, they had pointed to one of those plants and said, "That's epina," and I had wondered why they pointed it out and thought that plant was important.

The plants were scattered and were among other larger plants, so we had to search for them.

They told me to only pick a plant if there were two or three together. "If there is only one, and you pick it, no more may grow there. We don't want to end up with no epina."

I only picked three, to be sure they knew I was cooperating, but not overdoing it.

That night they dried the bean-like seeds we had gathered over a fire, so they could grind them between two smooth stones until they became a very fine powder. When they finished grinding it, one of the men put a little of the powder into the end of a hollow reed. The reed was about three feet long, and less than a half inch thick, but hollow all the way through.

After the man put the epina powder in one end he stuck the other end into the nose of one of his friends, then put the end with the epina in it in his mouth and blew the epina powder through the tube and into his friend's nostrils.

That man gave a whoop, jumped up, threw both arms up and danced in a circle then sat down with a big grin, waiting for another shot of dope.

Four of the other men then took the hollow tube and gave each other shots of epina. A couple of others just sniffed the epina powder. They were soon all staggering around, shoving each other, and yelling at each other. I wondered how many hours of drinking whisky it would have taken to get them acting like that.

Then the man who got the first shots of epina walked over to the hammock of the man who was sick and had stomach pains. He squatted down put his mouth over the man's throat, and began to suck. He then moved up and down the man's throat, still sucking on it. Another man came and sucked on his stomach and his chest.

Hekura explained to me that the purpose of the epina was to release the spirits that some enemy's witchcraft had sent to make the man ill. If the men who were treating him had enough epina in their systems they should be able to suck out all the spirits that were making the man sick. He said it gives the men who take it all kinds of wild visions. They believe they are making contact with the controlling spirits of the universe. They imagine they are making flights among the stars and the clouds. It leads them to also tell their feelings about others, or their plans, or other things they normally would not tell others. Sometimes their epina visions even lead to war.

Hekura and I went back across the shavano and laid down in our hammocks. We didn't get a lot of sleep, partly because of the yelling, laughing, and other noise that continued all night on the other side of the shavano. For me the loss of sleep was mainly because of my concern about what crazy ideas about me some of those doped men might get. I thought that some of them had an evil look on their faces. What could their hallucinations cause them to do?

In the early morning when we got up, Hekura told our hosts that we could only take time to eat a couple of bananas as we had to be on our way because there were other places that he wanted to take me.

I wondered if part of the reason we were leaving was because he also was concerned about what might happen there, but I couldn't ask that question. That would sound as if I thought he might be afraid, and there could be no worse insult to a Yanowamo man.

I was surprised that we were going east, instead of west toward our homes, but after about half an hour Hekura sat down on a log and motioned for me to do the same. He said, "We have to make a decision about where we are going. I'd like to go to a village of people I have never met, except when two of them came to a leajou at Hill Top village a couple of years ago. Those two became good friends, and they begged me to come and visit them in their village but it is over a mountain range from here. No one from Hilltop Village is willing to go there. But you are like me. You like to take long hikes, explore, see new places, and meet new people. If you are willing to go that far I would like to take you with me to visit those people. I know the location and the route because I was there years ago. I saw the village but stayed hidden because I was alone, and at that time I knew none of them. Do you want to go there?"

I hesitated because I knew how far and how fast Hekura could walk, but I gave him an enthusiastic "Yes. If you won't walk off and leave me when I get too tired to walk."

Hekura laughed, and said "I'll drag you." Then he went on seriously and warned me, "We have to get there unseen and surprise them, because if others who do not know me see us coming, they will assume we are enemies, as all strangers are. But perhaps you are like Wally. He says because of Gods care he's not afraid of dying,but I don't think you want to be killed, do you?"

"Not today!" I said.

195

Several days later, the Orinoco river, which we were following had become a fairly small stream and ahead of us we could see that it came out of a canyon with perpendicular sides and the mountain ahead was mostly cliffs. We could see that we could not get out of the canyon if we went that way, so we started climbing up the steep mountain side we were on.

I was hanging on to the small trees to pull myself up where the footing was unsure, but I quickly learned that I had to look carefully at every handhold to avoid getting my hands penetrated by thorns.

I also learned that there were two kinds of mosquitoes, the little ones that we were used to, and some twice as big, with white abdomens. There were also plenty of flies, chiggers, and occasionally

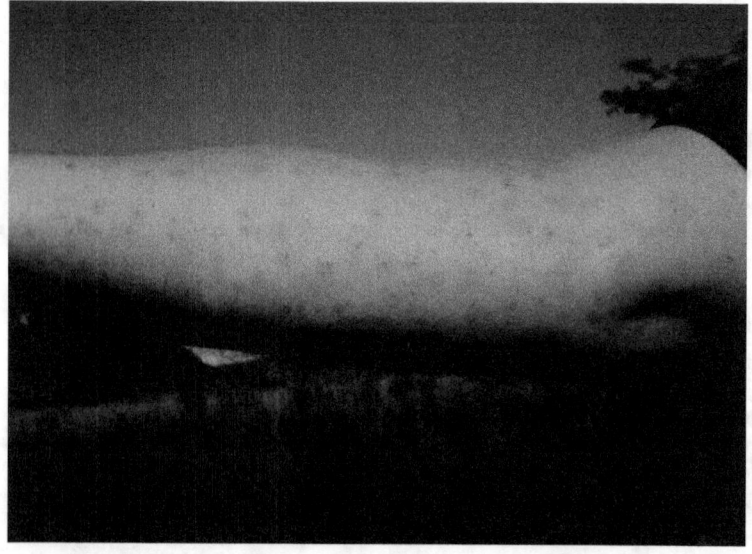

those little insects that are so tiny you can hardly see them, but they sting like wasps. But what was worst was the persistence of the little gnats that kept biting all day. My arms felt like nothing but red itching bumps.

As we walked I didn't notice an ant nest and three ants jumped clear above my shoes and bit me on the ankle.

I yelled and, at the same time, jumped clear beyond that ant hill. I squatted down and pulled off the ants that were still biting, then I sat there a minute rubbing my ankles. Hekura squatted down there and laughed at me. Then he asked, "What animals do you think are the most like us humans?"

"I thought a minute and said, "Well, wolves I guess. They work together and cooperate. When one gets some game, they willingly share with all the others. When a mother has pups they know she should be home taking care of them, and the males, even those not related, go out and hunt, and bring back the food for her and her pups. They do a better job of cooperating and sharing than most of the humans that are not Yanowamo do."

"Well, for the same reason, I think it's the ants."

"Ants? Like those that just bit me?"

"Yes. They, too, set an example for us. They are very brave, like we should all be. Think how much nerve it took for something the size of those ants to attack something your size, just to protect the rest of their colony. We should all be that brave and that protective of each other. They, too, all go out and hunt for food and bring it back and share it with everyone. The leader never has to do anything but provide the babies and care for them. That's the way it should be with us.

"Like the Yanowamo, they all cooperate, and help, and share with the others in their own village. And, like us, they consider all others outside their own village their enemies. If other ants, even the same kind of ants from another ant village come into their territory they are considered enemies to be killed. That, too is like us Yanowamo.

"And there are other ant tribes that are like nabas. I've heard that there are nabas who will blow themselves up and kill themselves to kill those who they consider enemies of their people. Is that right?"

"Yes. There are some people who do that."

"Well, if you look closely at one ant tribe, you will see that there are some that have big long bodies trailing out behind their legs."

"Yes, I saw some of those yesterday. They were well over an inch long. But the other ants were small!"

"Yes. Those long ones are the guards, They protect the others. If other ants, other insects, or small animals invade the territory of their village those big ones will keep puffing themselves up and if the invaders don't leave they will puff up till they explode. The poison that fills those big bodies is sprayed in all directions. Everything in a space

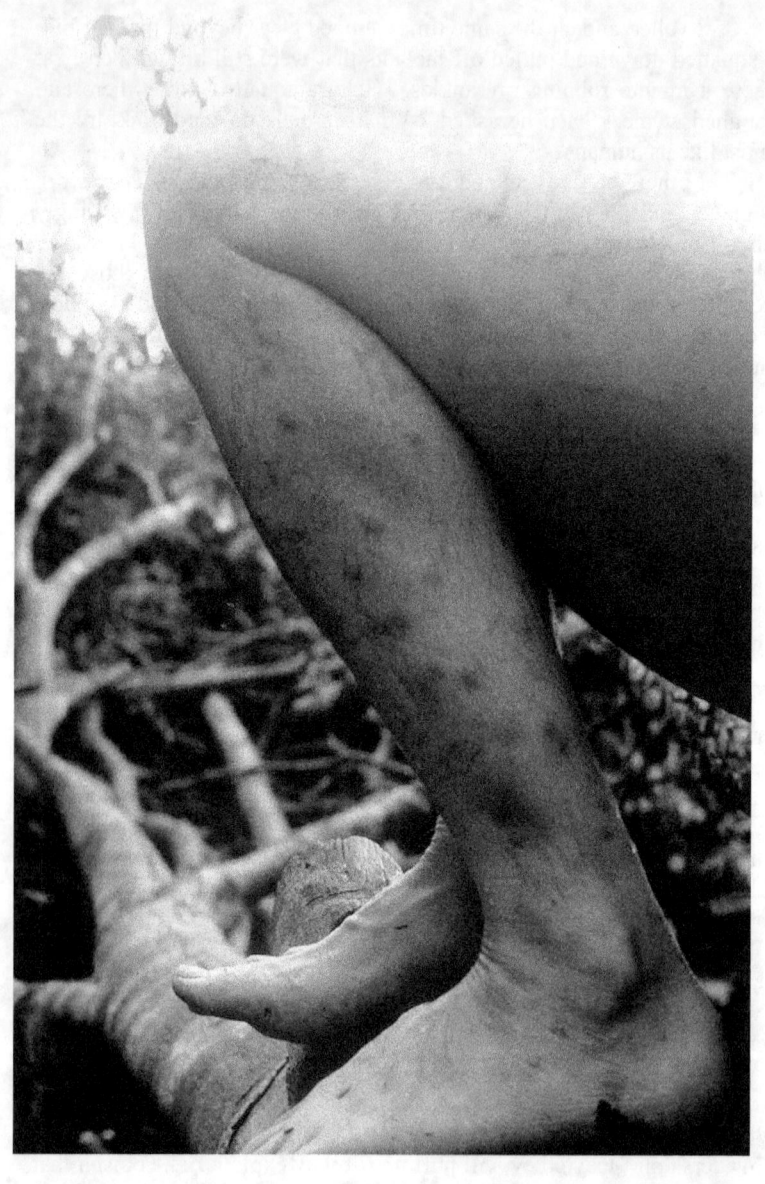

about as big as the length of your arm gets some of that poison, and it is deadly."

"I guess I better watch for those ants."

"Well, I don't think they effect people, at least I don't think any of our people have been harmed by them, but I've seen the dead insects that were killed. I didn't pick any up or even touch them.

"But some of our men are like those big ants. They are willing to get themselves killed to protect the rest of our people."

I looked down at the many bites on my legs and feet and said, "Maybe those ants do live like people, but I'd rather that they and all the other insects would find something else to bite and sting, instead of me."

We struggled up that steep mountain until we found a faint trail that led us along the top of the deep canyon. At the upper end of the canyon a small stream flowed over the brink into the canyon. That had to be the beginning of the Orinoco River.

The rest of that day we followed the narrow trail that climbed and climbed. The narrow stream we followed became smaller and smaller as we climbed until we reached the spring where it started. I laid down on the rocks, stuck my face in the spring, and enjoyed a big drink of the cold water.

Shortly after that, we reached the top of a mountain pass. There was an opening in the forest, so we could see for miles in each direction. It was a fantastic view.

"Do all the rivers ahead of us run toward the east?" I asked.

"Yes. Of course. This is the top of the mountain range."

"Well! Then we are going from Venezuela into Brazil. This is the border, but neither of those countries knows yet where this border is."

Hekura shook his head. "I don't think either of those places you call Venezuela and Brazil is near here. I've never heard of either of them. If they were villages, places where people live, the names would end with be-te-ri, to say there were people there."

"Well, they're real places, and I'm sorry to say that someday people from one or the other of them will come to your village and tell you it belongs to to them.

"Not our village. We're too powerful. No one can ever conquer us!"

I knew that from now on I'd be in Brazil but Brazil would never know I'd been there. I wondered how long it would be before some expedition would explore this area, and find out where this border was. I thought we were abut fifty miles from the location of the dotted line on Peter's map that showed where they had guessed this divide would be.

We continued on downhill the rest of the afternoon. We picked some pupugna to eat then moved a little way off the trail into the dense jungle to hang up our hammocks.

Shortly after we started on the next morning, the trail passed a small spring, then followed the small creek that flowed from it. That creek was joined by a number of others, and in a couple of hours the creek was already about twelve feet wide and appeared to be deep. We crossed where a large fallen log made a bridge across the creek.

Hekura pointed down at my shoes and, as always, held out his hands to take them and my camera across the river for me. This log was about three feet wide, and although in the middle it dipped clear under the surface of a deep, still water hole I wouldn't have any trouble balancing on that. My shoes were already wet so I just left them on and my camera on my belt, and stepped up on the log and, started across the river. What I didn't know was that the log, where it was under water, was covered by that very slippery moss. When I stepped on that wet part my feet flew out from under me and I was swimming.

When I got to the shore. I took my camera out and looked at it, but it was already soaked. I knew I would not get any more photographic records of this trip!

Hekura said we were getting near the village that was our destination so we stopped and he got out his paints and painted both of our faces red, with a few black lines across our cheeks. I took my shirt off and hid it with my hammock inside my backpack.

From there on, instead of walking down the trail we stepped off and made our way through the forest, near the trail but out of sight of it, just in case someone came down that trail. We did not want anyone to discover that there were strangers in the vicinity.

Hekura said, almost in a whisper, "It's just ahead. We're almost there!" We stepped onto the trail and started on toward the shavano.

A woman carrying a stalk of bananas stepped out onto the trail. She glanced in our direction and screamed, "The enemy!" She dropped her bananas and ran.

We dashed full speed after her.

Fortunately she lived in the far end of the shavano and had to use only the entrance near her family's home, so she went tearing down the trail that went around the shavano.

We did our fastest possible dash to the nearest gate. We could hear talking inside, but it stopped suddenly when we stepped through the gate and slowly walked toward the center of the shavano carrying our bows and arrows down at our sides. We were half way to the middle when the woman we had seen stepped in the gate on the other end of the shavano.

We stopped in the center of the circle of lean-tos and immediately did the visitors pose. We stood back to back, with our long arrows perpendicular, the feathered ends on the ground and the front tips straight up. Our heads were back, with our chins against our arrows, a most defenseless position.

The tension grew as a minute passed in total silence, then another. Suddenly one man began the welcome chant, and immediately all the others joined in. As soon as the chant ended, men came from all directions to welcome us. One of the men had finally recognized Hekura as the man he had invited two years earlier.

With everyone trying to greet me at once, and my problems with the language I didn't understand much of what was said, till one man who's face and chest were painted a bright red pinched my arm and asked what I used to paint myself so white. He took my hand in his and turned it over to look at the untaned underside of my wrist, the whitest spot, then he licked my wrist, to see if that white paint would come off.

The man who had invited Hekura led us to his lean-to, and hung our hammocks on two sides of his fire. His wife took hers and her daughter's and hung them in the neighbor's lean-to, about ten feet away.

That evening after we had filled our bellies full of anteaters and berries, several of us men were squatting in front of that home talking. I reached into my pocket and brought out one of my tiny boxes of matches. I took out three matches. All the men looked at them curiously. Three hands reached out, and each took one.

One of the men slipped the little reed out of the hole through his lower lip, and replaced it with a match. He turned and looked at his friends, with a big smile on his lip. He liked this new lip decoration with the little red ball on the end.

I scratched another match on the side of the box and it burst into flame. Shouts of excitement burst from several mouths. One man didn't believe it could be real fire and reached out to take it, and burned his fingers. I thought there was anger, as well as surprise, on his face.

The man who had put the match in his lower lip quickly jerked it out, fearful that it might burst into flame and burn him.

I gave the man who had burned his fingers another match and showed him how to scratch it on the side of the box. He proudly held up his flaming match.

I gave the box of matches to our host and suggested that he share them, but only use them when they were away from the village. That way it would save them the long effort it took to start a fire by rubbing sticks together.

As we moved around and visited in the different lean-to homes, I was astonished to see that three different families had boa constrictors for pets. Two boys and a girl, all about ten years of age were walking around with those huge, beautifully colored snakes (that I had always assumed were very dangerous) draped around their waists. When I asked about them, the parents said those snakes liked to be handled by the children, and they kept the shavano clear of mice and rats.

Two days later, when we were about to leave, I heard Hekura telling our host and three other men that there were three people like me in Niyiyobateri, the much heard of village in the big Savannah, and that they were teaching about a new way of life that they said might someday lead to peace among all the villages.

They all laughed at such a notion, but our host finally told him that someday he would like to go and visit that village and meet more of these strange-looking people and learn more of their strange ideas. Since they had always considered that savannah to be the source of all life, perhaps it could also become the source of a new way of life.

28
REVENGE?

Marg and Wally Jank appeared to be very glad to see me return. I think they were getting concerned because I was a few days later than they had expected me to be getting back, even after Rosito had told them I was traveling with Hekura. Now I had only a little over a week till the Mission Air Fellowship had promised that their pilot would pick me up.

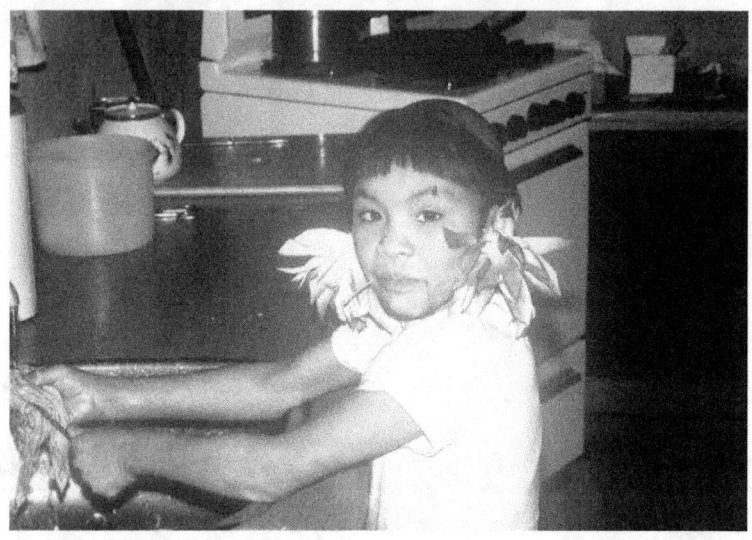

I noticed only one real change in the Jank household. That was Valentina, who Marg had hired to come in for a couple of hours every morning and do the housework for her. She was a pretty girl who looked to me to be about 12 or 14 years old. She would come in wearing only a string around her waist, but as soon as she entered their home, she would slip on the dress Marg had made for her and wear it till she was ready to leave. She had a very friendly and cheerful personality and was always willing to answer my questions about what was going on.

After those many miles of walking, I enjoyed having some time to "relax". It seemed that nearly everyone in the shavano thought they should welcome me back. Some of them had been very concerned that I was in "enemy territory" and they were sure I would be killed, or injured. Wally seemed to be immune to attack. He said God would protect him, and so far it seemed to be true, but they were not sure that would apply to me.

It was the third day after my return that I woke up with a lot of pain, and a high fever. Marg's thermometer said 106 degrees. I was sure it was malaria because I had gotten malaria when I was in the South Pacific during the second world war, and knew what it was like.

I was glad that Marg had a good supply of quinine to treat malaria. During the war the U.S. did not control a source of quinine so we only had atibrine which was not nearly as effective. I started taking that quinine right away.

When some of the Yanowamo people came to the house they saw me lying in my hammock. One of them said, "Look. Abufidoblau looks like he's really sick."

They, of course, were very familiar with malaria, and believed it was caused by the spirit of the mosquitoes. But in spite of what the Janks tried to teach them about germs, they still believed that all sickness other than malaria was the result of witchcraft.

Enrique said, "He never lies around in the daytime. He's always on the go unless he's too sick to be able to get up. This is too serious to be malaria. It has to be witchcraft. Witchcraft always takes three days to take effect. Someone in Mountain Top Village did witchcraft against him when he left there."

I wanted to get up to relieve their concern, but I didn't have the strength. I told them emphatically, "No! It's not witchcraft. It's malaria."

But they didn't agree with me. After they checked me over, and discussed all the symptoms, They said they were sure it was not malaria.

"Who could it be? Who would do witchcraft against him?" They left the house, still discussing the question.

All morning, different people kept coming in, talking to me, checking my symptoms, and discussing who could be to blame.

Finally I understood from what I overheard, that they were organizing a war party. They thought they had figured out who probably was to blame and they could kill that person. If they couldn't get him, they would kill someone else. That would punish the village for doing witchcraft against me.

They didn't waste any time. It was still morning when I overheard someone saying the war party was leaving that afternoon. I was really worried. Someone who was not at all to blame was about to be killed. Not only that, it would start a war with the people of Mountain Top Village, the one village that, at present, had no enemies. Then Mountain Top Village would have to return the raid. And that would necessitate a return raid from here. There would be no end to it. Once one of these wars got started, there was no way of ending it.

I asked the people who were there to please get Edwardo to come see me right away.

When he got there, I told him, "I appreciate the fact that the people are so concerned about me. I know they are planning this raid, because they value my friendship. But maybe you could all be mistakened. Maybe it really is malaria You need to wait till tomorrow to find out. You know that malaria is an every other day disease. You are very sick one day, feel much better the next, and are sick again the third day, and every other day, till you recover. Please, if you are really my friends, wait and see how I feel tomorrow. Tell the men that if they are really my friends, they will follow my request and stay here with me today, then promise me that the war party will not leave until they talk to me tomorrow morning."

Finally he agreed to that. He would go and talk to all of them right away, and try to convince them that since they valued my friendship they should follow my request.

The next morning I didn't feel well, but my fever was down. I was able to get out of bed and move around. I went right down to the shavano and let people see me moving around actively, and being cheerful. The way I felt, this was a real struggle, but I managed to appear to be well and keep on the move nearly all day, and made sure everyone saw me, and saw that I was cheerful.

I was sure glad I could lye in my hammock and rest the third day, when my fever was back.

It was in the afternoon, just a couple of days later, that Fast Man and two of his friends stopped in to tell us they were leaving the next morning to go and visit another village.

When he saw my look of concern, he assured me that it was not Mountain Top Village that they were going to, and it was not going to be a raid. This village was three long days journey south and east.

I had gone northeast, and they were going southeast, but I was sure that, too, would be in Brazil. "I thought that was all enemy territory," I said.

"Yes there is a tribe of deadly enemies one long day's walk from here. That's where Big Feet came from. One of our men captured her from that tribe. You know Big Feet, don't you?"

Yes, I remembered her. They had told me before that her big feet showed she was from a faraway village. They had also used my small feet as another proof that I was a Yanowamo.

They went on to tell me, "Beyond that enemy tribe there is another Yanowamo village. They are friends because Fast Man's sister lives there. They captured her from here, long ago. Because of her, we and that village, have become friends."

"But is it safe to cross the territory of the big-footed enemy tribe?"

"No. Well, yes. If we stopped overnight in their territory we would be killed for sure. But we know where the edge of their territory is. We camp just this side of it. Then we have a very long day's journey to the other side. As long as we don't stop, they will not harm us."

One of the other men said, "With Fast Man leading, we go fast." His hand motions and, the way he said it, told me it wasn't easy.

"Well, I'll have to tell you goodbye for good before you leave, because the pilot who brought me here is picking me up and taking me back to my own village, just a few days from today.

"But you're Yanowamo now. You're one of us. This is your home. You can't leave!"

"I have to. I still have another home, and I have a wife and children. They need me."

It was a sad goodbye, but they were soon on their way.

Throughout the time I had been with the Janks, and in the short time they had been in the Parima Mountains before my arrival, Wally and Marg had been trying to interest the people in the message of Jesus. This was the purpose of their being there. At first the people had seemed to have little interest in learning the ways to peace, and the ways to eternal life that the missionaries were trying to teach. Then, during the short time I had been gone, they had begun to show a real interest in the teaching.

I attended one of the sessions when Wally had called together those who had expressed an interest in learning about belief, faith, and prayer. After the meeting a small group of them came to me and asked me to teach them. "What Wally and Marg tell us is wonderful," they said, "but we want you to teach us too. Since you are one of us, we might understand it better if it came from you, than from one of the Nabas."

I appreciated that and tried to tell them so, but I didn't feel capable. I hadn't had the training, and my ideas and what I taught might conflict with what the Janks were teaching. For the first time, I was sort of glad I was not fluent in their language. I told them I could listen, and I could understand most of what they said, but I often had to ask them to repeat. They were glad to do that, with a little stretching of what they had meant the first time. But I couldn't really express myself. I told them so, but I think they still did not understand what there being another language really meant. They still thought the problem was with my ears, that I just couldn't hear well, and maybe that was why I had never learned how to speak well.

29
FAMILY PLANNING

One of the ladies who was very obviously pregnant stopped by to tell us, very happily, that she was on her way out into the forest to have her baby.

Marg told her she was happy for her, then put her arm around her as she prayed to God that everything would go well, and that it would be a healthy baby.

I was sure that was why this lady had stopped by, but I was also somewhat alarmed. After she left, I said to Marg, "I thought a woman always had to have an attendant to help her, either a doctor or a midwife, when she had her baby. I thought she had to stay in bed till she recuperated."

"Yes, that's true back home in the U.S., but apparently it's not absolutely necessary. Not as hardy as these people are. I was alarmed at the first one, but this is the third baby since we arrived. Here, the expectant mother goes alone into the forest to have her baby. They tell me that instead of lying in a bed the mother sits in a squatting position to have her baby, then she studies it carefully to see if it is a complete and healthy baby that should be brought into her home."

It was not until the next morning that this lady came strolling out of the forest, singing happily, a smile on her face, and her new baby nestled up against her breasts. She came directly to the Janks house and held the baby out as Marg came out the door to meet her.

I stepped forward to see better. I had never seen anyone so dirty. She had been lying in the dust and dirt, and and, with her sweat, her whole body had become almost completely black, the color of that dust, and the baby was at least as dirty.

Marg hesitated a moment, but then she stepped forward and took the baby in her arms and nestled it to her. They talked a few minutes.

When she turned to leave I expected her to head for the stream to wash off but no, she couldn't wait. She headed directly into the big shavano, to show her new baby to her family and friends.

Marg turned and headed into the house to change, laughing about at the black mud covering the front of her dress.

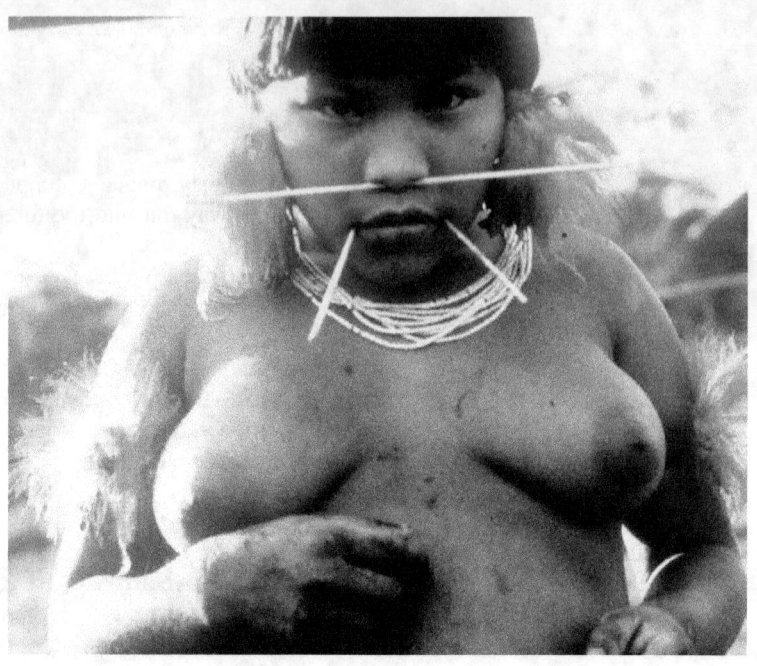

Catling was another pregnant mother who already had two daughters about four and eight years old. She was so obviously pregnant that we had expected her baby to arrive before the other new mother had hers. She had been stopping by every morning hoping Marg would have some work for her to do so she could earn a carrying strap for her baby soon to arrive. Most of them used a bark strap, but Marg had made one out of cloth for another lady. Marg finally told her, "I'll have one for you when you come in, bringing your new baby.

"Yes," she said happily, "and it will be a boy. I know it will. I already have two daughters. I need a son."

It was just the next morning that she waved cheerfully as she headed into the forest.

"It looks like you'll need that carrying strap," I said.

"I sure hope so!" Marg looked very worried.

When I asked why, she said, "You heard what she said about hoping for a son. If it's a daughter she may destroy it."

"Destroy it! Someone would destroy her own daughter? Why?"

"In their old age, every couple needs a son. Their daughters will probably be gone, married to someone in another village. A son will be here, and can help to provide food and protection. The mothers nurse their babies till they are three years old, so they never have another child till the last one is four years old. Since their children are four years apart, no one has more than four children. If a woman has three, or even just two, daughters, and the next is another girl, if she gets rid of it, she can have a son within a year. If it's a girl she may smother it, or just leave it lying where it was born. If she picks it up, she has to keep it.

"If she carried it back to the shavano she couldn't give it away, because she would become too emotionally attached to it. In our discussions of the moral values of Christian life, I have talked about that, but the one time when Catling was there when I began talking about it, she got up and walked out!"

"That must make an oversupply of men, who may not be able to get wives."

"Not really. More boys are killed by the hazards of life in the jungles -- jaguars, snakes, raiders -- and some baby boys may also be destroyed, if there are already two or three sons, and no daughters. Although the sons may provide for their parents in their old age, the daughters do it earlier. The daughter will probably marry a man from another village, who will then have to bring food for her and her parents for several years. They think they have to have both a son and a daughter."

Wally had gone to Hulacobateri, the one nearby village, early that morning. So, since Marg was so worried about the baby, I kind of stuck around near the house that day.

It was the middle of the afternoon when I saw Catling come out of the forest and head for the gate of the shavano, apparently keeping as far from the Jank's house as possible. I hurried in and told Marg. She grabbed her hat with the mosquito net on it and dashed down to the shavano and straight to Catling's home. I followed behind, trying to stay just near enough to hear any loud speech.

Marg rushed into Catling's lean-to and asked harshly, "Catling, where is your baby?"

Catling looked up, with an innocent expression on her face, and said calmly, "I didn't have a baby."

"Yes you did! Your were pregnant and now you're not!

"Maybe you thought I was, but you were mistaken! I didn't have a baby!"

After her denying it two more times, Marg headed to the other side of the shavano and gathered four of her friends. They listened to her, shook their heads and looked very doubtful. Finally they hesitantly followed her out the gate of the shavano.

Once outside, one of the other women took the lead. She knew where the women were most likely to go to have their babies. I followed, but stayed at a distance from them, just close enough to keep track of them.

When we got to the area where they thought the baby might be, the trees were somewhat scattered and the women spread out so they could search the area more thoroughly.

They had been hunting for a while when suddenly the women farthest to the west called out excitedly, "She's here! Right here!

The others started hurrying over to see it. So did I.

The baby was lying on the ground with her eyes open, squirming around a little. I thought I heard a whimper. The women all stopped about ten feet away, like they didn't know what to do.

Marg had been the farthest to the east and there was a whole bunch of dead logs and brush that she had to make her way through to get to us. She could see us just standing there and called loudly, "Pick it up! Pick it up!"

But they all stood still and shook their heads.

Why wouldn't they pick it up and care for it? Were they afraid of getting a little dirt on them? Most of them were already very dirty. I couldn't understand. I stepped forward and carefully picked the little baby up and cuddled it up to my chest.

When I did this I felt something hard at the back of it's neck. I held it out so that I could see it's back. What I had felt was a knot in a vine that had been tied tightly around it's neck. After one of the women stepped forward and untied that knot, the baby could breathe well enough to begin crying.

Suddenly all the women were grouped tightly around me, admiring the baby, reaching out to touch it, saying "Isn't it beautiful!?"

"It's really a charming baby"

"She looks healthy too!"

"Aren't you lucky!"

"Your wife will love you for bringing home such a beautiful baby. It will be a blessing."

When Marg walked up, she saw that I was a little perplexed, and laughed at me. After she took the baby and looked it over, and cuddled it for a minute, she too remarked about how beautiful it was, then she handed it back to me, and said, "Yes, you're really fortunate. It's a wonderful baby."

I was still mystified, as we started back toward the shavano, with *me* carrying the baby.

As we walked, Marg explained: "The women wouldn't pick it up because the baby belongs to the first person who picks it up. If one of the women picked it up it would be her baby. It would be a life time commitment. She would have to raise it because it would be her own baby, not the baby of the woman who bore it. That's why Catling never picked it up. If she had it would belong to her. And she would become emotionally attached to it. But since she never touched it she doesn't have to be concerned with it, because it is not her baby. It's yours!"

Marg helped me take the baby down to the stream and give it a bath. She had baby bottles that she had used with her own children, and had brought them along when they moved here, just in case. So she helped me mix powdered milk and feed this one. And she made a nice soft pad for it to sleep on.

As I carefully laid the baby on her pad, Marg said, "You act like you've really accepted the baby, on their basis. If you took it home, do you really think that your wife would accept it?"

"She'll love it once she gets acquainted with it. She loves babies and enjoys taking care of them. But if she doesn't there are plenty of people around Billings who would adopt it and give it a good home. But I guess I better try to call her from Puerto Ayacucho or somewhere and let her know, so she'll be prepared."

"Well, if you do, don't tell her the truth."

"Why not!? Not tell her what?"

"That it's really YOUR baby! She might not understand it the way the Yanowamo do." We both got a good laugh out of that.

That morning, when Valentina, Marg's young helper, came in to do the housework, she was excited and thrilled when I told her that for the next three days she was employed full time, not just two hours a day. I told her I would give her the trade goods I had left if she would help me care for the baby. She was pleased with that but said she would have done it for me without any pay, just to help me out, and she liked being part of the family. "What are you going to call her?" she asked.

"Well the women we were with called her a blessing for me, and they said it was a blessing that we got to her while she was still alive, I guess she's already been named, 'Blessing'."

Two days later Valentina came in carrying a basket that her mother had woven especially for me to carry the baby in.

Valentina was in for a little more responsibility than she expected because, when Wally left the next morning to go back over to Hulacobateri, where he was trying to get some of the people interested in his teaching, I went with him.

Three of the men there had some games they wanted to teach me, but they also wanted to listen to Wally, so when Wally went back home, I stayed there at Hulacobateri and spent the evening with them, then waited till the next morning to go home.

30
ANOTHER INVITATION

I had only been back to the Janks home a half hour and was sitting out in the visitor's room listening to Marg and a group of women who had come to visit with her, when suddenly one of the women jumped to her feet and started yelling, "Look! Here they come! It's Fast Man! Look!"

I knew it couldn't be Fast Man! Just six days ago, he and his friends had gone to visit a village in Brazil that would take three days of fast walking to get there, and they had planned for a long visit.

I dashed to the wall at that end of the room so I could get a better view through the spaces between the bamboo slats. Sure enough, it was Fast Man and his two companions. In a minute they came bursting thru the door. "Abufidoblau! It's you! You're still here! We've come to get you. Our friends are waiting. We told them all about you. They had never heard of the nabas, the outside people, the giant white skinned people who made all kinds of stuff, and did all kinds of things none of us had ever heard of. We told them you were the one they had to meet. You could tell them all about the other nabas--warn them what to expect from the nabas. You're the one who has to do it because you are one of us even if you are a naba, too."

Oh how I hated to disappoint them, especially since they had rushed for three days, and given up their visit, and because it would have been the kind of opportunity almost no one had ever had. But I had to tell them my plane was coming tomorrow, and I had to be on it.

Fast man broke in, "Wally has that thing he calls 'radio.' He can talk to anyone. Tell the plane to wait and come later."

There was no way I could tell them about a job, or that I had to start teaching at the University on a certain date, so I just said, 'He can't do that."

"Then just stay, and build your own plane. We can build anything we need. Can't you do the same?"

"But I don't have the materials. You've seen the plane. You know we don't have the materials."

"Then just tell the pilot to bring the materials. Then you can build your own plane, and we will be glad to help you."

I had to admit, "I'm not as smart as you. I can't build everything I need!"

"But you're Yanowamo now. You're one of us. This is your home. You can't leave us."

"I have to. I still have another home, and I have a wife. She needs me."

31

BLESSING

That afternoon, I went back to the shavano and visited with the different families. They were all looking very sad and sorry that I was leaving. Men came up and put their arms around me and gave me big hugs. The women just stood and talked, some from a distance, others would come up very close to my face. Unlike other societies, with the Yanowamo, there is no personal space custom, no particular distance that a person stands to talk.

They were all asking me when my plane was coming, and how many wives did I have, and how many children, and was I coming back?

They were also asking if I was going to take "my baby", Blessing, home with me. They all assumed I would because, since I was the one who picked her up, she was MY baby. Valentina was hoping I would leave her with Marg because she had so much enjoyed taking care of her for me. I really hadn't had much time with the baby because those few days had been so rushed with other things. But I said I couldn't leave it because Marg had too many other responsibilities, and had her own children to care for.

I told them my wife, Erma, loved children and would probably fall in love with this one and thank me for bringing it home--after she got used to the idea.

The next morning when we heard a plane fly over we all rushed outside to watch as the plane circled around and came gliding in. When the pilot got out, I was glad to see that it was Peter, the same pilot who had brought me in for the first sighting of the big Savannah, and had brought me here three months ago.

When we were ready to load up, Peter was surprised at the changes in my baggage. He was especially surprised when I showed him the baby. I also showed him that instead of my big backpack I had my baggage in two lady's burden baskets, and I had a bow and a dozen long arrows to try to get into the small plane. The baggage section was just long enough for those seven foot arrows. It was lucky there were no other passengers. I got in the copilot's seat and held Blessing and the bottle of milk that Marg had given me, on my lap in the beautiful carrying basket that Valentina's mother had made for me.

I was surprised to see tears on the faces of some of the group who had come out to see me off. "I'll be back," I called to them, but I wondered if I could ever actually do that.

When we landed in Tamatama two of the teachers at the boarding school that the missionary's children attended came out to meet us. I handed the basket with the baby down to Gloria Parker.

"Oh what a beautiful baby," she said, then looked up and asked, doubtfully, "Is this your baby?"

"Yes!" I said. Then I told her how it had become mine because I was the first person to pick it up when it was born.

"Oh, can I keep it for you till tomorrow?" she asked.

"Yes. I'd really appreciate that!"

"What's her name?"

"I named her 'Blessing' because it was such a blessing that we found her while she was still alive."

The next morning, when I went to Gloria and Henry Parker's home to pick up the baby, Gloria was sitting there with the baby cuddled up to her. "Oh, are you here already? Please don't take her yet, till your plane's ready to take off. Don't take her at all. We've become so attached to her, we love her so much, we just can't stand to see her leave. We'll give her a good home, and we'll love her forever. She'd be such a blessing to us."

I didn't want to leave her. I'd become pretty attached to her, myself. But I didn't know what her future would be if I kept her. If Erma didn't feel up to raising another baby, and I had to give her to an adoption agency, what kind of home would she get. If I left her here, it would really be a blessing for her, and for Gloria. I held her a few minutes before I left with tears in my eyes, but I knew it was a blessing for Blessing.

When I got into Peter's plane to leave, he asked if I thought I could actually take that bundle of bows and long arrows onto an airliner. After we landed in Puerto Ayacucho, the pilot of the mail plane that took me from there to Caracas asked me the same thing, and I told them both, "I don't know, but I'm going to try."

When I checked it at the airline desk in Caracas the clerk hesitatingly checked my two burden baskets through but told me my bundle of long bows and arrows couldn't be checked baggage. "You might be allowed to carry them on," she said sympathetically, "Just try."

I carried them up the steps to the door of the plane and asked the hostess, "Can I get these on the plane?"

She looked them over and said, "I sure wouldn't make you leave those valuable artifacts behind. Just let me put your camera on a seat to reserve your isle seat half way to the back of the plane. Keep them with you and wait out here till everyone else is on the plane, then get on." (At that time, no seats were reserved ahead of time.)

When the plane was loaded, she motioned for me to come up, and she laid my bundle of arrows on the floor on my side of the aisle, then warned the passengers next to them to remember to step over them if they got out of their seats.

When we landed in Miami, there was a little building about three hundred yards out from the main airport building. The plane pulled up beside it and all the passengers and their baggage were unloaded there, then they had a limousine that made two trips taking the rest of the passengers to the main building, but the customs agents wouldn't let me get on it.

They made me untie the cords that held all my possessions in my burden baskets. They took everything, even the smallest item, out and carefully inspected every detail. They also made me take every item out of my pockets so they could inspect them. Then they asked, "Are you sure your don't have anything else?"

"Yes, but what are you looking for?"

"Why were you in Venezuela?"

"To live with the Yanowamo Indians and learn their culture and way of life. Were you looking for insects that could invade our land and cause trouble? Or what else could you be looking for?"

"Diamonds. Raw uncut diamonds. About two months ago someone discovered diamonds back in the jungles of Venezuela. There was a sudden rush of people going out there to look for diamonds. Even doctors and other professionals were just walking off from their duties to go diamond hunting. Just a glance at you told us you had been out in the wilderness for a very long time. You didn't list diamonds on the import form you filled out on the plane so we were sure you had diamonds that you were trying to import without paying duty on them."

When I got home I told Dr. Waterman, the Dean of Education at the university about the invitation to go into another unexplored area, that I had to turn down. He said, "You could have gotten someone on the radio and had them call me on the phone. I could have gotten some others to teach your classes the first three weeks of the semester." And my wife said, "You'd been gone three months, if you had let me know it was important to you, I could have waited three more weeks."

During the next three years, I was thankful that the Janks and the Dawsons kept me informed about their activities, and their progress in working with the Yanowamo and Yanomami.

I also got three letters from Gloria and Henry Parker telling me about their daughter, Blessing. Shortly after I left Blessing with them, they retired from their duties teaching missionary children in Tamatama, and were now living in Seattle, Washington.

When I went to Seattle to speak at an educator's conference, I went a day early so I could have some time to spend with the Parkers.

We were siting out in their back yard having a barbecue dinner. Blessing, who was then three-years-old, was playing on the lawn, and they were telling me what an intelligent, happy person she was, and how appropriate her name Blessing was for them.

Suddenly Blessing jumped up and, pointing north, said, "Look. A plane."

We all looked but saw nothing, but Blessing was still staring. Gloria asked. "How come you noticed it?"

"I heard it. Don't you hear it?"

None of us did, but less than a minute later there was a dot in the sky, then the sound of the motor began to be audible.

Henry said, "She always hears everything, and notices every sound. She amazes me. I wonder if all her people hear and see like that."

"I guess they have to," I said. "If a child is walking those jungle trails, and he doesn't see everything, and hear the slightest sound, he's not going to grow up."

It was shortly after that when another tribe was discovered in Venezuela. A mission family was going down the river in their boat when two men sitting on the bank gave them a friendly wave. They stopped to talk. The men spoke a language very different from any the missionaries had ever heard. But through motions these people told them they lived about a half day's walk up a trail that they pointed out. Later, someone went up that trail and found a friendly tribe of about fifty people. As soon as they heard about that, Gloria and Henry Parker immediately volunteered to go and live there, as missionaries to that village. They were very happy with those people.

I was happy to know that "my baby," Blessing, got to grow up in an Indian community where she felt like one of the people, and had a happy childhood.

1969
THE OUTSIDER

32
AGRICULTURAL ANTHROPOLOGIST

Where ever I go, throughout the world, I try to live the way of life of the people I visit as totally as possible,, learning the culture of the people by living it. Most of the people I visit appreciate that, and give me insights into their feelings, and their way or life that they wouldn't give to tourists. For example, an anthropologist who studied and wrote about the culture of a tribe that I had lived with, disagreed with my observations of the people's feelings about, and attitudes toward several things.

Because he built his shelter a half mile from their village, and never accepted the people as friends and equals, they continued to consider him a stranger to whom they should never interpret their true feelings, but only the impressions they want to give the outsider.

I am not saying my way is better than others. I only explain these differences so you can understand why I may disagree with others on some points.

It was in 1969, just three years from the date when I had left home for my first three months with the Yanowamo, that I was able to take another leave of absence from the university and go back to visit my friends, and see how their lives were progressing.

Wally and Marg Jank had kept in contact with me, keeping me informed of their activities. They had taken a furlough the last six months of those three years, and had spent it back at their original home in Canada. Their furlough ended just about the time mine began so, at their suggestion, I arranged to get there for my visit just two weeks after they got home from Canada.

When the Mission Air Fellowship plane that was taking me in to Niyiyobateri took off from Puerto Ayacucho, the pilot told me that we would be stopping in Tamatama to pick up another passenger.

After that passenger loaded his baggage and climbed into the back of the plane, he reached up to the copilot's seat, where I always rode, and shook my hand. "I assume you are Hap."

"That's right."

"Well, my name is Andy. I'm an agricultural anthropologist from the University of Pennsylvania. I came down here to study the Guaica way of life, how they use the land to grow crops, and how that affects the environment, and all that. The people in Tamatama said if I wanted to visit the Guaica people and see their life as it has always been, the place to go was Niyiyobateri and visit the Yanowamo."

"You're about three years late for seeing the original culture, but yes, I hope you'll see it without a lot of changes because it's a very interesting culture. You'll find the people and their way of life one of the most unusual and interesting of any place in the world. Like you, I love to live the life of the people I visit just as it's always been."

"I don't want to live it! Just study it, but without the changes that outsiders bring. That's the trouble with letting the missionaries come in here. They have so much influence on the lives of the people that we can't see them as they have always been."

"Yes, and if the missionaries hadn't come here, do you think you would have had any chance at all of getting there?"

"Well, maybe not, unless I wanted to walk in a couple of hundred miles."

"And probably get killed on the way!"

As we visited I learned that Andy had really done his best to get what information was available on the Yanowamo and actually had information that I didn't have. A lot of information had been obtained from flights over their territory in southern Venezuela and northern Brazil.

He said that government planes had flown over the territory so they now knew that there were over 150 Yanowamo villages, and that they occupy an area roughly 500 by 300 kilometers. Their territory was bordered by the equator on the south, latitude 5 degrees on the north, and from longitude 60 to 66.30' west.

He even knew that these Indians differed from the Carib and Arawak, who lived close to them on the west, in the construction of their homes, and that their language was completely different from any of the neighboring tribes, indicating that, probably, they were all decendents of a small original group which arrived here, about four thousand years ago, and had remained relatively isolated from any others for centuries.

I agreed, and told him we thought that until we arrived there had been no major changes for more than a thousand years because with their way of life there was no need for change. Nature provides for all their needs, and since they do not cut down all the trees or do the other things that modern men do which destroy the balance of nature, they are part of that balance. I also pointed out that contrary to what other invaders did, the missionaries were careful not to pressure them to make any changes that would change that natural balance.

Andy said he had heard that there were a few women who spoke differently, and acted differently. I said yes, those were the women who had been captured from the distant villages of other tribes. I knew that very well, but I was surprised that this much information had already become available to outsiders.

Andy was surprised at the high, flat topped mountains we flew over. "Till I was coming down here, I'd never heard that there were other mountains besides the Andes in South America," he said.

"Most people don't know about these mountains," I told him, "But that's because this part of the world is still mostly unexplored. These mountains are not on any of the maps yet. Most people realize

that the Andes running all the way down the west part of South America, are much like the Rockies on the west side of North America only higher, but they haven't heard about these Parima mountains that are farther east like the Appalachian mountains in the eastern U.S. and these, like the Andes, are higher than the ones in North America."

I guessed that Wally and Marg Jank had probably told their friends that I was coming back, and I was sure of it, when a lot of the ones I knew, especially the children, came running out to meet the

plane. There were so many of them crowding around the plane, yelling their greetings, that it took a while to get through the crowd to where Wally and Marg were patiently waiting.

Wally welcomed Andy and told us he thought their small attic room would be space enough for both Andy and me to hang our hammocks. We were glad to share it.

We, only visited a few minutes before we took Andy down to the shavano to see the way of life there, and that also gave me an opportunity to be reunited with many of my friends.

As Wally translated some of the conversation, Andy was surprised to hear that so much of the Indians conversation was recalling interesting things I had participated in when I was there before. The people seemed to think it was important for Andy to understand that I was one of them, not a Naba. They talked about all the things I had done, the foods I ate, and the customs I had adopted.

Andy commented, "But he does look like us!"

Fast Man said, "No he doesn't. Look at your big feet. All Nabas have big feet. Abufidoblau has tiny ones like the Yanowamo."

When Wally went back to his house, my friends were so anxious to hear about what I had been doing, and to tell me all that I had missed out on, that I stayed to visit. Because Wally suggested it, Andy stayed with me in spite of his fears.

My friends told me about some of the changes that had taken place while I had been gone. They emphasized the fact that as they accepted some of the Janks teaching they had become less anxious to go and kill, and therefore they, themselves, had less to fear.

I translated as Rosito told Andy how frightened he had been as a child, when groups of raiders made their way clear inside the village and killed several of his friends, and how awful it had been to hear the screaming and moaning of the captured women as they were dragged away, and would never be seen again.

Even though Rosito talked about the changes the missions had brought, it didn't make Andy feel any more secure. He kept looking around like he didn't feel safe. I wasn't able to translate as well as Wally had done, so when we were doing a lot of laughing and fast talking, he felt left out.

35
LIE TO YOUR ENEMY

That evening, Andy and I were visiting, discussing the things he had seen. He asked me a lot of questions. "When you were talking with those men this afternoon, I know you were talking about Sherwood, the anthropologist who was here recently, 'cause I heard his name twice.

"Yes, they were telling me all about him, and the things they had told him."

"But you were all laughing your heads off."

I didn't really want to tell Andy why, so I just stated the fact, "The Yanowamo laugh all the time. They laugh at everything. You know that they laugh more than any other people. Most of that time, they were talking about all the things we did when when I was here before, the fun things, like when we were diving into the waterfall, and they gave me the name 'Split's the rock.' "

"But you were all laughing so much. What was so funny?"

"Oh, that's when they were telling me all the crazy things the Nabas do. Naba is their name for outsider. They think a lot of the things we do are pretty crazy. Since they consider me one of them, they don't want to believe I still do all those crazy things myself! "

"But how did Sherwood come into all that humor?"

I hesitated, but finally told him, "Well, yes. That was when they were laughing about all the lies they told him."

"Lies? You mean some of what they told him was lies? "

"Yes, nearly all of it."

"But why would they lie to him. I trusted the information I got because I thought they were honest."

"Oh they are. You came with me, and you acted like a friend, so they consider you a friend. They believe that you should always tell the truth to a friend, but you should always lie to an enemy. Whether the information is important or not, if he is an enemy, tell only lies. Sherwood didn't wait till they were friends and would want to help him. He burst in here demanding answers without taking time to get well acquainted and make friends. They think only enemies do that.

"With the Yanowamo most of the people in your village are considered good friends, but nearly all other villages are enemies, so any stranger is an enemy, till you are well acquainted. Sherwood could understand their language, to an extent, because he knew the Yanomami language which is similar. Like me, he had lived with that tribe six years ago. I was only with them a month, but he came there two months later and stayed nine months. He should have known what their reaction to a stranger would be. But then, I guess he never really became a Yanomami either. He built his house a half mile from their shavano, and he never considered them good friends and equals, so those people, too, always tried to show him how fierce they were, and never let him understand their close relationships, their tender care and love for each other.

"But he should have known that till he was acquainted with them enough to become a friend he would be considered an enemy, and you have to always lie to an enemy."

Andy just sat there and shook his head, then he asked, "Well, what kind of lies did they tell him?"

"He was trying to chart all their family relationships, so he would ask a person who his relatives were. That person would point out those who he said were his wife, his brothers and sisters, and his children. But none of the ones he pointed out were even remotely related to him. Since you are also never supposed to say anyone's real name, they gave him the wrong name for everyone. Then the person who told him the lies, or one of those who had been listening, would rush around and tell everyone else what they had told him, so that when Sherwood would go across the village and ask others questions, they would verify all the false information he had been told. And they lied about their activities, the things they like to do, too. That's why we were laughing so hard. They were telling me all the crazy stories they had told him."

When Wally came in and joined us, Andy asked him about Sherwood.

Wally said, "He brought lots of machetes and matches and other trade goods, so he could pay people for information, and they would let him take blood samples and urine samples to take home for analysis. He would say, 'Bring your people here and I'll give you an ax. Give us blood and we'll give you a machete.' We were glad to see that because people were furnished with things that they really needed. He got lots of information but it wasn't necessarily correct.

"Sherwood has done the same kind of studies in Brazil, and several other places, and his system worked fine, so he assumed the same actions would work here, but they didn't. He did find two boys who liked him and wanted to help him out, but still most of his information is erroneous. When he'd ask, "Who is your father," and the boy's father was dead, since you can never say the name of a dead person, the boy would just say the Naba name of another person who was no relation whatever.

"His studies of other places are exact, and well written, but when he would ask a person here 'What is your name?'" they would say 'Saveta,' or the name of some other enemy, in an enemy village, thinking that if he did witchcraft against them it would be against that person instead of them. When he would ask the same question of three different people here and get three different answers, he was ready to throw in the sponge.

"Sherwood was using the Yanomami dialect and getting what he could with that, but he didn't know that in the Yanowamo dialect the meanings of some words are very different, even maybe the opposite. Hap had a lot of trouble with that the first time he was here, didn't you Hap."

I laughed, "Yes, and I still do!"

"There is no doubt that Sherwood is a good anthropologist so we tried to help him, and we tried to get all his important information straightened out. But then, when he left here, he told the government a lot of the false information that he had been given, and he said that they should get rid of all the missionaries."

Andy asked Wally, "Why don't you expose him and his false information? I can tell you where to send your expose."

"No. An anthropological organization or magazine would not print it if it was written by a missionary and it was written against a famous anthropologist. But Sherwood should realize that if he is going to want the cooperation of the missionaries and rely on them to get the information you need for your work, then you shouldn't try to destroy them and their work."

I said, "Maybe it was not the Yanowamo, but the missionaries who should have considered him their enemy."

34
SHOULD WE BE HERE?

After Wally left us, Andy told me "I know Sherwood. He came to Pennsylvania University and spoke at an anthropology convention a couple of months ago. He's the one who gave me the information about how I could get down here to do my study. But in his speech he told the other anthropologists that the missionaries should be refused admission to the territory or any permission to work with the Indians because they are destroying the vast cultural and hereditary resources of the Indian people of Venezuela, and destroying their culture."

Then Andy looked me in the eye and said, "Most of my anthropologist friends think the government should kick all the missionaries out, and not allow them to work with any of the Guaica tribes, 'cause they are changing the way of life of the people. Sherwood, is really against the work of the missionaries."

"Yes, I know. When he came to Cosheroateri he told those Indians that they should refuse to come to any of the missionarie's meetings. He said if they did associate with the missionaries, he and the other anthropologists would not have anything to do with them. That was a real threat to them because he and his friends were so liberal with their trade goods."

"Well, you've worked with both anthropologists and missionaries, what do you honestly think?"

I thought a minute before I said, "The missionaries are here because they believe that saving the souls of people is the all important thing, and I can't argue with that. But let's look at it strictly from the anthropologist's viewpoint. I have to agree that there are good things in the culture that may be lost. Just like the Indian people of Montana lost some good parts of their culture when what we call civilization came in. People say 'but they are no longer at war with the other tribes around them.' That's correct. They are joining our army and fighting our bigger wars instead. But let's look at the Yanowamo. Their ways are very different from ours. I'm not going to say one culture is better than the other, but we know the ways of the outsiders are going to come to them whether they like it or not. Look at Brazil. They are cutting down thousands of square miles of rain forest every year. The Indians are losing their homes and their way of life. In both places many Indians were killed.

"The changes are going to come to these people, too. They've just been able to keep their old ways longer than the Cheyenne and the Sioux. Do you think it would be better that the army, and the prospectors go in and conquer the people and force the changes, like they did in the U.S., or that the missionaries come in and teach them, the ways of peace, and help them adjust?

"There was one tribe in Montana, the Salish, who heard about Christianity and asked that missionaries come and teach them. Those missionaries faced many dangers and took many chances, just like these missionaries, here, have done. But that tribe never had to fight the army. They adjusted more easily.

"The missionaries are teaching these Indians that they don't have to be continually at war with each other. The Indians are going to lose some good things, yes, but they are doing it a good way. Anthropologists like to know that there are at least some people where they can go to study the cultures of the past, but all primitive people are going to be forced to change, regardless of what we think, and the changes will be much better if they come through the teaching of missionaries than if they come by force, like they did for most North American tribes."

SHOW NO FEAR

The next morning Andy was very hesitant about going down to the shavano without Wally. He thought it wasn't safe. But I said, "Oh, come on and go with me. It's safe enough, and maybe you can get some of the information on their agriculture that you came after, or do some trading. You said you wanted artifacts, some of the things they use in their daily lives."

After a little discussion, Andy hesitantly decided to go with me.

"Fill your pockets with some of the trade goods you brought with you," I said. But don't let anyone see them, till you are ready to make a trade, or you'll get swamped."

As we walked along in front of the lean-to houses, I greeted people, and stopped to talk. Three of the men joined in and walked along with us. Andy saw a man with a black fur headband. He pointed to the man and asked, "What kind of fur is that? Do you know?"

"Sure. They gave me one of those last time I was here. They thought I should wear it all the time to make me look more like one of them, with their black hair. It's the tail of a big monkey that has a very furry black tail."

"I'd sure like to get one of them."

We all walked over to the man, who was standing talking with two others. I asked the man if he would sell the headband.

The answer was an emphatic "No!"

The way he said it, Andy thought he was angry, and still believed we shouldn't even try trading without Wally being there. "Let's get back to the house." He looked like he was ready to run

"Oh come on," I said. "I think Rosito has one of those head bands."

The three men still walked with us as we strolled over to Rosito's home. Rosito and his parents welcomed us and motioned for us to sit down on the hammocks and visit. Three of us sat down.

Rosito was glad to get the headband out of the little basket that held his possessions, and showed it to Andy, but then put it on his own head.

Andy pulled out a box of matches, and offered to trade.

"No way!"

"Two boxes?"

Still no interest. But then Andy pulled out a big pocket knife. Rosito watched excitedly as Andy opened the blades. He took the knife and examined it, opening and closing the blades, but he handed it back to Andy. Then he handed Andy the headband.

Andy laid the knife on the hammock beside him as Rosito's mother showed him some other trinkets she thought he might want to trade for. I translated as we visited.

A while later, when we got up to leave, Rosito took the headband off his head and handed it to Andy.

Andy smiled and reached down to pick up his knife to give it to Rosito, but the knife wasn't there. We looked under the hammock and all around, but didn't find it. I then realized that Chon, one of the men who had come in with us, was no longer standing with the other two. "Chon must have taken it," I said.

The other two looked as if they agreed with me, but neither would admit they saw him take it.

"Come on," I said. "I know where he lives." I headed across the shavano, but Andy said, fearfully, "No, no, forget it, let's get back to the house."

"We can't do that," I told him. "If he gets by with stealing from you, they'll all think you don't value your possessions, and won't protect them, so it's all right to steal everything you have. Besides, the men will think you are no good." No man should ever show fear. You've already shown too much. If you are afraid to protect your own property they will lose all their respect for you."

Andy hesitantly followed as I headed across the Savannah. Rosito and the other two men followed far enough behind to observe, but not participate.

When I entered Chon's lean-to, he greeted me as if nothing had happened. When I demanded that he give me the knife, he said, "I don't know what you're talking about. I don't remember any knife. I wasn't even there."

I grabbed the long bow that was leaning against the railing and swung it up like I was going to hit him on the head with it, and said, "You better remember or I'll beat you to a pulp."

He put his hands up, and backed off, but still insisted he didn't have the knife.

When I stepped forward and said, "This is your last chance!" he said, "All right, yes, I took it. But I already traded it off. Funte gave me this for it." He pointed down at a bucket and some string, both of which had to have come from Wally and Marg.

When I started for Funte's home, Andy looked scared to death as he said, "I'm not going. I'm going to the house."

"No! You can't. Come with me."

Funte tried to say he didn't know what I was talking about, but he kept one hand behind him, and I knew he was still holding the knife. With the the threat of my fist in his nose, he handed it to me.

Rosito gave us a smile and a wave as Andy and I headed for the house.

That same day as soon as lunch was over, Wally and Marg both went with us as we went back to the shavano to talk with people who Wally thought would be willing to take Andy out to see some of the gardens, which was his main objective in coming here.

We took our time and discussed with them the things Andy wanted to learn about.

Suddenly a group of young people came running to us with Antonio in the lead. "They're stealing from your house," Antonio said. "People from Hulacobateri are stealing clothes from your house."

They were disappointed when we didn't respond and furiously run for the house immediately. "I locked the door," Marg said in English. "They like to kid us, and try to get us excited."

We tried to just go on with our visit, but Antonio kept on insisting, so Wally decided they better go home and check.

When we got to the house, Antonio pointed out the place where someone had stuck a hunting arrow in through a crack in the wall. He showed us how he, himself could stick his arrow in and use the barb of the arrow point to hook onto some clothing in the closet of their bedroom.

Antonio said three things had been taken. He held up three fingers. Then he stuck each one into his mouth, to show that each finger represented a different item. This finger represented a red one, this was a white one, and this was a striped one.

The problem was that when they returned from Canada the Janks had piled their clothes in that space for storage, and hadn't yet sorted them. Some of them were their clothes. Some were things they had brought for trade, since some of the women now wanted some naba clothes.

Marg said that to tell Antonio that they had so much clothing that they did not know what was missing did not seem like a good idea. It would indicate that others could get by with stealing from them.

They looked through the clothes and tried to decide, as well as they could, what exactly was gone. After looking them all over they didn't think anything was actually missing, but they were bothered that Antonio still insisted some had been stolen. "Do you just say to let them have it?"

They told him that whatever was stolen they would get back, but they were still uncertain about what they should do.

Finally he changed his attitude and I heard him tell his younger brother that people who were not really concerned about having things stolen from them were not worth helping. He said, "These nabas just say 'Let it be' when something is stolen. I'm going to steal something, too."

So Wally and Marg decided to keep checking into it and show that we really were concerned and believed that the Hulacobateri people really had taken something.

The next day, a group of Hulacobateri people came back for a visit. About twenty minutes after some of them left to go home Marg discovered that her dress that had been drying on the clothesline had disappeared.

That settled it. They apparently had decided these Nabas were easy to steal from. That meant there would be no end to it. We were going to have to make a trip over there.

Some of the Hulacobateri were still there, in the village visiting and Wally told them the others had stolen things from him.

One of those sitting there denied it would happen. Then the others said to forget it because they would never get anything back.

Wally said they would get it back, and that afternoon, too. The time for action had arrived.

The Hulacobateri people who were still there jumped up and started to run down the trail to warn their people that the Nabas were angry and were going to come and try to get their property back.

We insisted that the one couple from Hulacobateri who were still there go with us and we were soon on our way.

235

Andy stayed at the house, using as the excuse, that someone should be there with Marg, and assured us that he wouldn't go down to the shavano, or even outside, while we were gone.

Wally and I tried to hurry as fast as we could, but as always, with the swamps and the so-called floating bridges, hurrying was practically impossible.

Just past the swamp I saw a peccary. It looked very much like the wild boars I had seen in New Guinea, except that it was little smaller. I wished I could take time to watch it, and learn more about it, but just taking a moment got me behind, so I had to run to catch up with the others.

As we neared the village, the young couple who had come with us started to run, to get there ahead of us. Wally loudly insisted that they should not to go ahead of us, but they ran ahead anyway, obviously to prepare the rest of the villagers.

Just as Wally and I stuck our heads through the gate screams and shouts came from the Hulacobateri men. They didn't know what to expect, but they were prepared to defend themselves. Fighting with Nabas would be something new.

Men stepped to the entrances of each of the living areas to guard their families. Some men danced back and forth in the middle of the village, screaming and waving clubs. Others put arrows to their bow strings in readiness.

Wally headed for one of the houses, where a man had his bow and arrow pointed straight at him. Wally didn't slow down. He quickly walked far enough so the man had to lower the arrow to keep Wally from banging right into it.

Ignoring the ranting and raving, Wally pushed his way into the house and demanded the stolen clothing.

"We don't have it. We don't have it," was the cry, but it didn't slow Wally. I followed his example and we began looking into and behind baskets and palm leaves, and everything in the home. Then we moved on to the next home, as Wally kept demanding that they give the clothing back.

We were followed by the armed guards, who kept threatening to shoot us.

Wally kept repeating, "We came here to be your friends and you're acting like enemies to us. We don't steal your things, so why do you take ours?"

A man whose pet monkey I had played with three years ago called to a child and ordered him to go get the Naba's things.

Off he ran, into the jungles and soon came back with Marg's dress.

Another man called, and two more children headed out to the jungle. They both came back carrying clothing.

The trouble was that Wally didn't know exactly how much had been stolen, so he couldn't know how much to insist on being returned.

He decided to call it quits, and we both started laughing and smiling at our acquaintances so as to leave on a friendly basis.

All the time we had been gone, the Niyiyobateri who knew what had happened and where we had gone kept telling Marg and Andy that there was sure to be a big fight. "They'll kill them, they'll club them. You should just let the people keep the things that they steal."

Marg told us that part of the time she was almost able to laugh at their wild predictions. "Maybe some of them just liked to frighten Andy. Maybe they wished we would give in, like they told us to, so they themselves would feel free to steal something." But she added, "As time went by, once in a while I did feel a real pang of fear ."

36

MEASURE THE GARDENS

I had told Rosito that Andy's main purpose for coming here was to see their canugos (their gardens), to learn about how they got their food, how much land they used, and what effect that had on the rain forest. So I was glad when Rosito came to the door first thing the next morning and said he and three of his friends were willing to spend the day taking us to his family's canugo.

When I translated for Andy he was very pleased, but he was also concerned. "Do you think it is safe?"

"Yes. And this may be your only oportunity. It's only two days till the plane is coming to pick you up."

We had walked about a mile when Rosito and his friends stopped to show Andy one of the places where the moth larva had their cocoons on the side of a tree.

One of the men pulled the whole plaque off the tree and tied it on his back with a vine.

"How much farther is it to what you call a canugo?" Andy asked.

"I've been to this one before. I'd say it's about three more miles."

"Why in the world would they put their gardens four or five miles of mountain trails away from home?"

"They just put them where they think the soil looks good, and they can manage to cut down the trees. It does seem like a long walk for us, but it doesn't seem far to the Yanowamo. To them walking distance means nothing."

"Well if it's that far, why is he carrying those cocoons all the way there and back? Why didn't he pick them up on the way back?"

"Because we always come back a different route."

"You do? Why?"

"If the raiders see our tracks, they'll probably lie in wait for us to come back. So will the bushmaster snake, if it smells the tracks."

That answer really alarmed Andy, but he knew it was too late for him to turn back now.

When the men stopped to eat some berries, Rosito said, "There are better ones just ahead, let's go on and pick those."

The others trailed behind, and we had just walked a little ways when I was very excited by the sight of a puma. It was very much like the mountain lions I had seen in Colorado, except it's coat had a more gray color and it had a noticeably white chin. I thought that it must not be hunting men, but it wasn't afraid of them either, because it just laid there on a big rock and watched us go by. Our presence didn't seem to bother it at all till I swung an arrow up to firing position, then that puma was off and gone in a second. It must have been shot at before!

Just after that, the men behind us started yelling at us. We turned and yelled back at them. At that particular position, there were two high perpendicular cliffs a short way off to our right, and another to the left. They were at different distances, so we clearly heard echoes of our voices three times. We all laughed and went on.

Twice more we stopped and yelled where we got good echoes, but only one echo instead of three.

When we got to the canugos, we saw that there were three different gardens, close to each other, Andy pulled his 100 yard tape measure out of his pack.

Although they couldn't see any object in doing it, the men were very willing to run across each of the gardens, leaping on or over the old logs, carrying one end of the tape, so Andy could get exact measures of the size and shape of each garden. He had a notebook on which he took a lot of notes of the details.

An hour later, when we were ready to start back, he asked me. "Why were you doing all that yelling on the way here? You did it three different times!"

"You heard the echoes didn't you?"

"I sure did. It sounded like people all over the place!"

"That's the whole idea. These guys know exactly where those echo cliffs are. There are also a lot of brushy places along that trail, good places for raiders to hide. If there were raiders lying in ambush, waiting to attack us, they would hear all those different voices and they'd think there were twenty of us coming instead of just five, and they would get out of our way."

That explanation didn't help Andy's comfort at all.

As we started down the trail toward home, the boys broke into laughter a couple of times. I couldn't hear what they had said to each other, but I was sure they were laughing at Andy's frightened look, and the way he tried to keep his eyes on everything at once.

The last part of the trail we took was through very dense jungle, where the trees leaned across and hid the sky, so there was barely enough light to walk by. It looked almost like we were in a tunnel.

Finally we came to where we could see the bright light of the open savannah ahead. Andy said, "We made it! And we're all still alive!"

"Although the men didn't know English, his meaning was pretty obvious. The man farthest back hit himself in the chest with his fist hard enough make a loud thud, and he screamed as if in pain.

Andy almost passed out!

MACHETE FIGHTS

I had told Andy about the chest pounding and he had seen the man I called Elo-Kawi and me close our fists and threaten each other, then laugh together. But I didn't expect him to see the real thing, or discover that since the introduction of machetes it had now developed into a much more dangerous game. But that was until Thin Man's relatives came to visit.

Thin Man had been given a wife by one of the upriver villages. But after a couple of months the man who had her before, and some of her friends and relatives from that village changed their minds and decided they were going to come down and get her back. So they came after her.

However, she liked Thin Man, and the other people of Niyiyobateri. She felt she belonged here, and she didn't want to go back. She was even wearing a shirt she had gotten from Marg, which made it obvious that she was from Niyiyobateri. Those from the other village had never even seen a shirt before.

So the leader of the group who came after her challenged Thin Man and his friends to a fight. But they didn't hold up their fists in a challenge to a chest pounding. Now that most of the Indians had machetes, they all brought those out instead.

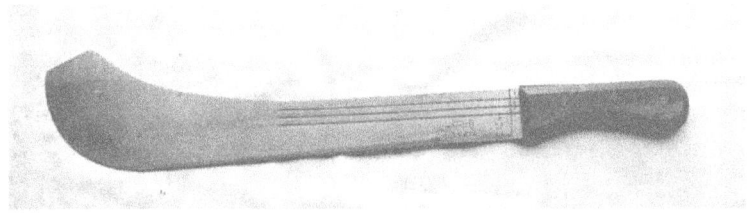

The men from both groups formed one big ring. One of the visitors walked out to the center of the ring and held his hands straight up over his head.

My scars

242

Thin Man walked out and slapped him on the chest with the flat side of his machete. When he fell to the ground, and began to crawl Thin Man walked out and slapped him on the chest with the flat side of his machete. When he fell to the ground, and began to crawl away, not seriously injured, Thin Man dropped his machete and stood there with both his hands above his head. Then the man from whom he had gotten his wife came out and did the same to Thin Man.

This continued until three more from each side had been knocked down and one of the strangers had been knocked out. When no one else from the other village stepped forward, the men began dropping their machetes, then they all stepped forward and started slapping each other on their backs, apparently congratulating them on their bravery.

They were soon all laughing together, acting like old friends; all except the girl's former husband, who went and sat down sullenly, knowing that they were not going to capture his wife and take her back.

I pulled out my handkerchief and joined the women who were pushing in, trying to examine the bruised backs and heads. and began to wipe off some some of the spots of blood. No one had serious injuries, but there would be a few new scars and bumps.

After watching all this from a distance Andy said, "Now I think I understand why all the men have the hair practically shaved on the tops of their heads. It's to show all their scars!"

"That's right," I said. "And I'm glad I have a scar on my head. I'm also glad I have this." I pointed to my tummy so he would see the huge scars. "It's from an appendix operation when I was 12. I was backpacking and I had to walk out twelve miles with a ruptured appendix. When the doctor operated a day and a half after it ruptured, the nurse that prepared me told me I didn't have a chance. When these people see those big scar they can only assume they are from from more than one one of their long arrows."

Andy grinned. "Do they ever ask about it? What do you tell them?"

"I do exactly what one of their warriors would do. I laugh, and refuse to talk about it. They do that because they can't brag about the dangers they have faced.

Thin Man's wife could see us when we were talking about my head. She stepped over and said, "You'd look more like a man if you had your hair cut on top." I had to agree and said I had thought about doing something about that.

An hour or so later, Andy and I were standing just outside the Jank's house talking about all that Andy had learned, when Thin Man's wife and two of her friends walked up to me and said, "I brought this out to cut your hair."

In her hand, she held a little knife made from a part of a turtle shell.

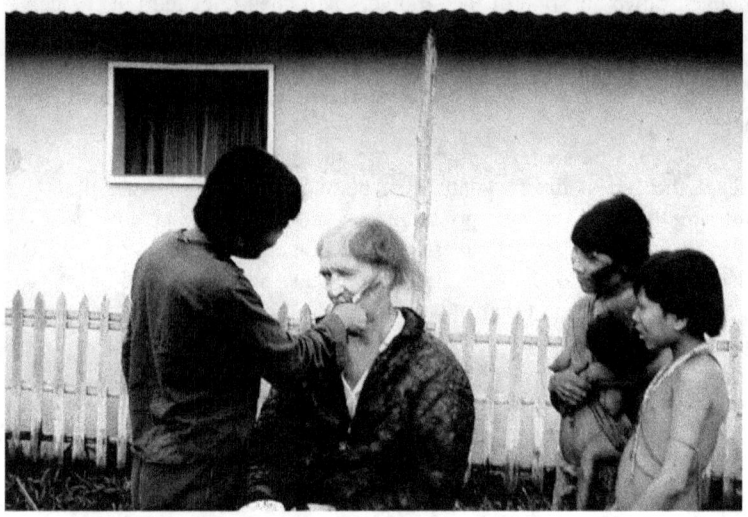

I said, "No, wait."

I went in the house and borrowed a pair of scissors from Marg. After I showed Thin Man's wife how the scissors worked she trimmed my hair very short, and even did a little work on my whiskers. They were pleased to see that I had a big scar on the top of my head. Until now I had always been glad my hair hid that scar.

38
EXPANDING MISSIONS

It was not until the plane Andy had chartered came and picked him up that I really got to see how much the teaching that Wally and Marg Jank were doing had changed the ways of the Yanowamo. Now that the visitors were gone, I could observe, and learn how much the Janks had accomplished in the way of teaching the people during the three years since my previous visit, and before the Janks took their recent furlough in Canada.

Since the Janks had been in Canada and hadn't returned until a few days before we arrived, most of the time since their return Wally had been concentrating on getting their home repaired. Now that their home was back in good enough condition to make it livable, they could concentrate on their work as missionaries. They were anxious to get classes started again, and I could see that some of the Indians were just as anxious to get back to learning.

Each morning the village was practically cleared out as nearly everyone left to hunt, work in the gardens, or gather wild roots and fruit. But mid afternoon brought an end to most of the work, and many of them gathered for an afternoon or evening meeting. Sometimes Wally and Marg led them in singing hymns they had translated for them, then discussing the meanings of those hymns. Other times Wally spent the time teaching them stories about the life of Jesus. Sometimes they each talked with individuals, or groups, discussing with them how faith in God, and in Jesus' leadership, could guide their lives as well as give them confidence in the decisions they made when problems arose, then explained to them different teachings of Jesus that would be helpful to them.

Marg told me about the months before they had gone on furlough. She said, "Enrique is one of those who really took our teachings to heart and learned everything he could about the teachings of Jesus. He is the one who started a series of evening meetings that took place at dusk every other evening for prayer and singing the hymns we had translated into their language.

"Enrique knew that some of the people would be hesitant to attend because of certain taboos. For example, in-laws are to be avoided, and women and men don't just all mix in, close together. But they had a good crowd anyway and the children were always eager to gather.

"Sitting on the ground, Enrique began teaching them the Yanowamo version of the song 'I've Got a Home in Glory Land.' Progress in learning music was slow, but interest was high and they liked shouting it out.

"After a few meetings the group was smaller, but some of them, like Thomas, Striped Shirt, and Nice Old Man tried to be there every time if they could. It was obvious from their comments and questions that their interest was growing.

"I tried to sit in on some of those meetings, and saw the sincerity that some of them felt about the things they were learning.

"They asked questions of each other. Did God actually know about all the spirits that caused them trouble, that sent them fevers, that gave gave them pains, that terrorized them in their sleep?

"Enrique said that God knew them all, and would help the people avoid them.

"One evening at the end of the meeting one of the young men spoke up and said he wanted to make a confession to God. He bowed his head in prayer, and said that he once thought that being the bravest and greatest raider and defender of his people was his ambition. He had already killed two men but he now understood that God had other plans for him, he thanked God for bringing peace to his heart, and said he believed that God could bring the peace that would make fighting and raiding unnecessary.

At the end of another session one of the men said, "When I hear about God's teachings, I am convinced that as Christians, we should no longer be cracking our wives over the head or threatening to kill them. Just slapping them and yelling at them is enough."

39
CHANGING WAYS

Now some of those who had already learned a little about reading, before the Janks left, wanted to learn to read better. They were anxious to get back to having more practice and instruction in reading, so the Janks restarted their reading classes.

Of course, during the six months the Janks had been gone, they had forgotten some of what they had learned, but it was surprising how many came for instruction, and how interested they were in learning to read, even though the only time they had ever seen anyone read, or had seen any printed material was when the Janks read from their translation of the Bible. And that translation was the only material they had to read, but it was one way they could learn about God and Jesus teachings when the Janks were busy with other things.

The Janks encouraged the children to come to their reading class every day at 3:00, and the women came at 4:00 to read, then worship together. At about 5:00 the men came and had a short service.

The people were anxious to try to read the additional portions of the the Bible the Janks had translated while they were on furlough. Their daily reading classes served a double purpose. While they taught the people to read, they also helped the Janks check their translations, to make sure that what they had written correctly interpreted the ideas of each passage so that when the Yanowamo people read it, they would be sure to interpret the meaning correctly.

I was surprised at the number of adults who felt that they could take that much time away from their hunting, gardening, and other activities to come regularly.

I tried to help them practice their reading. While it helped them to learn to read the words, it helped me to learn the words I didn't know, and become more fluent in the language.

I listened to them read, and helped them with recognition of some of the words. And I sat and talked with them. They couldn't

247

understand how I could tell them what those words were, when I saw them, if I didn't know those same words when I talked to them.

While they learned to read the words, I was learning the meaning of some of those words. But I was trying to learn too many words and was forgetting most of them. I finally decided to make myself a dictionary. So I began writing the most essential ones in the little notebook I carried in my shirt pocket.

When I couldn't understand what they said, or couldn't think of the words I needed, they would reach out and pull my notebook out of my pocket, thinking that if I looked at it I could think better.

Saturday evening Wally told me that he had led a church service each of the three weeks they had been back, before I had arrived, but he had asked Enrique to lead the service tomorrow, Sunday morning. "Since he has been the spiritual leader while we were gone, we will get to see how he conducts a service, and what kind of message he brings."

We met on a sloping hillside outside the shavano, and I was surprised that nearly everyone in the whole village showed up. Everyone found a place to sit, mostly in groups of either men or women. They wouldn't want both men and women crowded that close together.

I sat down in a little open space. A minute later, Marg and a very pretty young lady came and sat near me. Marg introduced me to Uishiquini. Then she told me in English that she and Wally didn't use that name. They just called her Beauty Queen.

Uishiquini had come with Marg because if she came alone, her husband might come and try to drag her away. Uishiquini had been one of the first Yanowamo to declare herself a Christian, and she was so joyous and wanted to to get in on all the things that would teach her more about the Lord. But her husband had beat her, saying that he hated God, and telling her that her faith was taking too much of her attention away from him.

There was much loud talk and laughter until Enrique, who had actually put on Naba clothing, stood up in front and started motioning for everyone to stop talking. Then he started singing the Yanowamo translation of "Jesus loves Me." When he got to about the third word some others started -- from the beginning. Then individually, each person joined in when he felt the urge or had heard enough to help him remember the words. Soon they were all singing, each at his own key, and each starting at a different time, but all starting from the beginning, and all singing with enthusiasm. When those who started first had sung it through a second time, that meant everyone had had a chance to sing through the whole song at least once, so Enrique motioned for everyone to quiet down, which they gradually did.

When it was finally quiet, Enrique started, "Softly and Tenderly Jesus is Calling" -- the translation that Marg had given me to help me in learning the language three years ago. Like the rest, I joined in with enthusiasm, at my own time and tone!

After the third hymn Enrique began praying, thanking Jesus for coming and teaching them that there was another way of life where the emphasis was on peace and love instead of hate and revenge. He was thankful that he himself might know God and eternal life, and for the privilege we have of serving Him.

When he stopped, another man stood up and prayed, thanking God that he himself had resisted the urge to kill the Nabas when the first ones arrived. "All the wonderful faith and hope we now have would have ended with them."

When he stopped, everyone started their own prayers, all praying aloud.

Enrique's message was long, but expressed with enthusiasm, and with complete confidence that Jesus could change and improve the lives of every one of them.

He even hinted that maybe, some day, he or another of them could actually go to other villages and teach about God's saving grace, just as Wally and Marg had come to them.

At that statement I saw a lot of shocked expressions on the faces of his listeners, but two or three were nodding their heads, "Yes".

I was getting restless. For me, who had grown up sitting in chairs, sitting on the ground an hour and a half was difficult.

At the end of his message, Enrique invited anyone who wanted to give their life to Jesus, but had not done so, to come forward.

A woman got up and, stepping over and around all those in front of her, made her way to the front.

As she turned to face the crowd of over a hundred and began telling them how sure she was of Jesus love and guidance, I was shocked to see this woman standing their in front of the congregation wearing absolutely nothing but a string around her waist. But then I thought, why shouldn't she be dressed that way? She was married. It was only those who were from the age of puberty to marriage that were expected to wear the little fringed skirt. With a string around her waist, she was fully dressed. I should learn from them, that there   was nothing evil about the human body! Wasn't the human body God's creation? I was glad they hadn't been taught our concept of it.

40
COURAGE

As we were eating dinner I said to Wally, "Two different times, some of the men have told me that you, yourself have gone to the most dangerous enemy villages, places they themselves wouldn't dare to go. Is that right? Did you actually do that?"

"Yes, I wanted to keep peace."

He resisted telling me any more. I understood why. Obviously anything he told me would sound like bragging about his own bravery, and Wally had had become so accustomed to the Yanowama ways that he wouldn't want to do that, so Marg took over the conversation and told me about it.

She said that it was just a year and a half after they arrived here that Samuel told Wally that their perpetual enemies, the people of the Balafili valley, had said they were coming to kill Wally, because they knew about his shotgun, and that he intended to use it against them.

She said, "We knew that if they believed that, they would attack us first when they came on a raid. And our being here might even cause an attack on the village, instead of preventing one. Wally knew that the only thing to do was go and visit those people and let them know that our gun was only for killing birds for food, and that we intended to bring peace to everyone.

"Wally asked Samuel to go with him as a guide, because Samuel had once lived with the Balafili. But Samuel said that since he had moved to Niyiyobateri, the Balafili considered him an enemy. He didn't think he should try to go back there.

"Wally radioed Paul Die, who was one of the two who had made the first contact with the Yanoamo people three years earlier, and had, at that time, made the first contact with both the people here and the Balafili people. Paul agreed to come and go with Wally to talk to those people. When Paul flew in, they finally talked Samuel into going along to show them the way.

"When they entered the village, warriors surrounded them, intending to take them captive, but Wally and Paul finally convinced them that their intention was to bring peace and friendship.

"Most of those people scoffed at the possibility of ever becoming friends with the Niyiyobateri, their traditional enemies, but

251

they finally accepted the idea that Wally and Paul would always be friends to everyone, and were teaching the Niyiyo people new ways that should bring peace.

"By the time they left there, they had several good friends who told them they wanted to hear more of this God who had taught them the ways of peace. Those men said they could not promise that there would be peace between the villages, but said they thought that the other men of their village would agree with them, that if they attacked Niyiyobateri in the future, the attack would not include the homes of the Nabas.

"Wally realized that to really gain the friendship of the whole village, he should be inviting them to a bone drinking ceremony that would include both groups dancing, fighting, and chest pounding. That was the way friendships were usually renewed. But he didn't know of anyone who still had powdered bones to use for that purpose."

I learned later that Wally had actually gone and made friends at two other villages that were known only as enemies only because they were strangers, and from whom Niyiyobateri men had captured wives.

When I was getting ready to leave, and head back to my home in Montana, several of my friends tried to talk me into staying. "You are one of us. You shouldn't be going back to your Naba village."

"But I have a wife and three children, and they need me."

"You have a wife? How did you get her? Did you have to give her parents lots of gifts, or did you capture her on a raid?"

"Neither one. We fell in love and agreed we wanted to marry."

"She already loved you, before your were married?"

"But you did have a girl-pulling didn't you! Was it a tough one? Was it exciting?"

They couldn't believe that her parents actually wanted to let her go. I reminded them that Olaluca, one of the members of their village, and his wife had fallen in love before they got married.

"Yes; that's true," they said, but they were still astonished that it could have happened to me, too. And they were more surprised that my wife's parents would actually let her go without a fight, or else many gifts.

I realized then, that my telling them that there was no resistance was, in their opinion, an insult to my wife. They thought that if she knew I had said it, she would be angry about my telling them.

I was so moved by all the weeping and wailing as I was getting on the plane to leave, that I actually broke down and shed a few tears, myself.

FLOOD

41
A NEW OPPORTUNITY

When I again took off on a plane to South America, I assumed that I would have no difficulty getting back to Niyiyobateri, to have another month or more with the Janks and my Yanowamo friends. I was already in Venezuela, on the flight from Caracas to Puerto Ayacucho when I developed a bad case of diarrhea and began coughing.

I remembered what one of the men down on the Orinoco had told me last time I was there. "All illness begins with the whites. They are the ones who invented it. If there were no whites there would be no diseases in the world."

I realized the truth of that statement. Because of our worldwide travel, we have picked up the diseases of the whole world, and after having many generations of them, we have developed immunity to some of them. When the first people had arrived in Hawaii, they had been in their canoes for weeks. Anyone with a disease was already dead. So there were no contagious diseases in the Hawaiian Islands for centuries, until the first ships landed there. During those centuries the people had lost their ability to resist disease, so when the first outsiders arrived, about half of them died from the common diseases that were not serious for others. I knew the history of North America was almost as bad. In North America, almost half of the Indians had died of smallpox. Some of the U.S. Army officers intentionally gave blankets that had been used by soldiers with smallpox to the Indians, knowing it would wipe out two thirds of the members of those tribes.

My cough and diarrhea might mean I had some kind of disease I might pass on to my Yanowamo friends. For them it could be a disaster. I canceled my flight to Tamatama and got myself a room in Puerto Ayacucho.

My symptoms only lasted a day, so after three days of feeling well, I decided I could go on to Niyiyobateri. I went over to mission headquarters to see if they could get me on a plane that would go there.

It had been raining hard ever since I arrived there. It was really a drenching rain, and I was told that it had been raining like that for a couple of weeks before I got there.

At the New Tribes Mission headquarters, the Baxters welcomed me, but they said my chance of getting to Niyiyobateri was almost nil. The Janks had called on the radio and informed them that two of their friends were deadly ill from injuries and they really needed a doctor, but their airstrip was covered with water and they doubted that it was safe to land there. However, Jim Hurd and a doctor who had been there before were so determined to get there that the pilot had gone ahead and flown them in. The plane had nearly turned over when they landed.

"Are they still stuck there?" I asked, "Or were they able to take off again?"

"Oh yes," Bill said. "After several days there, the pilot finally managed to take off, and they got back this morning. He was only here for an hour, before he took off again to take the sick people he had brought out to San Fernando de Apure. Before he left, he warned everyone that no other plane should even consider flying in to Niyiyobateri while the rains last, or for quite a while after that, because the landing strip will take weeks of drying before it will be safe for anyone to land there. But before he took off he handed me this letter. It's from the Janks. He said they thought you would be arriving here in Puerto Ayacucho, expecting him to take you back to see them."

It looked like my chances of getting to Niyiyobateri were nil, but I was glad to at least get some communication and know what was going on there. I ripped the letter open.

Dear Hap,

Greetings from Niyiyobateri!

We're very sorry you can't get here to visit us, but the pilot who brought Jim Hurd and the doctor says that if he succeeds in taking off tomorrow morning, he's definitely not going to try to bring you here, and nobody else should either, not till we've had a long dry spell. It probably means that you cant visit any of the Yanowamo , but if you can't get here, we hope maybe you can at least visit the Dawsons, or one of the other Yanomami villages.

We sure wish you could be here 'cause things have really been popping around here lately, with all kinds of excitement. Television crewmen filmed Niyiyobateri life for a Caracas TV studio. The enemy village came over to declare an end to the war. A man from Joorocobateri was here and was bitten by a huge snake, and is still trying to recover. Juancito's foot was smashed by a falling tree and necessitated calling in the doctor to look after it. So we've been busy, to say the least.

You'll remember Uishiquuimi, who we used to call the Beauty Queen. She lives in Mayubateri now. About two weeks ago she had her leg almost chopped off by her husband for running away on him. Then when he saw how serious it was, he was too scared to come over and ask for help, so we never found out about it till three days ago. Then Jim Hurd flew in with a doctor to look after Juancito's foot. While the doctor was taking care of Juancito, Wally and Jim made the long day's walk over to Mayubateri to give polio vaccine to the people there. So they found Uishiquimi lying in a hut behind the shavano with her leg terribly twisted and badly infected. They loaded her onto a hammock and two men helped them carry her all the way back here so she could see the doctor. She just laid on the hammock groaning and crying and praying all the way over here. The doctor gave her a quick examination and said that the leg was already rotten so she'd have little chance of living, apart from and amputation.

So after a tearful and fearful consideration, her relatives agreed to send her out for the operation. Her uncle, is going along to try and cheer and console her; and Paul and Marty are going with them as interpreters. They'll be to Puerto Ayacucho tomorrow morning, if the pilot manages to get the plane out of this swamp, but they will be flying on to San Fernando de Apure tomorrow, where they're better equipped for major surgery. As you know, she made a profession of faith when you were here before, and her faith is sustaining her. Nako will go along and try to keep her in good spirits so she won't lose heart and quit eating, as Guaicas are prone to do when they're lonely. Nako said, "I have Jesus now, and I really think we'll help her, but she's scared, and so am I." So that's the story up to now.

Well, I've got to get to bed, but realizing that you know the people but can't get here as you planned, we knew you would be really concerned about all of these things. I assume you must be at the mission headquarters in Puerto Ayacucho by now, and will get this letter.

Love to the family. Maybe we'll be able to see you when we're on furlough in the U.S. and Canada later this year.

In His care, Marg & Wally

I looked at Bill and said, "Well, even though the rain stopped this morning, it looks like there's no chance that I'll make it to Niyiyobateri, but do you suppose I might find a way to get up to the Dawsons, on the Padamo river?"

Bill looked at me and shook his head. But then he grinned at me and said, "Always looking for a way to get somewhere, aren't you, and something always shows up. And maybe it will again. You know these floods that are blocking you from going to Niyiyobateri have drenched the whole upper Orinoco. The rivers have risen so high that they have wiped out most of the gardens of nearly all the Indians who live along the rivers. Well, the U.S. government has learned of these hungry people and they sent a big shipment of rice and sugar, to be distributed to all those villages, to save them from starvation. A large boat came up the Orinoco river, carrying lots of sacks of rice and sugar donated by the U.S. government. They have been stopping at all the villages below here and giving it out. When they arrived here yesterday, they learned that they couldn't go any farther because they couldn't get their boat up through the sixty miles of rapids above here. We told them about the boat the Indian commission uses when they go up from here."

"Yes," I said. "That's the dugout canoe the commissioner used to take me up to Tamatama the first time I came down here."

"It's a bigger one now, and there's now a good road to get up past the Rapids of Death to the boat. They were trying to make arrangements for that boat last night. They shouldn't have much problem, 'cause they're doing it to benefit the Indians. Jump in my car and we'll dash down to the dock and see if they're still at the boat they came in."

When we got there, they were just loading all the sacks of rice and sugar into a truck that was to take them up to the Indian Commission's boat. I got acquainted with the two men as I helped them load the truck.

When I told Marquis about my wanting to visit the Dawsons at Cochilowateri on the Padamo river, and asked if there was a possibility that I could ride up the river with them, he said yes, they could take me there. But they would rather take me all the way to Mavacateri, the farthest village they would be going to.

At each village they were putting someone in charge of seeing that some of the rice and sugar was given to each family, preferably a little each day. They knew about the Dawsons and their ten children. One of them would be glad to take that responsibility. But they hadn't been able to contact anyone at Mavacateri to see if there was someone there who would take that responsibility.

I really jumped at that opportunity. I told him, "That's where I first met the Guaica people. I was with them for three weeks in '63. I'd love to go back there."

As I climbed up on top of the stack of rice bags for my ride up to the boat, I thanked Bill for his help. "Every time I get here, I'm stranded, and don't know any way to get to my destination, and you always know someone who's ready to go there and wants to take me. It's miraculous."

"Have you thought about the fact it might not be accidental? Maybe the Lord's taking care of your needs."

The new motorboat Bill had told me about, turned out to be two very large dugout canoes placed side by side, attached by a wooden platform. That made plenty of room for the sacks of rice and sugar, and for two 50 gallon drums of gasoline. There was not a lot of space left for us to sit, but we managed.

42
MIKERETARI

After our boat landed at Tamatama and Marquis talked to one of the teachers there, he told me we would be there three days, while they made arrangements to get the rice to the nearby Mikeretari villages who needed it.

One of the Mikeretari Indians who I had gotten acquainted with on my former trip, because he spoke English, was listening to our conversation. He turned to me and said, "My family is out of meat so I have to go hunting tomorrow. We Mikes usually hunt alone, but since you have to wait, I'd be glad to have you go with me. I have an extra bow you could use."

I really jumped at that opportunity.

The next morning when we got ready to go, we had to cross the river by canoe before we started out. As we crossed the river, I watched some dolphins in the water, swimming, dodging around, apparently chasing each other. They swam in groups ot two or three, often making high jumps out of the water.

I said that seeing dolphins really surprised me, since we were about a thousand miles from the ocean where they are normally found.

My Mikeretari friend told me there were freshwater dolphins which often go far up the rivers, and when there was a flood they would do more swimming and much more traveling around than they normally did. It was only in flood seasons that many of them got this far up the river.

As I got out of the canoe, my friend was looking critically at my tennis shoes. He smiled at me and said, "Maybe those will be quiet enough! Most whites make much too much noise. You can't walk quietly in their big, stiff, hard soled shoes."

When we got on the trail I understood what he had meant. With his bare feet he could walk absolutely silently, never stepping on leaves or stems, or anything that would make a sound. I tried my best to do the same.

He stopped, sniffed the air, and whispered, "There's a deer near here."

All day, I was impressed by his ability to know what was nearby through smell and understanding of the animal habits, and his silent

259

travel. The duck and the parrot that he shot never knew we were there till his arrow went through them.

The next day our supply ship was on the way up the river again. In the afternoon of this, our fourth day traveling on up the river, our leader told me we were nearing our final destination, the last village we would try to reach. Soon, our boat pulled into the mouth of a large creek that flowed into the Orinoco. There was a little dock there, with three canoes pulled up on the bank beside it. Just above that was a small house, and a hundred yards back in the forest I was glad to see the shavano, the Mavacateri village.

Charlie and Carol Caldwell came running down from the house to welcome us with open arms. It was they who had first informed the missionaries at Tamatama, by radio, that the floods had destroyed the Mavaca gardens, and the people were having a great deal of difficulty finding enough food to keep them alive. They had, since, received the news that a boat was coming up the river with emergency food, but they had been unsure as to whether it would get thts far up the river.

We unloaded all the bags of rice and sugar that were still on the boat and stacked them in the end of the "guest room" in the front of the Caldwell's two-room home, then we hung my hammock beside them.

The men running the boat told me to share that food in a way that would, make it last as long as possible. I should give each family a little rice and sugar each day. I told Charlie I would probably need his help in rationing out the food. Since I didn't know the people I was sure some of them would try coming back for a share more than once a day, and I wouldn't be able to recognize everyone.

Charlie laughed then made a very good suggestion. He said, "They love to paint themselves up, with marks all over their bodies. I've got a black felt tip marking pen. I'll give you that and you can mark everybody you give rice to. Use a different mark each day."

"Are you sure that won't wash off? If it will, they could take a bath and come back two or three times every day."

"It's indelible ink. Besides, who takes baths? Not these people!"

As soon as the boat left, Charlie, Carol, and I took a kettle of rice and walked into the shavano. It was very much like the shavano at Niyiyobateri except that it was smaller. We went into a home that had a fire burning and Carol put water in the kettle with the rice and cooked it. When it was done, I said I wished we had a lot of spoons so we could give a taste to each of those who had gathered around to watch.

Carol said we didn't need that. She held up three fingers and said, "Everybody take one scoop, no more!"

She was nearly knocked down as everyone crowded around her, all trying to be first to get their taste. No one was bothered by the fact that the fingers of a dozen others had been in the goo before them.

Sure, the Caldwells had told them about germs, but they didn't believe a word of it. They knew all sickness was caused by witchcraft, not by some invisible thing the Nabas had dreamed up.

I held up the little gourd dipper Carol had given me, and told them that every morning someone from each family who wanted food, should bring two gourd bowls to the Caldwells home, and I would give them two scoops of rice and one of sugar for each member of the family.

I pulled out Charlie's black felt tip pen and put a mark (a number one) on the shoulder of each of the three members of this family where Carol had done the cooking. Then I told everyone that if they wanted rice they had to go home now and we would bring it to their homes. We went to the next home and I put number 2 on the left shoulder of each of the family members, and a 4 on their right shoulder to show there were four in that family. When we got to family number 10, their little girl jumped for joy because that family got two marks on their left shoulders instead of just one.

I usually get up at dawn, so the next morning, I was awake and ready when the first couple came for their rice and sugar. Before the Caldwells got up two hours later, I had given out most of the day's rations. The second day, someone from nearly every family was back for more rice. They were all very appreciative of the fact that once again they all had something to eat. They all wanted rice, but no one asked for more sugar. When I asked a man why they didn't want it, he said they didn't know what to do with the sugar I gave them yesterday. They each enjoyed eating a little dab, but what could they do with the rest? They couldn't just eat it, like any other food, and they wouldn't think of asking for more till they had eaten up what they had.

I had wondered why the government had sent the sugar anyway. I never did figure that out.

43
SNAKES

On my third day in Mavacateri, five men came together to get their ration, then they asked Charlie if he would pass out the ration to those families who had not gotten theirs yet, because they wanted me to go with them. They were sure the berries would be starting to ripen on a grove of trees a half-day's walk south of there. They could pick what were ripe, and hunt for meat on the way.

I hesitated, because four of the people had come down with cerebral malaria, the kind of malaria that kills many of those who get it, and the Caldwells were very busy trying to take care of them. Fortunately I had already given the food ration to most of the people early that morning, and Charlie assured me that it would be all right for me to be gone the rest of the day.

The men took their rice home, but they were back in a few minutes, each carrying a small basket like the women's burden baskets on their back to put the berries in, and they each had their bows and arrows in case they found game on the way.

They put me in the middle as they made their way up the trail, close enough together to hear each other talk. There was seldom any silence, because one or another of them was always thinking of something funny to say, and the others would sometimes whoop and holler in addition to their laughter.

I had to laugh to myself at the difference between their noisy, laughing way of hunting, and the absolutely silent way of the Mikeretari hunter.

In spite of all their noise and laughter, they did shoot one small bird on the way, and they did get one snake that was slithering into the brush.

When we got to the berry trees, we each filled our tummies full of berries, then they picked the rest of the ripe ones to put in their baskets to take home.

We didn't go back to the village on the same trail we came on. We followed a longer, harder trail. When I asked one of the men if we were on that because maybe we could collect more food, he said, "Oh no. We have enough for today. We did it for safety."

"From possible raiders?"

"Yes, partly, but mostly from snakes. There's a big poisonous snake, what the Nabas call a bushmaster. If it crosses the trail and smells your tracks, it knows you came down the trail. It assumes you are coming back the same way. It hides in the brush along the trail, where you can't see it, but it can strike when you pass, and try to kill you, The same thing applies to the raiders if they see our tracks."

They may have been fearful and by the time we got back to the shavano on this longer trail, we were all hungry again, but neither of these facts decreased the amount of noise and laughter all the way home.

When I got back to the Caldwell's home and I was telling them about our day, I commented, "You know, if a man and woman from Montana were down here and were going to marry natives, the woman would want to mary a Mikeretari man. They are bigger, stronger, and more interested in and capable of doing hard work. And the men are expert hunters who go out alone and move silently, so they can get lots of game and keep the family well supplied. But the Montana man would want to mary a Yanowamo girl because they are such cheerful, happy-go-lucky people who keep you laughing, and they expect the men to be very sociable and be more concerned about enjoying life than being a good provider."

It wasn't more than half an hour after we got back when one of the men with whom I had gone berry picking, came to the house and asked me to come and eat dinner with him and his wife and two children.

With my handful of extra rice, the meal was still small, but adequate. It was mainly an opportunity to talk and laugh about some incidents on the trip, but also an opportunity for me to hear more about their children, and the things they liked to do.

When I got back to the Caldwell's home, Carol asked me if I had a good time.

"Oh yes, it was great."

"Well, tell us all about it. We've been here two years, and have never been invited to eat in an Indian home.

44

STARVED INFANT

The Indian men who had taken me hunting kept telling me about a village that was up the creek that joined the Orinoco river in front of the Caldwell's home. That was the one village who's people were friends, not enemies of the Mavacateri. No Naba had ever been to that village, but those people had heard all about the missionaries, and how they had brought new ideas as well as trade goods and medicine to the Mavaca people. They had said they were anxious for some one of the Nabas to come and visit them. The men I was talking with were sure I was the one who should make that first contact, and they wanted to take me there.

I was anxious to go, and the Caldwells said they would take care of the distribution of the rice for three or four days, because my visit would make sure the people of that village would welcome them, or other missionaries, later.

The men who invited me said that we could get there by canoe, but because paddling a canoe upstream would be hard work. It would be easier to walk. We spent an evening talking about it and planning to go "soon." Setting definite dates was not a part of their way of life, and one of the men who wanted to go was just recovering from malaria, so I said we could wait.

The next morning, as usual, I was up a couple of hours before the Caldwells. This particular morning I walked down to the dock and was sitting there watching the birds and fish, when a canoe came floating down the creek.

It appeared that the man in the back was weak and was having trouble paddling it over to the dock, to keep it from being swept on down the Orinoco. I jumped up and helped him pull the canoe up onto the shore beside the dock. The woman managed to climb out of the canoe, and showed me the baby she was carrying in her arms. The length of the baby told me that it must be about six months old, but it was nothing like any baby I had ever seen. That baby looked like nothing but a skeleton with skin stretched over it. There was no flesh on it at all.

The parents told me they had come down the river because they had heard about these white skinned people who had done medical miracles for the Mavaca people, and they hoped maybe we could save their baby's life.

I took them in the house, sat them in my hammock, then woke the Caldwells, telling them to come out as quickly as possible.

I told the visitors that I was planning to go to their village in a couple of days.

"There's no use going," the woman said. "Since we left, there are only two men left alive in the village."

As the Caldwells and I talked with them, we learned that almost everyone in the whole village had come down with cerebral malaria, and this couple had been trying to take care of all of them. All of the others were so sick they could do nothing, and several had died, before this couple, too, had come down with it.

For what must have been two or three weeks, this couple had laid in their hammocks, unable to get up or move around, or even take care of their baby, and the three or four still alive were not well enough to help them.

When they finally recovered somewhat, the baby was in its present condition. It had not taken the malaria. It had just starved. Because of her illness the mother's breasts were no longer producing any milk, and they could find nothing else to feed the baby.

Finally they decided yo get in their canoe and head downstream, in hopes that those outsiders they had heard about could save their baby.

The baby was so weak it could not move. not even a finger. It could not cry. The only things it had the strength to do were open its eyes, and breathe.

We mixed powdered milk and put it in a baby bottle Carol had. But the baby could not suck on the nipple. So we took a spoon and put milk in it's mouth. It nearly choked because it didn't have the strength to swallow.

Charlie and I decided that even though there was no way to get food into its body, we could give it a shot of vitamins. Maybe that would help. We filled the hypodermic needle, but nowhere on it's body was there flesh enough to insert the needle.

We took the family to the shavano, and the people said there was one vacant home. The family who lived in that lean-to had left two hammocks when they went to visit another village, and their neighbors didn't know when, or if, they were coming back. To me, it was just as if preparations had already been made for the guests.

We left them there, wondering if there was any chance the baby would still be alive when we came back a couple of hours later.

We went back four times that day, but there was no change. We could feed the starving parents, but there was nothing we could do for the baby.

That night, before we went to bed, we went back, and each of us prayed for the parents, for comfort in their sorrow. We could have prayed for the baby's survival through the night, but we knew that was impossible.

We hesitated to go back there the next morning. Carol said she was surprised that we hadn't been awakened by the wailing. Of course it was a tiny baby, and a total stranger to most of the people, but still, any death would normally bring out the loud wailing. Everyone would take part, and it would last for hours.

"Yes," I said, "I've heard it before, and you would be able to hear it plainly a half mile away. Maybe, just maybe that baby is still alive."

Carol was sure there was no chance of that.

When we got there, the mother was rocking the baby in the hammock. It could no longer open it's eyes or show any signs of life, except that by feeling and listening closely, we could detect that there was still breathing and a faint heartbeat. When I put my hand on it's leg, and spoke softly to it, I thought I felt a slight muscle movement in that leg.

"That's just wishful thinking on your part," Carol said.

Throughout the day and the next night there was still no change. The following morning the heart beat was so weak we could barely detect it. But I was sure it was still there even though the family in the next lean-to said we were just imagining it.

About the middle of that morning a dozen canoes, each filled with Guaicas came paddling up the river and docked along the shore. Joe and Millie Dawson jumped out of one and greeted us. All the Indians stayed in their canoes until Charlie and I went into the shavano and told the people that these were not enemies, but friends from a Christian village, who had come to help them learn about the Lord, and a better way of life.

When one of the Mavaca leaders from the shavano came down and let them know they were welcome, all the Indians piled out of their canoes and headed for the shavano.

Joe and Millie Dawson were anxious to tell us what had led up to their visit. As I knew, their village was the first Guaica village to be contacted by missionaries. The Dawsons had gone there soon after the tribe was discovered. The people there had listened to the teachings of these missionaries and eventually all of them had become convinced that Jesus was their savior. They had sworn their allegiance to Him, and were happy with their decision.

It was not the Dawsons, but the Indian people themselves, who suggested this trip. They said that they appreciated so much the missionaries coming to them and teaching them, that it was time they themselves went out as missionaries to teach others. They had chosen Mavacateri because it was right on the Orinoco river and, in their terms, "easy to get to." Since it was seventy miles up the swift Orinoco, and they had to paddle against the current, it had taken them five days to get there.

They had all brought their hammocks, a week's food supply, and some little gifts, so each family moved in with one of the local families and planed to spend the next three days telling them about their own Christian beliefs, and the great improvement in their own lives since the Dawsons had been there.

With all those visitors, and the excitement of visiting, sharing foods, and listening to descriptions of the Christian life, as told by other Yanomami, the couple with the starved baby was left alone in their corner of the village and was pretty much forgotten.

In the evening Carol and I went to see them, and once again tried to give the baby a few drops of milk with a medicine dropper, but it was hopeless.

The Dawson parents hung their hammocks in the kitchen of the Caldwell's home, and their children hung theirs in the guest room with me.

It was just a little past midnight when I heard the beginning of the wailing and I knew that had to mean the death of the baby.

The wailing began to increase rapidly, as I expected. I knew that with the members of both villages wailing, the sound would be deafening for the next few hours. But then, to my surprise, it faded away.

The Caldwells and the Dawson parents and I were quickly on our way up to the shavano to see what was going on.

All the members of the guest families were gathering around the hammock on which the baby lay, and the mother lay curled around it weeping uncontrollably.

The guests had convinced all their hosts that they should not begin their wailing until they had all had a chance to pray for the soul of the baby. Several of those around the hammock were praying softy but steadily.

I stepped over them and felt the baby's neck and was certain there was no pulse. Joe Dawson did the same, knowing that he had more experience checking pulse and breathing at the clinic they had set up at their mission. We were both certain the baby was dead.

The Caldwells said "The wailing will begin again soon, and they returned to their home. But the Dawsons and I just stepped back out of the way, and waited.

The praying went on and on. No one took charge in any way. Everyone just prayed in his own way. Occasionally only one was praying but most of the time many or all were praying aloud, individually, but all at the same time.

This praying had been going on for over two hours. There was a time when only two were praying aloud, and most of the others had raised their eyes and were looking at the dead baby for which they were praying. My eyes were on it, too.

Then the baby raised its head! It opened its eyes. One of the women laid her own baby down, picked up the starved one and nestled it to her breast. It began nursing.

My leave of absence from Montana State University in Billings was about up, so two days later, when all the visitors went home, the Dawsons took me with them down-river to their home. A visitor then gave me a ride to Tamatama, where I could get on a series of planes that would get me back to my home in Montana.

Three years later, the churches and friends who had supported the work of the Caldwells decreased their support of the mission work, to the extent that they could hardly pay for the food that the mission supply boat brought them every three months. They decided that it was time to quit the mission work and go home. The only trouble was that they had no money at all to pay for their flight back to the U.S.

They decided that in spite of that, when the mission supply boat came with their supplies they would have to just get on the boat, and ride to the mission base in Puerto Ayacucho, even though they had no idea how they could ever get home. Perhaps they could find some kind of work there to support themselves.

When the boat arrived, along with the food, it brought their mail. In that mail was a. letter from one of their supporters. With that letter was a donation check. It was for the exact amount it would cost them to fly home from Puerto Ayacucho. They left everything they had and thankfully got on the boat going back to its home base in Puerto Ayacucho.

When the boat stopped at the Dawson's village, Carol informed Joe and Millie that the baby who had nearly starved to death, but had been saved by prayer, was growing into a very active boy, always cheerful, happy, and full of fun, with no indication of his having ever been starved when he was a baby.

MY NEPHEW VISITS
1972

45
LYLE

It had been three years since my last visit with the Yanowamo people, and I was anxious to get back and enjoy another visit and see what changes had taken place. I knew that Wally and Marg Jank, and their son, Davy, were on furlough in Canada and were about ready to head back to Venezuela so I wrote to them telling them the dates of my summer vacation from the university, and of my plans to go back to visit Niyiyobateri. Their immediate reply said that, just like the other two times when I went there, they would be getting to Niyiyobateri just shortly before I arrived.

My nephew, Lyle Moss, was very interested in medicine and all through high school and college he had spent much of his time as a volunteer in a hospital, where the doctors appreciated his desire to help the patients and to learn everything he could about medicine and surgery, as he assisted them. Because those physicians and science teachers all highly recommended him he had been accepted as a student in medical school, where he planned to enroll next fall.

He was also a very adventurous person who loved to explore caves and climb mountains. He was an expert rock climber, and liked the challenge of climbing anything that had never before been climbed. His parents had written to me telling of his experience climbing one of the two highest rock spires near their home in Grand Junction Colorado. He had started his climb early in the morning thinking that he could be at the top before night. However, when it got dark he was only half way to the top so he had to tie himself to iron spikes that he drove into the rock and he hung there all night. It was in the evening of the second day that he finally made it to the top.

That didn't discourage him. There was still one rock spire in western Colorado that everyone was convinced could never be climbed. Climbing that was a challenge he couldn't resist. He planed to do it in June, as soon as school was out.

270

Since he was so adventurous, I thought that maybe visiting an almost unknown primitive tribe of Indians might also be just the kind of challenge that would really excite him. I wrote him a letter and told him about the Yanowamo, and said that I was leaving for another visit with them as soon as spring quarter was over at Montana State University Billings, where I was a professor. I told him that if he could postpone his climb until we got back, I would love to have him go with me.

Three days later I had his answer. The Idea really sounded great. He'd do almost anything to get to go, but it was totally impossible. The cost of the airfare getting there was completely beyond any possibility for him. Registering for medical school in the fall would take every cent of his savings, and everything he could earn this summer.

I was sorry to hear that but understood, because it was difficult enough for me, with a family to support to buy my own ticket. I immediately went ahead and made my arrangements to make the trip alone again.

A few days later I got a long distance call from Lyle. He had showed my letter to his parents. Almost immediately, his mother (my sister) had told him that if he would promise that he would never attempt to climb that rock spire that he was planning to climb, then she would pay the cost of his trip.

Two weeks later, Lyle was sitting there beside me on the plane to South America.

46

WELCOMED BY THE DAWSONS

I had been able to schedule a regular airline flight to Puerto Ayacucho, Venezuela, but could not contact the Mission Air Fellowship until we got there. When we arrived, the mission headquarters informed me that they had a plane going to Tamatama that day, but that plane would have to to come right back, to bring two teachers out so they could catch their plane to the U.S. for their summer vacation. It would be four days before they could get us to Niyiyobateri. We could wait in either Puerto Ayacucho or Tamatama.

I said, "We'll go Tamatama. There's a lot to see there."

When our plane landed in Tamatama, Joe Dawson was at the airstrip to welcome us. He had come down from their mission on the Padamo river to pick up three of his children who were attending the Tamatama high school.

Joe told us that their seven younger children were being home-schooled at their mission on the Padamo river, but they thought Velma,

Lyle on the plane

Mike, and Susan, who were high school students should get the broader experience of a larger school.

Joe suggested that Lyle and I come with them to their mission on the Padamo river. I was glad when Paul Johnson, the Mission Air Fellowship pilot, agreed that would be OKay. When he came back to take us to Niyiyobateri he could pick us up at the mission there, just as well as here in Tamatama.

Joe explained to Lyle that when the "Guaica" Indians were first discovered in the late 1950's he and his wife, Millie, had been the first people to offer to start some mission work with them. They had then started a mission at Cochilowateri, a village on the Padamo river, a branch of the Orinoco, about fifty miles above this Mikeretari village of Tamatama.

When I had come to Venezuela the first time, there were only two of the Yanomami villages that had any outsiders living with them. The Dawsons had started a mission, working with the first one and had been there four years. Because I wanted to visit the the Indians with the least contact with the outside world, I had gone on up the Orinoco to a newer mission. I had spent a month there then, on the way out, I had a week at the Dawsons mission.

Joe and Millie Dawson and four of their children had visited me and my wife in Montana, while they were on furlough last year, so I was anxious to get this chance to spend more time with them.

The next morning the three Dawson children and Lyle and I were with Joe in his motorized canoe, heading up the river.

Lyle was enjoying seeing the rain forest along both sides of the river and watching closely for any wild life. There were a lot of water birds and we could see pigeons and other birds in the trees. Mike, one of Joe's boys, excitedly pointed out a huge snake on the shore.

Lyle was surprised at the size of the snake. I had told him that we would have to watch out for the bushmaster, because those snakes often hid beside the trails waiting for people or animals to come by. So when he saw the snake he said, "Is that a bushmaster? I didn't know they were that big!"

"They're not," Mike said. "They're usually no more than six or seven feet long, and you'd seldom see one on the banks of a river. This is an anaconda. They're not poison like the bushmaster, but they're just as dangerous. Watch for them when you go swimming. That one there could easily wrap around you and squeeze you to death. Too bad Pepito isn't with us. He'd kill it for us."

"Who is Pepito?"

"He's one of the Indian boys in Tamatama. A couple of months ago four of us boys were going up the river in a boat like this and we saw an anaconda. We were so busy watching it that we ran our canoe into a big rock. I was sure we were going to get dumped out and maybe the anaconda would get one of us, but before I could say a word, Pepito grabbed his machete, dived off into the river, then dived under the anaconda and stabbed it. The anaconda made it to shore but Pepito followed and finished it off. The Indians had a feast that night.

That evening when we pulled up at the dock we saw the boat

the Dawsons used for their mission work. They had recently taken on the responsibility for a much larger ministry. Instead of just working with the people in Cochilowateri, they would be traveling to about twenty smaller villages on the Padamo, Orinoco, Mavaca, Manavichi, and Cuntinama, rivers teaching and encouraging those interested in the Christian way of life,.

Before building that boat, the Dawsons had not only built two houses, a church, and a school, but they had inspired four of the Indian families to build houses similar to theirs, where they could live more comfortably than in their lean-to homes in the shavano. I felt like it was beginning to look somewhat like a modern village.

Lyle and I spent our first morning at the Padamo mission with the Dawson family, getting acquainted with their ten children, and learning about their activities and interests. And the Dawsons also told Lyle about their experiences in those earlier times.

Joe told about a time right after they came here, when the

Indians told them that some white people had come to the river above there, and were spending a lot of time along a side stream hunting for yellow rocks. The Dawsons thought it best to report this to the authorities to avoid they, themselves, being incriminated for gold-mining without government permission. The accused turned out to be government workers who were doing this illegally. When those workers were confronted with the evidence they quickly claimed that they weren't the culprits, the missionaries were. Then they took the authorities to their own camp sight and told them that was where the missionaries always went to hunt for gold.

At the time when the Dawsons first started working with the people here at Cochalowateri there were two or three other villages on the river with whom they were friends, but most of the villages were enemies, and these people had often gone on raids.

Since that time all but three or four or the people in this village had become Christians, and they no longer wanted to kill off their enemies. But keeping peace was not always easy.

Joe said, "Since it is now safe to live near the rivers where people travel, several of the villages have now moved down to the river, so there are more people traveling in their canoes. There are often groups of canoes coming up or down the river past here, and our people can never be sure whether those canoes carry friends or enemies. Even though they now want to be friends with everyone, they know that more often the travelers are enemies, intending to raid them. So they still show themselves on the shore with their weapons when they see someone coming down the river.

"If the people going by don't want to fight they sometimes wait and go by during the night so that there will be no chance that fighting will break out as they go by."

He told us that one of the villages up the river, by the name of Shiloateri heard that the Cochalowateri had become Christians and didn't want to fight anymore, so they said, "Well, that will make it very easy for us to go down and kill all of the men and steal all the women. However when they got there the Cochalowateri were ready, and captured the ones who landed.

The captives were so surprised that none of them were killed, that they wanted to know more about this Christian idea, and that village was now one of the villages they were visiting, and teaching.

47

LAUGHTER

In the afternoon, I took Lyle down to the shavano and we spent a couple of hours getting acquainted with more of the people. Since the Yanomami language was similar to the Yanowamo I could translate for Lyle as we visited with some of them, and we could just wander around, listening, and watching the children at play.

That evening at dinner time Lyle told Joe, "I can't believe the amount of laughter I was hearing all afternoon. When Hap talked to people, I couldn't understand the language of course, but it seemed like they spent at least half their time laughing. And the children were doing the same. Three little boys not more than four years old were chasing each other across the savanna and one of them stumbled and fell flat on his face. I expected him to lye there crying, but he jumped up and laughed his head off."

"Yes," Joe said, "I'm sure the Yanowamo and Yanomami laugh more than any other people in the world, and even after all these years, working with them they still surprise me. If someone falls, like that little boy you saw, or makes any kind of mistake, in our society other boys might laugh at him or make fun of him, but here, he's the first to laugh, because he considers it a joke on himself.

"About three months ago, I was with a group of men, hunting. We had taken a canoe up one of the rivers that flows into the Padamo. When we came to a long series of rapids and falls, we took the canoe out and all five of us carried it up the bank till we got above the falls, then put it back in and paddled on up the river.

"That afternoon we were coming back down river with an alligator and a wild boar in the canoe. When we came to the top of the rapids we stopped and discussed what we should do. I didn't think we should even consider going down through those falls and rapids, so I took my pack and my shotgun out and put them on the bank ready to carry them. But we all agreed it would be a big job carrying our game and our canoe down the shore, and we had hoped to be home before dark.

"Two of the men said they thought they could take the canoe anywhere, even down those rapids.

"I told them, 'That's crazy. You'll wreck the canoe, and might even kill yourselves.' But one of the men laughed at that. He puffed out his chest and said, 'I'm an expert. I can take a canoe anywhere!'

"The two of them pushed that canoe out into the river and jumped in. They did great for a ways then we saw the front of the canoe fly up in the air and the whole thing come down on top of a big sharp rock and split open, and both men were sprawling on the rocks. They both managed to grab a hold and stay on top of the rocks. The men and the broken canoe were right above some falls, so to me it looked impossible for them to swim to the shore. They jumped up on top of those rocks and laughed and laughed. The whole thing was a big joke on them.

The two men still on the shore with me immediately started gathering vines from the nearby trees and tying them together. Finally they had a vine rope long enough to reach the men.

"They tied it to a chunk of wood and one of the men swung that around his head and let it go so it flew across just above the men on the rocks and floated down to them.

"They pushed the canoe off the rocks so it tumbled over the falls and floated on down the river. Then one of the men put the vine rope around his waist and we ran back from the shore to pull the rope fast, and with his swimming and our pulling we got him to shore without his going over the falls. He got on the shore and jumped up and down and shouted for joy. Then he tore off, running down the shore, trying to catch up with the broken canoe, while we used the vine rope to get the other man ashore.

"The four of us picked up my equipment and the gourd they had brought their lunches in, and headed down the shore. Eventually we came to where that first man had actually been able to pull the wrecked canoe ashore. All four of them laughed and laughed about the appearance of the wrecked canoe, and about how scary the whole experience had been.

"It took them more than two hours to tie the split canoe together, and use sap from a tree to try to fill in the cracks enough so we could use it to get home. Of course the paddles and the two animals we had killed had floated away.

"Fortunately home was down river so with four of us using our hands as paddles and the other using the gourd to bail out the water that rapidly leaked in, we arrived home by the middle of the night

"All the way down the river the four of them told about other such experiences and laughed and laughed about them."

Lyle said, "Wouldn't it be great it we could all learn to see the humor in everything we do, and laugh at all our problems, like they do!"

48
BACK TO NIYIYOBATERI

After three days with the Dawsons, the Mission Air Fellowship plane picked us up and we flew on to Niyiyobateri. When we arrived, there was a dense cloud cover that made it look to me as if we might not be able to land, but the plot circled around, dropped down so we were in the small space below the clouds, and flew a few feet above the river till he got to the landing strip.

Lyle was astonished when dozens of Yanowamo Indians rushed out and started hugging us as soon as we started to climb down from the plane. My Indian friends were so anxious to welcome me back, and to meet the "strong young man" that came with me, that it was a while before I could get us through the crowd and introduce Lyle to Wally and Marg Jank, and take our baggage into their home.

Lyle is on the right next to the plane.

Reconstructing that home was Marg and Wally's main occupation at the time, because the heavy rains had taken much of the clay out from between the bamboo slats of their walls. Also, they were often not able to keep open the ditch that drained the water away from the front of the house, so that water had rotted the bottoms of the poles that secured the walls, so the weight of the roof was causing parts of the walls to buckle. Apparently, six years was about the limit for that kind of construction, in that climate

Wally was having a hard time finding workers willing to help. These people had always met all their own needs with their gardens, and gathering in the forest. Why should they work, just to get trade goods that were not necessary to their simple way of life?

We spent that first evening sharing some of the Jank's and my experiences while we were away, in Montana and Canada, and how we had all looked forward to renewing our relationships with the "Real People," as the Yanowamo called themselves. And we talked about how glad we were to be back where everyone had a sense of humor and could laugh at their hurts and problems, and where sharing and helping others was the natural way.

Young mothers, with tear stained faces were bringing their babies in asking her to pray for them. The Janks had brought a lot of food with them, but it was supposed to last a long time as they expected to get bananas and yucca root and most of their other food in trade, but this year the crops were not growing, and there was not enough food available to even keep some of the Indians from going hungry.

When I told the Janks about Lyle's background, they were glad that he had some knowledge of medicine. He hadn't been to medical school yet, but six years of volunteer work in a hospital had given him knowledge that would be a good supplement to their short course in emergency medicine that was included in their preparation for jungle missionary work.

They had built a small 'clinic' building behind their house and the next morning Lyle found himself there, in that clinic, already practicing medicine.

There was an epidemic of falsiferous malaria going around. It is the deadly kind and more than ten percent of the "real people" had been killed by it before the Janks got back. There were several who were still seriously ill.

The Jank's clinic

Marg said she and Wally had both been very glad get back from Canada to their "home sweet home," but the sentimentality of that reunion had only lasted about one day. The second day after their return, a teenage girl was bitten by a snake and they were struggling to save her.

49

PROPERLY DRESSED

When we finished breakfast the next morning, one man and four women, along with their children, were already waiting outside the door of the clinic, and they said more were coming.

After Wally had taken care of the man, he told us that not more than two people could be working with patients at the same time in that little clinic, so he suggested that Lyle could help Marg take care of the patients, and he and I could spend most of the day working on the reconstruction of their house.

He said we should go into the jungle and start cutting poles. He couldn't get the Indians to go and cut them because they were afraid to go into that area. The trees where those poles grew were so thick that we wouldn't be able to see more than three of four feet in any direction, so the Indians wouldn't be able to see anyone who was trying to ambush them.

That sounded a little alarming, so I asked him if that didn't make it unsafe for us, too! But he assured me that we didn't need to worry. He said, "Any raiders that come will only be planning to kill some member of the Niyiyobateri village. They couldn't possibly confuse us with the Indians who never wear any clothing when they go out into the jungles."

I thought about that a little, then hesitantly concluded that if I was going to be one of them, as before, I definitely couldn't act like a coward and refuse to go.

For the walls and floor that Wally wanted, we could only use the trunks of a certain kind of tree that grew in a spot about half a mile away from the trail south of the village. This kind of tree is very strange because the trunk next to the ground is only about a half inch thick. That tiny trunk grows straight up three or four feet, then sends out limbs on all sides. From those limbs it sends down aerial roots which grow downward all the way to the ground, then into the ground, and they support the tree as it grows. From those horizontal limbs, held up by the ariel roots, new tree trunks grow. As the straight up tree trunks grow, they get larger, and the aerial roots grow larger to support them. Six feet up there are a half dozen very straight trunks three or four inches in diameter. It was those trunks we were after.

The aerial roots that support the the trees are covered with long sharp thorns. But there are no thorns on the long straight trunks above them, that go straight up another thirty feet or more.

We managed to chop through the thorny ariel roots of one of those trees till there were not enough left to hold the tree up. When it fell, we cut each of the long straight trunks into sections fourteen feet long.

Then we had a problem. The forest was so dense that we had to cut a lot of other trees down to make a trail straight enough so we could carry those long straight poles down to the main trail.

After we got two of those out we went back and spent the rest of the day chopping down and cutting up more trees.

The next morning, since they knew we had cut that wider, straighter trail, and they wouldn't have to go winding through the dense jungle, four of the Yanowamo men were willing to go and carry out all those logs we had cut.

We split each log down one side. On the inside, down the middle of the log, was a soft pith. The outside surface was very hard

284

but flexible. We spread each log out, doing what Wally called "unrolling" each one, then we turned them over and each log made an almost level, smooth surface ten to fourteen inches wide and fourteen feet long. Laid side by side, those unfolded trunks made a much better floor than the dirt floors Wally and Marg's house had always had before.

For one of the walls that was practically falling apart, Wally made two layers of those unrolled logs, with a space in between, that we filled with mud.

There were two men and one woman who Wally had hired to help, and was paying them with trade goods. The men each stayed for an hour or two, but the woman stayed and was willing to work hard

all day. Lyle and I had started working on the wall just before she arrived. I was standing on an upended barrel and Lyle was on a ladder, using a trowel to press new wet clay in between the slats of the wall.

Lyle was a little shocked when this nice looking young lady about his age came in and started to work. She was wearing absolutely nothing except a tiny string around her waist.

Lyle, speaking in English, said to me, "I thought all the girls wore the little red fringed skirts. I didn't know they went naked."

"They don't," I said. "Never. But she's properly dressed, in her work clothes. All the girls have to wear the little skirts from puberty till they're married. Most of them continue to wear those after they are married, at least part of the time. But that is only to make them pretty, just like their ear plugs and necklaces. You wouldn't expect a girl at home, when she's on a labor job, to wear her jewelry and her prettiest fanciest dress. She'd wear her jeans. That's what this girl is doing. Didn't you see the string around her waist? She's in her work clothes.

The subject came up again, that evening, at the dinner table. Lyle said it embarrassed him, working alongside what looked like a naked girl.

Wally said this particular girl bothered him a little too. She was taller than most of the women, and because she was one who didn't spend a lot of time out in the sun she was lighter complected. She looked too much like like our North American friends.

I admitted that the almost naked condition of all the people had always bothered me a little for the first three days of each of my times down here, but after that it just seemed natural, and from then on, I hardly even noticed it.

I told Lyle about the time I had been sitting in the visitor's room writing, when six women came in. Marg came out and we both sat and talked with those women a little while. Then another women came by. She stuck her head in the door to say hello, then went on her way down to the shavano.

It was a few minutes later that I decided I should go back into the kitchen and do my writing. In Yanowamo society it was not proper for one lone man to be sitting there with a group of women.

When the women left, Marg came back in the kitchen, and she asked, "Did you see the woman who stepped in for a minute to say Hello?"

"Yes."

"Did you notice that she didn't have a skirt on.?"

"No."

"Well, she had been out in the forest gathering roots, and stopped to take a quick bath in the stream, before going home. When she finished her bath, she didn't want to put on her red skirt till she dried off, or some of the red die would come off of it and be on her, so she just draped the skirt over her arm, picked up the roots she had gathered, and headed for home. Then she saw the other women in the house and stopped to greet them. The other women who were in there were very shocked that that woman would actually step in there naked. Just like back home, no one should ever be seen running around naked!"

The reason I had not even noticed her condition was because three of those six who were so critical of her naked condition, three were wearing nothing except a string around their waist.

50
THE POWER OF EMOTION

Since the Janks had just returned from their furlough, the conversation soon drifted to some discussion of their experiences while in Canada. Their son, Davy, who was now 14, had been very glad to actually experience going to a regular public school. Wally told us about that. During the first couple of weeks Davy had developed a firm friendship with Roger, one of his classmates. But one evening he had come home quite upset, saying that he was wondering about that friendship, because Roger had such peculiar ideas.

After their physical education class, all the kids had gone to take a shower and get dressed. Roger had told Davy to hurry, he had something exciting to show him. Then he took Davy into the janitor's store room. In the corner of that room was a crack about an inch wide, through which they could see into the girls shower room. Davy was puzzled. He couldn't understand why Roger would have such strange ideas! How could he be so excited about watching the girls taking a shower, about seeing them naked. Davy thought the girls looked so much nicer when they were wearing their pretty bright colored clothes, with their hair combed and fixed up. Why would Roger have any interest in seeing them naked! To him that interest made him seem weird.

Wally went on to say, "Down here no one talks about sex. Sure it exists, but it's not important. It's not on people's minds. Back there in Canada, everyone's got their minds on sex. The girls choose their clothes to call attention to it, to make them look 'sexy'. The shows emphasize it. It comes into the conversation all the time. I'm sure glad Davy is growing up in a place where there's a sensible attitude about sex."

"Yes," I said. "Where love is important, but sex is not. I found out, last time I was here, that some of them have seen enough of visitors so that one of the reasons they disrespect the Nabas and their culture is their emphasis on sex."

Lyle shook his head in wonder. "But they don't seem to hide their other feelings,"

"Oh no," I said. "They learn to express them. It's something we lack. You've seen how much they laugh.

288

"Remember when we landed here, how everyone came out to meet us, so excitedly? They were overjoyed to see us. And in this culture, they should demonstrate that joy. They should have lots of emotion, and they should express it."

Lyle commented, "And the most noticeable thing is the laughter! I've noticed that it's not just the adults. The children seem to laugh all the time."

"Yes. They learn to laugh. Our children learn to cry. That's what we teach them to do."

"Not in my family!"

"No? Think about it. When the baby cries, he gets a lot of attention. His mother cuddles him. Maybe she gives him a treat, or a toy. When he stops crying, she leaves him. When he's happy, and cheerful, and laughing, he doesn't need anyone's attention, so he's left alone. So he's being taught to get attention by crying.

"In the Yanowamo family, when the baby cries, his mother checks to see if there is a reason, if he is injured, or in pain, she takes care of him. If not, and he keeps crying, she walks away. So does everyone else. No one likes to listen to a baby cry! But when he laughs, and smiles, and is cheerful, not just the family but the neighbors come to enjoy him.

You know that there are no walls. People see and hear all that goes on in the homes on both sides of them. All the people love children, and they have the leisure to enjoy them. So the cheerful, happy child is rewarded by having lots of attention, from both his family and his neighbors. He learns to act happy, and you know yourself, that if you act happy, you are happier. You move toward the emotion you express. And the Yanowamo child learns to not only have the emotion, but to express it."

"Does that apply to all the emotions?"

"Yes. When we were young, we were not supposed to show our emotions. To do that, we had to learn to suppress our feelings too. But people here learn to fully express all their emotions, and maybe exaggerate them a little. When was the last time you cried?"

"Quite a while ago."

"I haven't cried for years. That's because I was taught when I was young that men do not cry. That if we cried, we were sissies. And we learned from example. I never saw my father cry."

"Of course not. Neither did I."

"No. But every child here, has seen his father cry many times. When Jose was killed by raiders, everyone in the village cried for hours. They think if you don't express your feelings, you don't really care. And they care a lot."

"You sound like you think their system is better!"

"I sure do. In general. But it has some drawbacks to."

"Oh? How?"

"What applies to joy, excitement, love, humor, applies to the other emotions, to anger, to hate. When one of the women here in Niyiyobateri died people assumed it was caused by witchcraft, and since Balifilibateri was our enemy village they also assumed it had to be someone from that village who did the witchcraft. My good friend Jose wasn't just angry. He was so angry he had to go and kill someone from Balifilibateri in revenge. Then the Balifilibateri were so angry they came and killed Jose. Then everyone was so sorrowful they did nothing all the next day but cry. I spent all that day in the Jank's home, because if my friends had known I didn't spend the whole day crying they would have thought I was a terribly unfeeling person.

"If we could have the strength of their love, their joy, their humor, there excitement, but none of their anger and their hate, wouldn't we have a wonderful world!"

Wally brought up another problem he had with our culture. He said, "Marg and I had spent six years down here with the Yanowamo, so by the time we went home to Canada, I was so culturally oriented to this way of life that I didn't understand some of those Canadian people. They would tell a joke and I couldn't see anything funny about it. I found that I was judging everyone the way a Guaica would. I would look at people's eyes and try to understand what they were thinking. I'd get so upset by the false front that some of those Canadians put on! Maybe sometimes, back home, a false front may have a purpose and can be a good thing for some, but not when you are not accustomed to it."

51
FAMILY RELATIONSHIPS

The next day, it began raining, and there were several days that the rain poured all day, or most of the day. It rained so hard that we couldn't see the Jank's house if we were thirty feet from it, and the sound of the rain on the metal roof was so loud we couldn't hear each other even by yelling.

The rain would flood the landing strip and the kids would go out there and go swimming. Seeing them swimming on the landing strip made it clear to me, why the planes had not been able to land there the year of the big flood.

The rain, and the noise it made in the house, did give us a lot of time to visit with the people under the grass and palm leaf roofs of the shavano.

One evening, after a long day of visiting, Lyle said, "I'm confused about that family we just visited. Maybe it's your translation of what they said. I thought one man was talking about his wife, then another man was calling the same lady his wife. She couldn't have two husbands, could she?"

"No, not really," Wally said. "But she'll call them that. You see, if an older brother is married, until his brothers are married, each of them will call her his wife, and will treat her as such. The younger brother in this family always calls his brother's bride his wife. In their language, they don't even have a word for sister-in-law. They just call her wife, and she calls them all husband. They not only call her wife, they treat as such. They are part of her family. Their word 'chotee', brother-in-law, is only used when a man is speaking of his wife's brother.

"Also, there is no word for niece or nephew, because you think of them as your own children.

"Sometimes the older brother does get fed up with having to share his wife, so he goes out on a raid and captures a girl, or goes to a friendly village and begs a couple to give him their daughter for a wife, then when he gets home, she becomes his brother's wife."

I asked, "Is there a word for grandmother, I've never heard one."

"Not really. Grandmothers are usually just called 'mother', but some use the word that means older sister. They don't think it makes any difference. It doesn't matter which they say. Those words all mean they are part of the family."

Lyle asked if the missionaries being there had made any change in the family life of the Yanowamo people.

Wally answered, "The biggest change we have seen is in the way the men are taking care of their families. They now recognize their responsibilities for their wives and their children, seeing that they have a good life and enough to eat. They used to think that protecting them was enough. Of course that responsibility of protecting them is not as great as before, because the chance of raiders attacking has been greatly reduced."

He said that some of the people had really changed. Nobama was a good example. When they arrived the first time, Nobama and many of the others were very undependable, and they stole everything they could. Nobama wouldn't work. He didn't have any garden of his own. He would try to bum everything off of everyone else. He could get by with it because of the generosity of the people. He stole a lot and made no effort to do anything for himself.

He had a little girl about five years old, who was very sickly and unhealthy. She couldn't walk. The Janks doctored her. Now Nobama has a nice big garden and takes care of his wife and family. He has the cleanest house of anyone in the village. He's the only parent who comes and sees to it that his boy comes to the reading classes. None of the others do. Whether or not the other children go to class is up to each individual child.

52
DEADLY SNAKES

One day Wally and Marg went down to the shavano right after breakfast, so I told them Lyle and I would do the dishes and clean up. When I opened the drawer to put the forks away there was a snake sprawled across the silverware. I said, "What a funny place for a snake," and shoved the drawer shut as fast as I could. I ran down to the shavano and described the snake to some of the locals, and asked if it was poisonous.

"Oh yes, deadly."

They came up to the house with me and opened the drawer. No snake.

We should have expected that it would get out of the drawer the same way it had gotten in. But that didn't solve our problem. We assumed the snake was probably still somewhere in the house, so it wasn't safe to walk around, or do anything, in the house.

Several of us searched and searched. Finally one of the boys found the snake and killed it. It was under the wood we had been using to rebuild the floor.

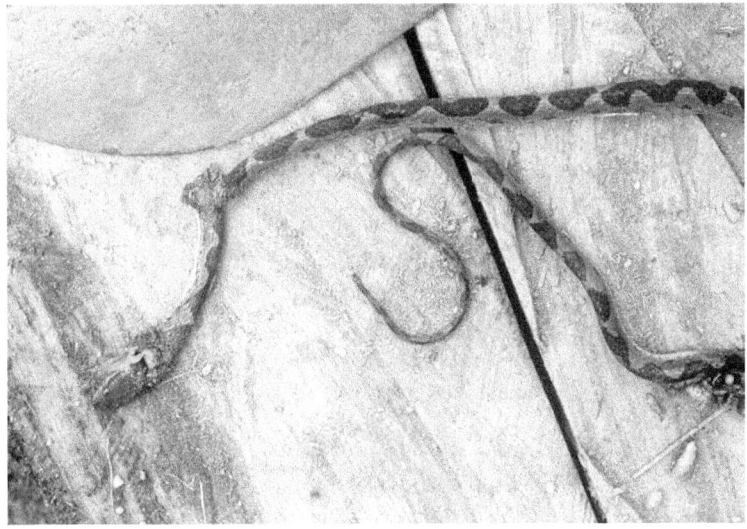

The next morning, Rosito offered to take Lyle and me out in the forest with him and another man. He told me we would gather a few roots and berries, but the main object would be for Lyle and me to see some of the wild life. When I saw that the other man who Rosito had asked to go along was One Leg, I quietly asked Rosito if his being along wouldn't keep us from going very far.

"On no! He can travel just as far and as fast as anyone else."

Rosito was right. One Leg didn't have a crutch or cane or any other assistance. He just hopped along on that one foot and kept pace with the rest of us, with no problem.

That evening, Lyle asked Wally if he new how One Leg had lost one of his legs.

Wally explained, "One Leg and one of his friends had both been out hunting and they had both been bitten by a bushmaster snake. He had, right away, used a piece of rope for a tourniquet that he put around his upper leg, then tightened it enough so that no blood with the poison in it could get to the rest of his body. Therefore he lived, but his leg rotted, and we had to cut it off. It took a long time for the stub to heal, but when it did, he was determined to live a normal life and started hopping as far as he could every day, till finally he could hop along just as well, and made it appear as easy as walking was for us."

Lyle said, "If I had been here and could have taught him about the necessity of releasing the tourniquet periodically to let the blood into his leg, he probably could have saved that leg."

"Yes," I said, "and maybe it would have let enough of the poison in to kill him. Here's what he needed." I reached into my pocket and pulled out a snake bite kit -- a hypodermic needle and a little bottle of antivenin, and said "I heard about how many of those bushmaster snakes there were when I was here before. So when I got home I looked it up and learned that the poison of the bushmaster and the rattlesnake were the same kind of poison, so before I came down here this time I bought one of these kits. I have carried them in Montana when we were going into the areas where there are lots of rattlers. And I've been keeping this one in my pocket ever since we got here, just in case."

"Where are the other three vials?" Wally asked. "It's true that it is the same kind of poison, but the bite of the bushmaster requires four times as much antivenin."

Lyle remarked, "I suppose the other man that got bit when One Leg did must have died."

"Yes," Wally said. "And his widow was a nice lady, so all the other women were trying to get their husbands to marry her. They like their husband's having a second wife. It gives them a constant companion, and someone to share the work. There's no jealousy. But most of the husbands aren't very willing. It means they have to provide twice as much meat. They have to feed two families instead of just one."

53
HULACOBATERI

Lyle says that the most memorable day of the whole trip was the day we walked to Hulacobateri. Rosito, three other men, and several young boys took us there. Some of the men walked ahead of Lyle and me to protect us as they watched closely for the poisonous snakes.

We took a roundabout route so we could also avoid wading through all the swamps that were between the two villages. That trail took us through the location of two former shavanos.

The men told Lyle that all of the villages move every few years. The Niyiyobateri shavano had been built shortly before the Janks moved there six years ago, so the boys took us to where their former shavano had been. We were amazed at how many trees had grown up in what had been all clear just six years earlier, and at how tall those trees were.

Then we went on to another location, where they had lived before that. It was a beautiful location, but there was nothing to indicate that anyone had even been there. We asked how long they had lived in each of the locations, but they couldn't tell us. They had no word for year, or any concept of what we meant. We understood that, because we use summer and winter to recognize years and they have only summer. Because of this, they had no idea of the age of any person.

We asked which of the boys who were there with us had lived in this village. The boys they pointed out looked like they were 12 or more years old. The ones they told us had lived in the other location appeared to be six years old or more. We judged that the pattern was to live in a shavano about six years and move on.

We asked why they would want to keep building all those new homes and all move that often. They said that after they had lived in one location that long most of the edible plants and roots within several miles of them were nearly all gone. The wild life was also getting scarce, so they were short on meat. And all the thatched roofs they had built for their lean-to houses were falling apart, and no longer shed all the water when it rained. Besides, there is a limit to how much junk you can store behind your homes.

Instead of rebuilding the old village, they could build new homes, so without all the work of trying to clean it up, they could be rid of all the junk and stink of the old village.

One of the men said they would be ready to move again now, if it weren't for the Janks. But houses like the Janks required so much work to build them they were sure the Janks would not want to move. The people of the village valued so much the friendship of the Janks, and all the things the Janks were teaching them, that they had recently gotten together and decided they would learn one more thing from the Janks -- clean up around your home and rebuild it instead of leaving it.

By taking that longer route to Hulacobateri, we had avoided having to cross most of the deep swamp between the villages, but we still had to cross a swollen stream to get there. Lyle got to try their kind of bridge, using a railing for balance while walking a log that was out of sight under the water.

One of the men used a stick to dispatch a poisonous snake that we almost stepped on.

Then we stopped in the jungles near the village and all of us, including Lyle and me, got painted up in red and black "war paint" before we went in.

Fortunately, someone in the village had just killed a tapir, so, as customary on such occasions, the whole village was celebrating. But it wasn't quite time for the feast yet. A crowd of the local people went with us around the shavano. When we stopped at each campfire that family would put on a show for us -- chest pounding, dancing with their weapons, or anything to show how fearce they were.

Then we all had a feast of tapir meat and plantain soup, which we ate out of big wooden bowls carved from tree trunks.

But tapir wasn't the only meat. As we sat on a log eating, Lyle remarked about the charred head of a monkey that looked like it was staring at us from the coals of the fire.

I assumed we would take the direct route through the swamp going back home, but Rosito suggested that, instead,we go up to the falls where I had earned my name, "Splits the Rock." We enjoyed a good swim in the lake, and I showed Lyle how we could swim around behind and look out through the falls. I told him the water was deep, and he could swim under the falls, but he didn't care to try it.

When two of the boys motioned for him to climb up the mountain beside the falls with them, he was about to go. But when I told him that what they planned to do was jump in the creek up above and come down over the falls, he pretended he didn't understand what they wanted him to do, and didn't go.

I was disappointed when the boys decided not to go without him, as I had thought we could both get to see what their dive looked like from below.

Nearly every morning while we were there, Lyle was in the clinic, helping with the medical problems. Wally told him how the Yanowamo used to flee from one village to another, slipping away quietly in the night, so the spirits of the sickness would not see them leave and, follow them. They had no idea that sickness was caused by germs, not spirits, and they had no idea that going to another village could take that same sickness to all of those people too.

Most of the illnesses that people had were not too hard to treat, and often all they needed was an aspirin or something else that the Janks had available. I just stayed out of the way, and Marg said Lyle was a big help in diagnosing and treating the people that came to their little clinic.

But there were some cases where the local medicine man was the one who could help. Some of the people had a disease Wally called Guasnos-del-monte. It was caused by the larva of a blow fly that lays it's eggs in the flesh, most often the flesh of babies. The bites turn into big open sores.

For this, the Janks learned a treatment from the local medicine man who went out into the forest and came back with leaves that, when broken, dripped with a white sap. He dripped this into the open sores. After the poison took effect he began squeezing the big ugly worms out of the sores.

It was the morning after our trip to Hulacobateri that I walked out to the clinic building with Lyle. There were three ladies waiting. All three had the same problem. It was another kind of parasite that penetrated people's skin, usually down low on the side of their feet, just above the calloused sole. The Janks had seen it before, but they didn't have a cure for it. They asked that medicine man, who had, himself, come for some aspirin, if the same treatment would work for those sores as the ones he had cured. He said "No. There is only one person in the village who can cure them. Since she can do it so well, I just leave it to her. That girl is Valentina."

"Valentina? The girl who helps me with the housework?" Marg asked, surprised.

"Yes, Valentina."

"I have a sore foot too," I said. "It was really hurting on the way back yesterday. I thought those sores probably came from thorns that penetrated my tennis shoes, but they keep getting worse instead of better. They must be from that same kind of parasites"

300

Valentina removes parasites from my foot

When Valentina came in later that morning to help with Marg's house work, she verified that diagnosis. She took me outside in the bright light of the sun, and removed several almost microscopic worms from under the skin of my foot.

The local people weren't the only ones getting medical help. A whole group from a Shamatari village many miles south came for help when one of their people died of malaria. They were carrying three members of their group who were very ill and didn't look as if they could recover, but with the Janks help they did.

TEEN AGE FUN

One morning Lyle commented at breakfast time that he hoped sometime he could do a little hunting with a bow and arrows he had traded for the night before. Davy Jank jumped at the opportunity and suggested that the three of us take off right after breakfast and spend the day hunting. I started to ask Marg if she had something we could take along for lunch but Davy said we didn't need to take any food, just some matches. We were sure to have some game before lunch time and, like the Indians, when they hunted, we could stop and cook something we had shot.

We had a great hike, and saw a lot of birds high in the tree tops, but by lunch time all the game we had was a tiny bird, the size of a canary, and a giant spider.

I built a tiny fire and Davy found a big leaf we could cook them on. We skinned the bird and saved the skin with the bright colored feathers on it, so we could give them to one of the girls for ear decorations.

After we cooked both items for a couple of minutes, we split the bird, which gave each of us two small bites. Lyle said he was adopting some of the other customs, but he was not yet ready to eat spiders, so Davy and I shared that and tried, by our actions, to convince him that he was really missing a treat.

We went on hunting and before it was time to head home, Lyle had proved he could use that new bow by shooting a beautiful toucan that Davy held up so he could take a picture of it. He carried it home to share with the family.

Some of the girls really paid a lot of attention to Lyle. When we visited the shavano they would have big smiles for him, but they couldn't be obvious about their interest right there in front of their parents and neighbors.

The room in which Lyle and I lived was on the back of the Janks home. It had one window, but of course there was no glass, just a square opening. The window was on the opposite side of the house from the shavano and the trail that most of the people followed when they were going out to their gardens, or where ever they were going. But three of the girls made it a point to always pass on our side of the house. They couldn't just come up to visit, and they couldn't come alone, but they made it a point to be just the three of them and they would always just happen to go by our window, and would stop to visit. Lyle enjoyed trying to visit with them and I sometimes got in on the fun because I needed to step over and translate for them.

But there was another girl who started breaking all the rules and slipping up there alone when no one was in sight to see her. She and Lyle couldn't understand a word of what the other one said, but they would both go ahead and talk as if the other one understood them.

They expressed their ideas by vocal tone and motions.

About the third time she came, Lyle was ready for her. As soon as she showed up Lyle handed her a little ear decoration he had made from the feathers of the tiny bird we had eaten on our hike.

That afternoon she was back with a big smile and two beautiful ear decorations for him.

56
WHY BEAT YOUR FRIENDS?

One morning a group of boys and I were out strolling around, and we came to a spot where there was grass four or five feet tall. A couple of the boys pulled up stalks of grass and, holding them in the middle of the stock, threw them like spears. With the root for a spear head and the stiff stalk they made pretty good toy spears.

Then some of the others pulled some up and acted as it they were all going to throw them at me.

I motioned for them to stop. I backed off, then pointed to three different ones, who I considered my friends, and motioned for them to come over to me. Then I pointed to the others and said "enemy village."

Those boys all started whooping and running, trying to hide then jump out and throw their "spears" at us as we came after them with ours. We played till it started getting too rough with some of them starting to use fists, then I suggested it was time to go home.

When I told Wally about it he thought that was a bad mistake. I should never play war with them.

He was probably right but the boys and I couldn't resist doing it again for a few minutes the next time we passed some of those tall reeds.

I had brought two balloons with me, thinking some of the kids might enjoy playing with them. I suggested to Lyle that we might be able to play volleyball with them. We put string between two trees to use as a net and tried to show some of the teenagers how to play the game of volleyball. They all enjoyed very much trying to hit the balloon across to the other players, so that they could hit it back.

We tried to show them they could jump high and hit the balloon over the net then down where the others couldn't hit it. But they couldn't see any point in making the other team miss it. That might make someone feel bad. To help them do well, and maybe feel that they did the best, would be fun, but you certainly wouldn't want to make them feel that they couldn't do as well as you did! That might disappoint them.

We developed our own volleyball game, always hitting the ball across the net, but trying to be sure we hit it to a spot where someone could be sure to hit it back to us. No one would want to do better than their friends!

When Lyle told Marg about that, she told us how she had unintentionally discouraged the students in her reading class from learning to read aloud. When she had them read aloud in class, one of the girls read so well that it sounded like she was just speaking. Marg complemented her on her reading, and said if the others really practiced and worked at it, maybe they could do as well. That ended the oral reading. That girl was being separated from her friends, like she was trying to show that she was better than them. So she quit and refused to read aloud. Then the others all had to quit reading aloud, because if they did, they might get the same treatment.

57

KILL THAT KITE

Lyle mentioned that most days the breeze was just the kind he and his brothers used to hope for every spring so they could enjoy flying their kites. He wished he could make some for the children here. Marg said she had some large sheets of paper she was using to print words large enough for her whole reading class to see. She could spare a couple of sheets if we wanted to use them.

We, right away, went out to find some small reeds to use and started making two kites. We tied on the last two balls of string from my trade goods. Some of the boys we had had fun with before saw us as Lyle held up one of the kites and I ran with the string to get it into the air. There was just enough wind to keep it there. The boys got all excited about those kites and for the next hour or more they took turns flying them, running forward to make them come down, running the other way to make them spin and dive.

Then they got the idea that those would make good moving targets for their arrows. The kites flew around like birds and shooting

at them would be good practice and lots of fun. They ran to get their bows and arrows.

We insisted they wait till we moved far enough down the airstrip so the arrows they shot wouldn't have a chance of hitting someone when they came down. Then we flew the kites and let the strings out so the kites were about as high as they could shoot their arrows.

They had a lot of fun shooting, as the ones holding the kite strings would jerk the strings or run with them to make the kites dodge around.

Two arrows went went through one kite without making holes big enough to bring it down. Others were yelling, "Kill that kite!" "Kill that kite!"

When an arrow did rip one kite enough for it to come down, we managed to patch it, then we flew them even higher, and tried to make them dodge around more, but it wasn't long till their arrows had "killed" both kites.

Anyway, we had an afternoon of fun that none of us will ever forget.

309

58

CAT FISH AND PIRANHA

The time seemed much shorter than we thought it would, till it was time for the Mission Air Fellowship pilot to pick us up. Lyle was impressed by the number of tears he saw on the faces of those who saw us off.

The pilot had to work our flight in between others he had scheduled, so when we landed at Tamatama, we had a couple of days to relax at that village before the plane came, that would fly us on to Caracas.

The morning after we arrived there, some of the boys from the mission school and some of the local Indian boys invited us to go fishing with them. They had fishing tackle their teachers had brought to them and taught them to use,so we all went down to where there was a small bay on the side of the river, and started fishing.

While Lyle and three of the boys continued to fish, the three other boys and I did a little swimming. They warned me that if I cut a foot on a rock, I should rush to get out of the water as quickly as possible, because if the piraña fish smelled blood, they would go into a frenzy and attack anything, any size, and they could devour almost any size of animal in minutes.

After swimming across the little bay a couple times, we climbed the very tall tree that leaned over the bay, to do some diving. The big branch about twelve feet above the water was plenty high for me. That's where I dived from. But the boys climbed to the the very top of that tree, nearly a hundred feet above the water, and they jumped from there.

After we had been having fun swimming and diving quite a while, Lyle and the other boys called us, and told us to come and eat. When we got to their fire we found that they had roasted eight piraña that they had caught right there in the bay where we were swimming!

They had cleaned out the insides, chopped the piraña along both sides, then wrapped them in a big banana leaf and roasted them on the fire they had built.

As we sat eating them, I translated as Lyle commented that it would be a lot safer if they could get rid of the piraña in these areas right near the village.

One of the boys said emphatically, "Oh no! Those piraña are one of our most important foods. We'd go hungry without them."

It was the next morning that the local Indians brought a sick baby to the missionary's home for help. This missionary thought Lyle might be a good resource for helping this small child.

They agreed that it probably had sepsis, or a congenital heart condition, but nothing they could do helped, and baby died that afternoon. They had a funeral pyre that night.

The next morning we went fishing again., but this time we took a long fish and cut it into six inch chunks. We put those on gigantic hooks and using six foot long leaders about the size around as pencils, we attached each of those hooks to a short part of a balsa wood log.

Then we rowed the canoe across the river dropping those balsa floats into the water as we crossed.

We rowed back out to the center of the river, where we could see all four of the floats, and we followed as they floated down the river.

Suddenly there was a big loud splash. Water sprayed in the air as one of those balsa floats went under water. A moment later it came up and went zigzagging down the river.

We paddled our canoe fast, chasing it and finally caught it. We pulled it over to shore and killed the giant catfish that was on the hook, then loaded it into the canoe.

We paddled down the river and caught up with the other three balsa logs, but the hooks were all bare. The piraña had beaten the other fish to the bate, and had thoroughly cleaned the hooks .

We paddled back up the river, and when we got back to the dock, we took our big catfish out of the canoe. We put a bamboo pole through the gills to carry it. When Lyle put one end of the pole on his shoulder, and I put the other end on mine, the head of the fish was higher than the tops or our heads, but eight or ten inches of the tail was dragging on the ground.

The next day we were on the plane, headed for Caracas with our long bows and poison tipped arrows. Lyle and I both wanted to see more of South America while we had a chance, so we took the long route home, visiting Peru, Bolivia, and Machu Pichu.

Here's how Lyle, later, described the trip home from Peru:

"When getting our return airplane tickets in Cusco, all the airport counter clerk could say in broken English was 'something's wrong.' It turned out that the airline we had tickets from Lima on no longer flew to South America. We did finally find a carrier that honored the tickets.

"New Orleans Customs sure didn't like our bows and arrows and almost took them completely apart. We were going to stay the night in the Big Easy, but realized the more civilized people in the world were in the jungles of Venezuela. Six weeks away from home was enough, so we flew on to our homes in the Rockies."

WELCOME CHANGES
1985

59
THROUGH MANY YEARS

By the year 1985, it had been nineteen years since our first visit with the Yanowamo Indians, and their first contact with the outside world. It was thirteen years since my last visit with them and I was really excited about finally having an opportunity to once again renew my friendships with the Janks and with my many Indian friends at Niyiyobateri, and to learn about the changes in their way of life that may have taken place. Although my time was limited I hoped perhaps I could also drop by for a short visit with the Dawsons in the village down on the Padamo river.

To me it would be a time to celebrate. I had no idea that it could also be a time of tragedy.

The Mission Air Fellowship plane that was taking me from Puerto Ayacucho up to Niyiyobateri flew up the Orinoco River, then followed the Padamo river, and glided right over Coshilobateri, where the Dawsons had started the first mission twenty five years ago, and were still working.

The pilot flew low enough to give me a good view of the village. It no longer looked like the Indian villages I had known. There was no longer any sign of a shavano. There were, instead, a number of houses, some of which had small windmills to give them electricity for lights. There was also a small school building, a storage building beside the dock, and other buildings.

I told the pilot that I hoped we could have time enough to land there for a couple of hours on the way out and I could at have a quick visit with the Dawsons.

He said that he didn't have anything scheduled for the day before my flight out. If I wanted him to, he would plan to come after me a day early, and we could fly to this village on the Padamo, that day. That would give me the rest of that day, and the next morning with the Dawsons. I was glad to hear that, as I didn't want to miss seeing them, and talking with their Indian friends about life in this new, more modern, kind of village.

An hour later we were landing in Niyiyobateri and in spite of the years since I had last seen them, I could recognize Rosito and Enrique right in the front of the crowd that came running as the plane rolled to a stop.

After all the hugs and greetings were over, the two of them wanted to immediately take me into the shavano to visit all the friends that would be waiting. I turned to Wally who laughed and said that was what they had assumed was going to happen. He and Marg would go along, then wait till evening for a good visit with me. "But don't think you are going to start with Rosito's and Eladio's families. They don't live in the shavano any more. They both have their own houses now."

The first two families inside the shavano welcomed me gladly, then commented to each other, "Oh, now we can talk about him again!" Since they hadn't seen me for so long, and they knew I was older than their parents, they had assumed I was probably no longer living, and the Yanowamo have a strict rule that after the day of the funeral, the bone drinking ceremony, the dead person's name can never be said again. The mother of one family said, "Now we don't have to be afraid to talk about the good times we had together."

Throughout the years, both the Janks and the Dawsons had kept me well informed of their progress, and also of some of the activities of my Indian friends. I knew there were bound to be changes in their way of life, but from all that I heard that afternoon, those changes had not been forced upon them like the changes that had been brought on the North American Indians during their first years of contact.

Yes, there had been some contact with government agents and with occasional visitors, but nearly all the actual changes in the lives of these Indians were the result of their acceptance of the schooling and the religious instruction brought to them by the missionaries, changes that the Indians, themselves, had chosen to make because of the examples set by the lives of the missionaries.

My friends were so anxious to talk about, and renew our friendships that nearly all my time for the first two days was used up, talking about the things we had done together in times past, and their continually reminding me that I was still considered one of them, but they did include some discussion of the changes during my absence.

The biggest change was their pride in the fact that the people of Niyiyobateri no longer considered all the other villages enemy villages. They were no longer anxious to go on raids or to kill their former enemies. Most of the people of Niyiyobateri had been really listening to Marg and Wally's teaching and had become Christians, so they wanted to live in peace.

In addition to the acceptance of Christ as their savior, they had taken seriously his teaching to "Love your neighbor, as your self," and had definitely agreed that they should no longer kill people just because they came from an enemy village.

The Janks had also taught them something of modern medicine and had finally been able to convince them that there were reasons for sickness other than witchcraft, so now, when there was a death, they no longer felt a need to try to figure out what enemy village had done the witchcraft, then go to that village and kill someone in revenge.

However, they told me they were hearing rumors that when some of their former enemies learned that the Niyiyo were loosing their interest in fighting, they had assumed that this meant they would not defend themselves if they were attacked. This had lead to Wally's conclusion that if they were to have peace he would have to go to some of the villages that had always been their enemies, get acquainted with the leaders and convince them that he and the people of Niyiyobateri really did want to be their friends.

Wally had been very much aware that going to any enemy village would be taking serious chances with his own life, but he let the people of Niyiyobateri know that it was his faith in the Lord, and the Lord's protection that gave him the courage. They had then agreed that if he arrived at the other villages alone, or with only one companion, those people would believe that he was not a raider, and they might possibly listen to him.

Depending, for their safety, on his leadership and their new faith, Enrique and Rosito and others who had, themselves, become teachers of the Christian faith, had agreed to take turns going with him, and with their help he had made trips, to several of the enemy villages.

They had actually been able to convince most of the leaders of those villages that the people of Niyiyobateri really wanted their friendship, and that the ways of God were ways of peace that would bring them much happier lives than their ways of war and killing.

Wally told those who's comments sounded as if they might be thinking of raiding Niyiyobateri because it was no longer prepared to fight, that his teaching brought strength, not weakness. The new knowledge had improved the health of the people, so they were now stronger, not weaker.

Rosito told me that the people of the Balifili valley, which was five days walk over mountain trails to the south, had always been considered deadly enemies. The Niyiyo leaders had always known that anyone who went into that area would assuredly be killed. Because of this knowledge, it had been many years since their last contact with any of the Balafili.

All the local residents who had ever had any direct contact with the Balifili were long ago dead and gone, so wouldn't the old leaders of the Balafili be gone also?

After much discussion, the Niyiyo leaders had agreed with Wally, that maybe, just maybe, it would now be possible to make friendly contact with them.

After making the long five days journey to that area, Wally and two friends had walked into one of the Balifili villages. The people there were so shocked that any Niyiyo would ever talk of friendship that they listened, and they agreed. Finally, members of three of the Balifili villages had become so interested in and curious about Wally's teachings that they had come all that way, in small groups, to visit and learn more.

Eventually Wally had also convinced Enrique and some of the other Niyiyo leaders that they, themselves, could actually teach the words of peace and the messages of the bible without his help, so they had hesitantly begun to make contact with other villages to the north. Their acceptance had been so successful that before long they were going to those villages regularly to teach the people of their new beliefs, and their new ways of life.

By this time, 1985, all of the villages with whom the Niyiyobateri had been able to make contact, were accepting them as friends, and individuals from more than half of those villages had expressed a desire to learn more about the teachings of the missionaries and the love of God.

Marg Jank was now leaving most of the teaching to Wally and the local leaders so that she could spend nearly all her time translating the bible into the Yanowamo language, with the hope that eventually the people would be able to study it themselves, and the leaders could use printed copies of the bible to aid them in their instruction.

Just a couple of days after my arrival, Enrique informed Marg that his young son Lujan, who was about eight years old, was now very interested in the teachings of the missionaries and wanted to be baptized. And he wanted to do it now, while I was still there, because he wanted me to take part in it. Marg told him that tomorrow morning, after their church service, would be a good time for that, but said, "Let's look carefully before we get into the water. Just this morning on the internet news we got the message that a bus ran off a dock into the Amazon river, in Brazil, straight south of here. 39 of the passengers were trapped, and couldn't get out of the bus, but some of the windows were part way down, so the blood thirsty piraña fish could get into the bus. Before the bus was discovered that afternoon, the flesh of all 39 of the passengers had been totally eaten up, by the piraña."

Enrique asked, "Were they still alive, or already dead before the piraña started eating them?"

"No one knows for sure, but they think probably they had already drowned. At least they hope so!"

Enrique just laughed at the idea that his family could be in any danger. "As long as there's no blood in the water the piraña don't attack. If we do see any, it's the piraña, not us, that will get eaten."

Lujan still looked a little doubtful.

Even as I lowered him into the water and he was baptized, Lujan stayed alert, and he did see one piraña in the water, so after his baptism, he and I were out of the water a lot faster than Wally and Enrique were.

60
FAMINE

Yes, I was seeing changes in the attitudes and ways of life related to war and peace. But this year, all the Yanowamo had another problem, much more serious than possible raiders. This had been the driest, hottest year any of these people had ever experienced. Because of the lack of rain their gardens had dried up. The vegetables from those gardens that they had always depended upon were not growing. And most of the wild fruits upon which they also depended were not ripening. Most of the people were near starvation.

I was shocked to learn that the situation was even worse than the year, many years earlier, when I had gone with them to hunt and to eat the big ashoa berries. That year our fears of going had been related to their enemies, who might find and attack us where we were camped. and when we were starting back, our leaders had feared that those enemies might be waiting for us when we got home.

This year there was no fear of enemies, but they had to go much farther to find food, and their fear was that when they got there they might not find enough food. If not, they could be too weak to walk all the way back home. However, just like the year when I had gone with them, Wally and Marg were surprised and glad to see that they came back in better shape than when they left. They had found roots to dig and a little fruit, and enough wild life so they could, again, bring back some meat to share.

This habit of sharing was one of the characteristics of the old culture that were misunderstood by many of the ever increasing number of outsiders who were coming into the area. I saw the same problems as I had worked with in the Montana schools, where many of teachers who came to the reservations didn't try to learn and promote the Indian culture, and adapt their teaching methods. so their teaching often opposed cultural traits that the teachers didn't understand. In both places the Indians willingness to share whatever they had was one of those very important characteristics.

One of the women who had come to Niyiyobateri to try to help with teaching the reading, and was enabling an increase in the hours of instruction that the children were getting, said to me, "We have to teach them not to give everything away. One of the families which has almost nothing, and sometimes has to go hungry is still always sharing. They are still giving food to people like Big Knees, who is too lazy to go out and find it for himself. Last time there was a leajou that family gave away the hammock the mother had made for their baby, and she had to start again spending weeks making a new one."

I told her that if the people learned her ways, and the type of wisdom she taught, then when that family was actually starving, no one would share with them. I told her I hoped she would learn and understand the many other good characteristics of their culture then help them maintain them, not change them.

The stream that flowed past the village had become much smaller because of the drouth, but there was still a little water, and some of the men decided that they should build a new garden down beside the stream and maybe they could run a ditch to it and irrigate it, then maybe that would be a place where they they could still grow some food. So they chose a low flat spot that had previously been a swampy forest area, and I joined them as they began cutting down the timber to clear a space for a garden, "Like you helped us do, long ago," Rosito said to me.

Just as they had always done, they let the downed timber get well dried out, before they went back to burn it. They had always known that if they let it dry out well, their fire could burn everything except the large logs, but it could never burn into the forest around their clearing, because a rain forest is always too damp to burn.

But this time, to their great shock, when they burned the dead timber in their garden area, the fire continued and spread into the forest. With this terrible drouth the whole rain forest had dried out. Before the fire finally quit spreading, several days later, it had burned the forest in an area more than a mile across.

Fortunately, the garden was east of the shavano, and there had been enough of a breeze from the west, so the fire did not spread westward and burn the forest next to the shavano. It did, however, catch the tall dry grass of the savanna on fire, and that fire was spreading in all directions. The Janks hurriedly got out the lawn mower they had brought when they first arrived there, for keeping the grass short around the house to protect it. Now they set it so it would do an extra short mowing, then mowed and raked away the grass around their house. They kept going and mowed all the way around the shavano, so when the fire reached their part of the savanna, it did not burn anyone's homes.

From Indian visitors, and from news on the Janks radio, we kept hearing of other fires and of places where whole villages had burned. People throughout the rainforest had always known the dense forest could not burn, so they were still burning dry timber to clear places for gardens, or were building campfires to cook their meals without ever being concerned about the location of their fires. The national news on the radio said that government planes flying over both Brazil and Venezuela had determined that more than ten percent of the entire rain forest had burned and many fires were still burning.

Except for the drouth and the resulting shortage of food, everything seemed to be going well for the Janks and the people of Niyiyobateri. They, and all the other villages with whom they had any contact, had been at peace for several years, and they were sure the days of raiding and fighting were long past. But they knew there were still people out there who had never had any contact with them, or with any missionaries, so the Niyiyo were always prepared for anything. With their history and traditions, who knows what may happen!

61

WHO KNOWS?

Late one evening near the end of my stay in Niyiyobateri, a couple arrived from one of the villages that had once been deadly enemies but were now friends. They said that when they neared our village they had seen a group of men painted like raiders, and they were heading our way. Two of those who saw then recognized one of the raiders as a long ago friend, and had been able to talk with him. Those people still believed that sickness, or anything else that harmed people, was caused by witchcraft, so someone must be responsible for the terrible drouth, and that should be revenged. Also they had heard that the people of Niyiyobateri had a lot of strange new ideas, so maybe they were the ones to blame. Besides, if the Niyiyo did not, and would not, fight any more, they should be an easy village to attack.

The Niyiyo men organized themselves, to have some of them on duty guarding each of the gates of the shavano, watching for the raiders, day and night.

It was just a day later that Marg started becoming very ill, and she spent the last couple of days before I was to leave in bed. I herd a couple of hints that some of the women were still not sure that her illness couldn't be caused by witchcraft from the approaching raiders, but of course they wouldn't let Wally or Marg hear them say that.

Wally and the others couldn't tell for sure what could be causing her illness, so they radioed the mission air fellowship, and the pilot who was picking me up. Wally told him that Marg would be going on the plane with me to Puerto Ayacucho, and she might need to go on to Caracus or somewhere else where there would be a better hospital.

The pilot said he would reserve time for the additional flight so he could take her there if it was necessary.

I talked to the pilot while he was still on he radio, and told him I thought that it would probably be best that we not make the planned overnight stop with the Dawsons on the Padamo river. He agreed but said he would be bringing mail for the Dawsons, so he would wait and land there to drop that off on the way out. That way, I could at least see their growing village up close, and give them my greetings.

Early in the morning of the day before I was to leave, I was in the back room, getting my pack ready, when there was suddenly a lot of yelling and screaming outside. I ran to the window. Coming running out of the nearest gate of the shavano came the men who were on guard there, and several others. And coming from the nearest timber was a group of men, all of whom had their faces and their chests painted black.

Then, out of the gate screaming and yelling their encouragement came a bunch of women.

The local men appeared to be holding off on their shooting until the first of those seven foot arrows came from the raiders, but they were still far enough apart so they were shooting very high. Soon there were a lot of arrows flying through the air. I saw one of our men drop to the ground before all the raiders suddenly turned and ran back into the forest. I was sure two of them were carrying wounded men on their backs.

One of the local men was lying on the ground, and others were staggering toward the house.

I was not far behind Wally as he dashed out to check on the injuries of the four men who needed help. Wally did a good job of patching up the two with wounded legs. And in spite of her illness, Marg carefully put five stitches in the shoulder of another.

One other man was in a much more serious condition. He had been shot in the abdomen. Since the arrow had already come out, we assumed it was a poisoned arrow and the head would still be in his abdomen. The poisoned tip, either a rodent's tooth or a piece of bone sharpened at each end, would have been fastened on in such a way that when the arrow was pulled out that tip would come off.

Wally had once before dug out a poison tip from a man's hip but this time, even with his long tweezers, he could get no feeling of contact with that sliver of bone. He had no way of knowing for sure that the poisoned arrowhead was there. If he cut the wound open in an attempt to find that tip, he himself, might cause the man's death. Since this wounded man was in very bad shape, and seemed to be getting worse, the only solution was to put him on the plane that was picking Marg and me up early the next morning.

Since the wounded man had never been outside Yanowamo territory, Eladio said he would go with him to help him adjust to the ways of the outsiders, and be sure he had food and other needs, as the hospital in Puerto Ayacucho expected the families of their patients to take care of those needs.

As we flew over the mountains the next morning, I was hoping we would be able to stay at the village on the Padamo River just long enough so I could see their new school building and other developments, and so I could have a short visit with Joe and Millie Dawson, and see what their younger children were like, now that they had grown up. I knew that a couple of the older children were now back as missionaries, but some of them were in the U.S. either going to college or working.

As we glided low over the Padamo river, I was watching closely, expecting to see the village looking just as it had been when we flew over it three weeks ago. I was shocked! Instead of the houses and buildings, all I saw was patches of white ashes. When we landed, there was no one there to meet us. We walked over to what had been the edge of the village. Several sad looking people were digging into the ashes, apparently searching for whatever belongings might still be there, unburned. Sticking up from the ashes were blackened stubs of trees, and blackened bodies of several animals we thought were goats and dogs.

The Dawsons youngest son saw us and came running. He told us about his family escaping from the fire by running and jumping into the boat they used for going to the other villages where they had been holding services. A few Indians had gotten in with them, and those with canoes joined them on the other shore of the river as they watched the village burn. Most of the people had just waded into the river as far as they could, and several of them had nearly drowned trying to get beyond the terrible heat.

He said his parents and several of the elders had gone down the river this morning, to a spot where the trees had not burned, checking to see if it was a place that they should consider, as a possible location for a new village.

The pilot felt that anything we tried to do there would probably just be getting in the way, and delaying the local people's progress. He left the Dawson's mail and I wrote a note for their son to give to Joe and Millie, and we were on our way.

The pilot radioed ahead, so when we landed in Puerto Ayacucho a doctor was waiting at the airport to check the man who had been shot with the arrow. After a careful examination, he told us that he had no way of knowing for sure whether or not there might be a poison tip in this man's abdomen. He did not have the equipment necessary to test for poison, or to do a possible operation, so he thought we should put the man back in the plane and take him to Carcass and the hospital that Marg was scheduled to enter.

Three hours later, we were at the Caracas airport. Marg, Enrique, and the injured man were climbing into an ambulance which would take them up the long mountain road from the airport to Caracas and the hospital. I had to stay at the airport so I could catch my plane home early the next morning.

Marg wouldn't check herself in for treatment, until she had made certain the injured man was checked in and being treated. The doctors soon assured them that this man did not have a poison arrowhead in him, and that he would be out of the hospital in a day or two.

Marg was diagnosed as having a serious kind of Malaria, along with two other ailments. She had to stay in the hospital five days, then stay in town in a rest home for a month, returning to the hospital every day for treatment.

All during her five days in the hospital, she kept asking about the injured man she had brought in, but all the nurses kept telling her they knew nothing about him. The day that she checked out, she went directly to the hospital office to inquire if he had been released, or if not, what room he was in. It was then that she was informed that their diagnosis had been incorrect, that he did have a poison arrow tip in him, and that he had died the day after his arrival.

2005

FORCED CHANGES

62
SHOCK

Throughout the years, Marg Jank kept me informed of the activities there, including Wally's heart attack and death on a trail to another village, and her continued efforts to finish her translation of the Bible.

In addition to Wally's absence, another big chnge in her life was the absence of her son Davy. He had heard that there was a Maco tribe about three days walk east of them that had had very little contact with the outside world. He decided it was time for him to be on his own, and sarting a new mission there would be his lifetime occupation. But first he would have to learn their language. So he had gone there, made friends with them, and was now walking back and forth, spending a total of about nine months each year with them, and three back with his mother and the Yanowamos.

The Dawsons had also kept me informed of their progress in their new village on the Padamo River.

It was April 25, 2005 that I wrote this e-mail letter to Marg about my possible return to visit her and my Yanowamo friends:

Dear Marg,

I have been planning for a long time to make one more trip down there, to visit you and all my Yanowamo friends. If I came back and refreshed all my great memories, perhaps I could write a good anthropological study of the Yanowamo people. I have boxes of notes and tape recordings to aid me in recalling many of my experiences there, but I want to bring all that up to date, and be sure I can correctly tell of all the changes in the lives of the people there, and their reaction to those changes. But most important of all, would be the opportunity to see you and the people of your village again, and to renew all those wonderful friendships

What do you think? Would this be a convenient time?

Affectionately
Hap

The answer came the next day:
Dear Hap,

I'm excited that you can come for another visit and I'm sure your Yanowamo friends will be too. It's been many years, and I'm sure you will be thrilled with the progress that is being made. Will I see you in a week or two?

Marg

I called Susan at AAA Travel to see if she could now arrange my flights all the way to Puerto Ayacucho, and I e-mailed Mission Air Fellowship to see if they could get me the rest of the way. I was all set to go.

But then, two days later, I got another e-mail:
Hap,

Stop! Drop everything. Don't try to come. You would probably get stopped by the authorities and not be allowed to fly out here at all. If you did make it, I might no longer be here!

Yesterday, I was notified that the president of Venezuela had stated that all missionaries would be kicked out of the country very soon, and they should be ready to scat any day now.

I hope it takes a while, but who knows? Maybe I'll be able to see you when I get back to Canada, or the U.S., or wherever I'll end up!

Marg

I was shocked and wondered what the reason was. I started checking with people who had Venezuelan contacts: former missionaries, anthropologists, businessmen. They knew about the plan but their opinions of probable reasons differed.

Eventually I was able to obtain a copy of the *Official Gazette of Venezuela*, which said, "A decree was published by the Ministry of Justice and Interior revoking the missionaries' indefinite permission for working in indigenous territory." But even that paper gave no reason!

A missionary who had been there in the 1960s told me the government had been very hesitant about letting them in the first time because the missionaries were Protestant and most of Venezuela was Catholic.

A man who worked with the CIA had a different idea: "That president has been very concerned ever since the New Tribes Missions got satellite connections and can now correspond daily with people in the U.S.

"The missionaries are obtaining some very unusual, up-to-date equipment, so that they can now teach by radio in very remote locations. Since that president hates the U.S. and thinks they are too powerful, he may judge the ideas of others by his own and believe that the missionaries are actually spies, that they are really there to get military information for our government."

I also learned that Venezuelan Government investigators had begun to show up in the villages where there were missionaries, and they were asking a lot of questions. But they were telling people that they were just getting the information the authorities would need when doctors or military personnel came in to help the Indian people and meet the needs that the missionaries had been meeting for years.

Marg kept me informed of what was happening, but always expecting that that e-mail might be her last one. Then I got one from Pepito saying that Marg was teaching him and other leader to use e-mail so they could keep in touch with her and others when she was gone.

The missionaries had to start rationing all the fuels, like propane gas and kerosene, that they had been using for years, because now the Mission Air Fellowship was gone and the government was controlling transportation and they could no longer count on supplies of any kind.

The Indians, who had learned to depend on many things brought in from the outside, began to say they should have stuck to the old ways, where they didn't have to count on anyone else. The government was now requiring permits for the travel that was needed for purchasing things. Everyone who had contact with the outside was now supposed to have a government-issued identification card, but those cards had to be obtained in the towns. Most of the people were very mystified. How could they possibly meet all these new requirements?

But Marg encouraged them, telling them to make every possible effort to get those government identification cards. The cards were going to be their ticket to the future. Eventually those who got the cards would be able to travel, study, work, and even vote.

Marg was still trying to put in full time doing her translations of the Bible, but was having to spend most of her time taking care of the new needs of the people. She wanted to do a good job of both at the same time, so she put in very long hours, knowing that her time to be there was getting short.

She kept thinking that even though she might have to leave and would not be there to continue teaching, she had the satisfaction of knowing that the people had now accepted the peaceful ways and were no longer considering every stranger an enemy and they were not going out to kill someone in revenge every time someone died of a disease they didn't understand.

But then someone found the body of Sedemi, the mother of three young children, brutally murdered in the forest nearby. Sedemi had been on her way to her nearby garden, through an area which everyone considered safe. Now the whole village was in an uproar, saying this was such a cruel, brutal killing that they had to go back to the old ways and revenge this killing. Different ones were blaming each of the nearby villages. Finally they found out the killers were from a distant village they had been at war with more than thirty-five years ago, a village that still had no contact with the outside world.

When Marg talked to the government representatives about the situation, they said, "We are not here to change the customs of the people. We are not supposed to do anything that will interfere with their ways, but to protect them from the influence of outsiders. Let them act according to their own customs and ways."

Marg wondered what would happen when all the missionaries were gone. Would their teaching of the Christian ways still influence the people?

I wondered if that was too much to expect when, by my observation, those Christian principles don't have much influence on the actions of a lot of the citizens of our own modern nations!

The village leaders in Niyiyobateri heard that there was to be a government registration in Coyowa, so the Indian people could register and get identity cards that would permit them to get government jobs. About 35 of the Niyiyobateri people took the four-day walk to Coyowa to sign up. They were told that now they could be included in government programs and, as they said, they would be "on the map."

Pepito told Marg that while they were on the trail, he and Teddy had done a lot of talking about the missionaries having to leave. "We decided we would be all right. We know things are going to be tough, but it will be our responsibility to carry on, to take leadership, both in the community and the church. Every time we have problems we grow stronger. Maybe this can even be a good thing for all of us. We need to grow up, to stop 'drinking milk' and start 'eating meat.'"

More than two-thirds of the adults in the village were now literate. Now they were told that if five of the best readers flew to Puerto Ayacucho, they could get their ID cards and work permits; then they would be given a short course in teaching and become certified to teach in the tribal situation.

Although for years, the only written material any of them had ever seen had been the Bible, most of the people wanted to learn to read. But Marg had been trying to also teach some of them a little Spanish, enough so they could communicate with the occasional visitors, and now this proved very beneficial because they could relate with the government employees who were coming in.

One of the men who went out to get teacher training was told to stay much longer, long enough to become fluent in Spanish, so they could add a Spanish class to their little school; then they would be able to read other things, mostly children's books that would be brought in for the school.

The government then began constructing a school building where they could have four classrooms and teach classes all afternoon, five days a week. Those teachers would actually be paid salaries for teaching.

The government began paying the local men who built the school building and other things the government wanted. So one couple was able to set up their version of a store where they could sell food and other things from the outside, things that some of the people were beginning to desire. And whenever there was extra room on their flights, the government helicopters would transport the supplies for that store

Most of the adults already had a much better knowledge of the Bible than the average American in the U.S. because soon after Wally and Marg had started the mission, they had not only talked their religion and started having church on Sunday, but they had also started having regular Bible study meetings. Some of the men who were really interested had soon started their own discussion group, meeting three or four afternoons each week, after the reading classes. They had said that since they had the leisure time, they might as well learn, and they had become very interested in the teachings of the Bible

When my nephew, Lyle Moss, had been there with me, he had compared them with an "upper middle class society" because most of them worked about five hours a day, gathering their food, then had the rest of the day to just visit, work on their crafts, or do whatever else they felt like doing, and for many, that was study the Bible.

Now, as Marg and three helpers still concentrated on translating the Bible, she would write her translation; then one of the men would review that first draft, checking for fluency and flow. Then the other two would check the revised version for comprehension, one of them reading several verses out loud and the other telling Marg his understanding of those verses. She would make any changes necessary to clarify the meanings, and then they would do the whole process again with different ones doing each part of the job, to make sure all the meanings were clear.

The villagers kept getting more and more concerned that Marg might soon be gone, permanently gone, and they might never again have the guidance of a missionary. They kept coming to Marg and telling her how upset they were about that, but she talked about the fact that not having an outsider there to lead their worship and other activities might promote their developing their own leadership and make them more able to do even the new activities in a more traditional Yanowamo way, so they would never lose the good parts of the Yanowamo culture.

They were inspired and, to an extent, they agreed. But they were also very fearful that the government officials coming in were going to force them to change and demand that they live more like the "modern" Venezuelan civilization.

Marg couldn't deny that she could see this beginning to happen, although, officially, the government had said the outsiders were not to force or encourage any changes.

Some government officials even told the outsiders who came to the villages that attacking other villages and even conducting return raids should not be discouraged, because it was the traditional way of the people!

Some said that anthropologists had encouraged the government to make those rules because the native tribal areas were now just about the only places where anyone could go to study and write about cultures that had not been completely changed by the promoters of European-type culture.

I wondered if Marg was spending all her time trying to finish up her translation and what other preparations she and her friends were making for continuation of her work after she left. Then I got this letter:

Samulito stopped in this morning to discuss the effect of prayer on his life. He said, "It works. Like when I prayed that you would write up something for us to follow in church, after you missionaries are gone."

Then seeing my blank expression, he laughed.

"I guess I never told you about that! Well one day after we found out that the president had decreed you would have to leave, I began wondering how things could continue on without you. And I began wondering if we'd remember how to use the Word correctly, and how we'd even know where to find the passages we had in mind. So I asked the Lord one night to put it into your heart to write up something for us so we'd know where to look for things in the bible. And I decided to ask you about it the following morning

"So I came the next morning, thinking I'd talk to you about it. And before I even sat down, you handed me some papers and told me to look at them and see if I thought they would be helpful. It was exactly what I had wanted. It was just what I had asked the Lord to put in your heart! And you did it before I even said anything! He just makes it happen."

Marg said that Pepito and the other translation coworkers kept coming to her and asking when they could get more copies of the books of the Bible that had been completed and only one or two copies made available.

Marg would tell them that as soon as she got back to Coyowa and her big printer, she would print more copies of those books and the ones they were just now completing. But then the tears would come to her eyes as she realized that she might not be able to get there soon, that she might never get there, or be able to supply them with the complete Bibles which they were working so hard to complete.

Then came that final e-mail announcement they had been dreading: **"In the spirit of compliance with a new declaration by the governor of the State of Amazonas, that the missionaries must immediately leave indigenous territory, New Tribes Missions of Venezuela has to have all it's missionaries out of its stations in the Amazon interior within two weeks."**

63
WE ARE ONE OF THEM

Of course, like all the other missionaries, the Dawsons on the Padamo River were given two weeks to get out of the country, but they ignored the orders and refused to leave. They told the authorities that many years ago, they had applied for and been given citizenship in Venezuela. They, like the Janks and other missionaries, had been sent there by New Tribes Missions, but they had resigned from that organization several years ago and were now supported by individual churches.

All of their ten children had been born in Venezuela, so they were native-born citizens. Two of the oldest had gone to the U.S. to get a higher education and had taken jobs there, but although four of the others had gone there and gotten their training to be missionaries, they were still citizens only of Venezuela and had a right to stay right where they were. Two of the boys, when they grew up, had married Yanomami girls, so they now had wives and children who were members of the tribe.

The government finally gave up and accepted the fact that they had a right to stay where they were, but told them to restrict their activities to their own tribe and their own area.

Their only problem was transportation. Since the Mission Air Fellowship had been kicked out, along with all the other missionaries, the Dawsons had no air transportation. Their only chance of getting any supplies was by traveling to Puerto Ayacucho by motor boat. That was almost two hundred miles each way, so they had to rely almost entirely on their Indian friends for food. But they were very glad they didn't have to leave their homes like the other missionaries had to do.

64

FORCED ABSENCE

When Marg arrived in Canada, she was very concerned. How was the big change, of the army replacing the missionaries, going to affect the lives of the Yanowamo people? Was the army sending in its forces immediately, as some had said they would do? And were those soldiers and the officials forcing any changes in the lives of the Yanowamo people? She wished she had some way of talking to the leaders and finding out.

And oh how she wished there had been just a little more time so she could have finished her translation of the Bible. The Bible had become such a very important part of the lives of many of the Indians. They were continually reading and discussing the parts she had finished translating and had printed out. For the past forty years, that translation had been her constant concern and her main activity.

She was sure that its teachings would be important to the Yanowamo for generations to come, if only she could finish the translation and get it printed in book form. And if only they had more copies of what they had finished! The three or four copies she had been able to print out would certainly not be adequate to give information and inspiration to all of the people.

Although she was stuck in Canada, she continued to try to finish her translation as best she could without the help of the Indians. She also kept herself very busy visiting churches that had supported her work, but she was continually wishing she knew how her friends, the Yanowamo, were getting along.

Then, to her surprise and relief, she got an e-mail from Cotabimi, a 23-year-old female doctor who had volunteered to go with the team the government was sending in to take the place of the missionaries. They were supposed to go as a team, but this lady had ended up there alone, ahead of the rest. She had taken over Marg's home and had found Marg's e-mail address there, so she was able to write to Marg. She said she felt completely overwhelmed by the situation. She was mystified and sometimes frightened by the strange culture of the Yanowamo people around her. Their lives were so completely different from anything she had known.

Of course, she knew nothing of the Yanowamo language, and although Marg had tried to teach some Spanish to the people so they could communicate with the authorities who visited occasionally or when someone had to go out to a doctor, none of them knew enough Spanish to really communicate.

This young doctor said she was very thankful that Pepito and his family lived close by and tried their best to help her.

It was only a few days later that Cotabimi allowed Pepito to use her computer to send his own e-mail to Marg, telling her that his friend Deno had died suddenly. Many of Deno's longtime friends from surrounding villages came rushing to Niyiyobateri for the funeral proceedings. Those friends were all sure that Deno's death was caused by witchcraft, and were insisting that it had to be revenged. But Captain Pedro refused to go back to the old cycle of death, which would result in a long chain of violence. He told them all that it was caused by natural causes, and they should not be overcome by grief, but learn the real cause and make the bone drinking a time to celebrate the good things Deno had done and his having accepted the ways that would save his soul.

The trouble was that the young doctor could find no evidence of any disease or accident and had no idea of the cause of his death. Finally Pedro had to settle for trying to convince his friends that since they did not know of a person who would have done the witchcraft, they should not go out and kill an an innocent person, and also have one of them killed in revenge. That last point had little influence, because in the Yanowamo culture, talking about it would make the speaker look like a coward.

A few days later, Marg sent me an e-mail telling me that the Venezuelan government had announced that she and the other missionaries could now go back into Venezuela, but only if they promised that they would stay in the city and never again go near the Indian territories. She already had her ticket and was ready to fly back to Venezuela on April 26, 2006, just two months after she had been forced to leave.

She was hoping that although she could not go near the Yanowamo territory, maybe, somehow, some of her people would be able to come to the city and help her finish the translation of the Bible.

65

HELP AND HINDRANCE

During the first few months after the missionaries moved out of all the Indian villages, the army cane in and set up a base right there in the village of Niyiyobateri. Many of the people were very frightened and were having a hard time adjusting to the big changes. They kept wishing that they had someone who spoke their language to help them understand and adapt. Then Cotabimi, the doctor who had taken over Marg's house, handed Pepito an e-mail, written in Yanowamo. It was from Marg, saying that she had finally been allowed to return to Venezuela, but she had to stay in the city. She had been in Caracas for quite a while, but although Puerto Ayacucho was on the Orinoco River, it was legally a city, so she had finally gotten permission to go there, but she could go no further.

Marg told him that she and her son, Davy, and his wife, Susan, had gotten settled in an apartment in Puerto Ayacucho, and although it was on the 14th floor of a big apartment house, it had a big back room in which they could accommodate several guests with their hammocks, or where they could hold small meetings, if any of her friends could somehow get permission to come there. She was again hard at work on her Bible translation.

A couple of days later, Pepito e-mailed her, saying that he was trying to get transportation to the city, to help her, and Marcelino, one of his friends who had not helped before, was anxious to come along and try to help, but they had to first get some kind of identification papers and a travel permit, and whether they could get a ride on the army helicopters, which were now making frequent trips, was questionable.

Pepito let her know that, in the meantime, he and others were keeping their worship services going. Some of those who she had been sure she could count on appeared to no longer have an interest, but others who she thought had only come to her classes for humor and companionship were really jumping in and helping teach the children.

Soon afterward, several local Christians of Puerto Ayacucho gathered in Marg's apartment. They were discussing the training they hoped they could give to some of the Indians who lived there in the city. Then, to their great surprise, Pepito and Marcelino walked in. With all the Yanowamo hugs, shouting, laughter, tears, and more hugs, all the work was temporarily forgotten.

Pepito explained that there had been orders that the Indians were not to be flown out, but there were helicopters bringing army officers in, and other helicopters for sick people that needed to be flown out. When one of those helicopters was ready to take off, the pilot had motioned for the two of them to jump aboard. "It was just God that got us here," Pepito kept saying.

It was in January 2007 that I got a letter from Marg, and I'm sure she won't mind my sharing it with you:

I've been here in Puerto Ayacucho for more than a week already. Today I decided to get back in gear and start writing again, even if it is just letters to "share life" with all its uncertainties. And I'd like to share some of our future plans.

The church here is setting up training classes, if the army will let the Yanowamo on their planes when they have some coming this way and have room.

Pepito and Marcelino arrived yesterday, unexpectedly, and already we have arrangements that while they are here, they'll be taking in a two-week workshop at our church for Indians who need help finding their way around this new world that is moving in on them: classes on Spanish, reading with comprehension, math and money matters, agriculture, health, government. I'm scrambling right now to get the schedule drawn up and find speakers for all the slots we hope to fill, and plan some field trips for them as well.

Samulito hopes to come out also, along with four or five others who have been going to other villages to teach the word in their communities. They're going to be participating in the workshops every afternoon, and we'll be having leadership training every morning.

I was very glad to hear that some of the Yanowamo people are going to get the training they need to fit into the modern world, training that they themselves really want. The plans seem so different, and so much better tuned to the needs and desires of the people than what the North American Indians had gotten when our army took over.

I couldn't help remembering what John Woodenlegs, great president of the Northern Cheyenne, told me when I was working with the Cheyenne in the '60s.

It was in the 1920s that John and his best friend, both six years of age, had been riding in the back of a wagon heading into the village of Lame Deer. Two government workers had grabbed both boys, tied their hands and feet so they couldn't run off, then without even informing their parents, put them on a bus with other children and sent them to a school over two hundred miles northeast of there. They were put in classes to learn to read in English, even though they didn't understand a word of English.

They were tied to their cots at night so they couldn't run off and were severely punished if they spoke even one word of Cheyenne, as they were to learn to speak only English, forget all their Cheyenne ways and culture, and learn to live, in every way, according to the ways of the European-Americans. John made a gunny-sack pad to wear inside his pants so the paddlings he got wouldn't be as painful, and for the first six months, he refused to speak a word of either language.

When John was in the sixth grade, he finally escaped. He nearly starved on his way, walking back home, because he didn't dare let anyone see him, or they might force him to go back to school. When he got home, he had to relearn the Cheyenne language.

Forty years later, in the '60s, he and I were working with the Cheyenne schools, teaching the non-Indian teachers enough about the Cheyenne ways so they could do a good job teaching the children and honoring their culture.

I was very glad that in Venezuela, the government, instead of trying to force the Indian people to completely give up their own culture, was insisting that no one try to change it.

I was also glad that instead of the first contacts with the Native people being made by the army and prospectors, who fought the Indians, as it had been in most of the countries of both North and South America, the first contacts with the Yanowamo and the neighboring tribes had been made by missionaries, and others who really wanted to help them.

I was also glad that again, now, forty years later, although the schools were to be taken over and run by the Venezuelan government, most of the teaching was going to be done by Yanowamo teachers, and I hoped that the non-Indian teachers who went to work with them would try to learn to understand and maintain their willingness to share and other good qualities of their culture, while also teaching them how to adapt to the outside cultures that were rapidly being forced upon them.

All through the spring of 2007, Samulito was managing to spend much of his time in Puerto Ayacucho, helping Marg with the final checking of her Bible translation, and Pepito managed to get there a second time.

There were two other questions still to be solved. One was that the Yanowamo language has nine vowel sounds, so they had to add two more letters. I understood that because both the Crow and Navajo languages have three vowels that are not in English or other European languages, so they have problems finding printers or computers that can print books in their languages, with the three additional letters.

The other problem facing them that all of them were very worried about was the possibility that when those Bibles were printed, the Venezuelan government might make it almost impossible to import them into the country.

Marg had to be very careful what she said or did that the local authorities in Puerto Ayacucho might misinterpret. Those authorities were still very vigilant, trying to make sure that no New Tribes Mission personnel tried "sneaking back" into Indian territory. They said they were controlled by the president's efforts at building a very strong nationalistic spirit and his growing disdain for anything North American.

In addition to the three men from Niyiyobateri who spent as much time as they could in Puerto Ayacucho helping her, Marg got some help from Henrico, a young Yanowamo who the government had allowed to come out and get some training as a doctor's assistant at the hospital. Although they kept him very busy on week days, he would come and help Marg on weekends. When Henrico had been there three months, the people at the hospital still couldn't tell him when his course would be finished. Marg suspected they were making it as long as possible, just to continue getting his help.

Henrico was very concerned about his fifteen-year-old wife and their new baby, who he hadn't seen for three months, so he asked his teachers if he could have her come and stay in Puerto Ayacucho if she could get a ride out, but they said there was no room for her and the baby in the apartments where the medical students were staying. So Marg told him she would mange to make room for the two of them in her apartment.

Others, who came to her home often, were five of the Yanowamo people who had, for a long time, volunteered their spare time, helping with the reading classes Marg had set up. Now they had been given an opportunity to come out and get some instruction in teaching. Then they would be able to go back and teach, and actually get paid as teachers. But before they could get paid, they had to have a birth certificate made for them, then get a national identity card, a medical certificate, psychological certificate, identity photos, a letter from Marg describing the work they had done, and a certificate stating they had completed the teacher training program. They were learning that there was nothing simple about modern life and living in town.

When Marg and her coworkers walked down the street, she had to laugh at the fact that her friends still walked one behind the other, as they had always done on the jungle trails. Only now she was the one in the lead, the one who "new the jungle." And they were especially glad to have her help when they approached the busy intersections, with the confusion of all the cars honking, the red lights and green lights, and the crowds of people.

66

THE NEW WAYS

During the first year that the missionaries were gone, the people of Niyiyobateri found that with the army and the doctors and government supervisors jumping in to take the missionaries place, their lives were being changed much more rapidly than ever before.

The Venezuelan army had quickly taken over all of the facilities the missionaries had to abandon, all except Marg's house, which. Cotabimi, had made her home and office.

Although they were somewhat fearful of the army, the people were glad to see this doctor. Now they could get more advanced medical help than Marg could have given them, and since Marg was in Puerto Ayacucho, she could now make arrangements for those with serious illness to go to the hospital there. That's if the army had a helicopter going out and had room enough for a patient, and if the patient had a friend who had been "outside" before and could go along and translate the Spanish language, and help the patient understand and adjust to the very different world outside.

But many of the Yanowamo were very concerned because they did not want to give up any of what Marg and Wally had taught them.

Pepito and Eladio and Samulito kept trying hard to make arrangements to visit Marg and help with her Bible translation. But to get on the helicopters when there was no one who had to fly out to get medical help, they had to try to find other reasons for the pilots to let them go aboard. The pilots knew very well that they would be in trouble if what they were doing was providing help for missionary work!

Then they learned that there was one great way that those three, and others, could get to town. That was for them to apply to attend the teacher-training sessions. If they could just get their citizen ID cards, then attend some government-approved teacher training, they could come back and spend much more of their time teaching reading. And while they were in town, they could buy things that their families would find useful. Then, while they were there, they could slip over to Marg's place and help her with the Bible translation.

After they returned home and had taught for a short time, and so had earned a little cash, they asked for and got an opportunity to go back for additional training. This time, when the training session ended, they didn't ask for an immediate helicopter ride home. They signed up for a plane that was going three weeks later. That way, they were able to stay there and help Marg for three extra weeks.

During that extra time, they walked around and saw all the interesting shops. They found a lot of clothing, tools, cooking utensils, and other things they decided they just had to have. So they spent every cent they had. But when they got to the airport they found that the pilot had let soldiers take the space they had been promised on his helicopter. They would have to wait, maybe for days, for a ride home on another helicopter.

When they went back to Marg's little 14th-floor apartment, sure that she would somehow make room for them, they found that they were too late. Two doctors who had been assigned to work in Niyiyobateri had found that even doctors had trouble getting on the helicopters. So they had gone to talk with Marg, and she, in her usual hospitable way, had invited them to stay with her till they could get on the plane. The woman was sleeping with Marg, in her bed, and the man was sleeping on a pad in the living room.

With a few phone calls to members of her local church, Marg was able to find a place for the three men to stay. Three weeks later they did get permission to get on a plane back to Niyiyobateri. But the plane made an overnight stop in Tamatama. When it was ready to take off again the next morning, the pilot informed them that he didn't have room to put their extra baggage back on the plane, so they had to leave all the things they had purchased setting on the airstrip. Naturally, their possessions wouldn't still be there when they got back again, maybe months later.

People I talked to expressed their opinion that the pilots must be under orders not to do anything that would promote the Indians adopting a new way of life.

When the men got back to Niyiyobateri, Cotabimi, the young lady doctor, told them that one of the Indian couples had a newborn baby who really needed to be rushed to a hospital. But when the helicopter took off, the family did not show up to get on it. When Pepito went to check, the mother told him that she was very concerned about her baby, but she said she was even more afraid that if they got on that helicopter, they would never be able to get a ride back home and would be stuck in the terrible outside world forever. The men certainly understood and had to agree.

The three men were surprised to find that while they had been gone, the soldiers had been treating the people well, and some of the soldiers who came in were even bringing along school supplies for the Indian students.

Pepito immediately went back to working hard at trying to keep the church going without the help of the missionaries. Although there were some members who had dropped out, and told him he was foolish to continue what he called "living the ways of the Lord," many of the women and young people had become even more interested.

Later in the year, Pepito knew that Marg was still counting on his getting back to do the final reading and checking on the last books of the Bible that she and Samulito thought were ready, but he couldn't get a flight out. He offered to walk the five days walk to the Padamo river, if someone could pick him up by boat and take him all the way to Puerto Ayacucho. But his friends in the Dawsons' village radioed him and told him they couldn't pick him up because they could no longer buy any gasoline for their boats.

All the people of the Big Savannah were again having a very bad time, because this year, another famine was developing, just like the one we had twenty years earlier. The land had never been very productive, and once again, their gardens were not producing at all. Everyone was hungry and thin. They were worried that if the strangers brought in any kind of disease, they, in their weakened condition, would not have any resistance to it. Most of them again moved out into the jungle, where they could find a few wild fruits and wait for their scant crops to develop. Those who were left at home were working in their gardens even though they were weak with hunger.

At different times, three men were flown out to the hospitals with broken legs, arms, and one back, from falling out of trees. That man had fallen on a log, on his back. The authorities asked what had happened when men fell in the past, when there were no planes and no doctors. The people told them it had never happened before. Falling out of a tree was unheard of. But now they were weak and could not hang on, and they were so hungry they would try to climb out on the flimsy branches attempting to get the few wild fruits growing on the tips of the tree limbs.

67

THE ELECTION

Through the doctor's e-mail connection, and through officials of the Indian Commission, the Yanowamo people began to hear of an election coming up and learned that for the first time ever they themselves were going to be allowed to vote! This was exciting news. They were real citizens now! But they soon learned that only those with official government identity cards could actually vote. However, they'd all have a voice, because there were now several who had the cards, and the others could all talk to them and express their opinions!

"Is this to be a presidential election?" they asked.

"No, it is a special election to vote on a new constitution for the country." They were told that the president and a group of high officials had written a completely new constitution for Venezuela. This special election was to determine whether or not this constitution would replace the one which had, for many years, been controlling the way the government was run.

Since the government had become so anti-U.S.A., many Australians and New Zealanders had taken jobs in Venezuela, formerly held by North Americans. It was only a few days later that Kristi, a lady from New Zealand, arrived in Niyiyobateri, bringing a stack of Spanish language history books recommended by the government for school use.

As a group gathered around to look at them, Pepito asked Kristi if she knew anything about the new constitution they would be voting on.

She said, "No. But I do know there must be a lot of opposition to it. There have already been some small riots, and there may be more. All the New Zealanders, Canadians, and Australians have been given one of these notices." She handed him a copy:

The Embassy wishes to remind Canadians and Australians to maintain a high level of personal security awareness, avoid large gatherings and other public areas where disturbances could occur, and closely monitor news broadcasts.

Registered Canadians and Australians should report to their Warden any threats or trouble, and should avoid interfering in local disputes or appearing to take sides on any local issue which is caused by or is related to the Referendum.

In addition, they were warned to keep plenty of food and water on hand, and have all their travel documents ready so they could get out quickly if there was an uprising.

"Wow!" Pepito said. "They must be expecting some big, wild riots. I wonder what's in that constitution that people are objecting to. Do you think it's that bad?"

"Not according to the president," Kristi said. "He is emphatically telling everyone how much more easily and effectively the government could operate if the people would approve this new constitution."

The next day one of the doctors said he had acquired a copy of the new constitution on the internet. Everyone wanted to know how it was different. "I don't have a copy of the old one, to compare, but the only difference I notice is in the power of the president. I think with the present constitution, the president cannot make new laws on his own. He can suggest and recommend them, but then the congress must approve them before they become law. According to the new constitution, he can just sign any new law he wants, and put it into effect immediately.

"The president says it will make the government much more efficient. New needs can be met immediately instead of waiting through the long delays of legislative action."

Pepito said, "Well, I can see why people are drastically opposed to that new constitution. It pretty much makes the president a dictator."

"Yes," Samulito said, "And I know one of the laws he's been waiting a long time for congress to pass -- the one that says the missionaries he kicked out will not ever be able to come back. I sure don't want that law. I've got an identity card so I can vote. I'm sure going to vote against that new constitution!"

"A lot of people feel like you do," Cotabimi said. "That's why the riots. But I think many citizens are going to be afraid to vote against it. There may be records of how people vote, and the president has remarked that anyone who votes against the constitution should be considered a traitor!"

Pepito's wife suddenly broke into tears.

"Why are you crying?" Cotabimi asked.

Between sobs, Candace muttered, "Marg is never going to be able to come back."

NIYIYOBATERI NOW

2010-2011

68
MAINTAINING THEIR WAYS

This year, 2011, it has been 47 years since the Yanowamo Indians' first contact with what they call the "outside world." When they were discovered, the Yanowamo and Yanomami cultures were considered the most warlike cultures in the history of the world. Their culture was also more different from the European-American culture than that of any other American Indians. Yet, surprisingly, there have been less forced changes in their ways than in the lives of almost any other tribe. And the changes in their culture and life style have not been as large or as devastating as the changes forced upon most of the North and South American tribes during their first years of contact. This is because rather than being forced to change, like most others have, the changes that have come about have not been forced upon them,but have been made because the Indians themselves have chosen to accept ways they have seen in the lives of the outsiders who have entered their territory.

However, since 1995 when all the missionaries were forced to leave, the changes have been much more rapid because so many people have been sent in by the government officials to take the place of the missionaries. The number of soldiers, medical personnel, teachers, and others has at times seemed completely overwhelming to many of the Yanowamo people.

Many of us feared that when the army came in they would force the Indians to change their way of life, as has happened with many other tribes. But surprisingly, most of the army personnel have followed the orders that they were not to change the lives of the people in any way.

However, the Venezuelan army has influenced a lot more people throughout the whole area than the missionaries could, because they were told that they must now be in contact with every one of the more than fifty villages of the "Guaica" Indians (the Yanowamo and Yanomami), even those villages that had, up until this time, had no

346

contact at all with the outside world. And the army has the helicopters to make this possible. They were told to let all the people know that there is help for very serious medical problems, and all the people are being encouraged to learn the Spanish language so they can relate to the outsiders who do come in.

One government team began flying out to some of the villages to work on providing identity papers for the people because these are required for any relationship with government activities, including medical help. But the team bringing those papers to Niyiyobateri had helicopter problems and had to return home. They never did make another trip, so most Niyiyobateri residents continue to have trouble getting any needed assistance.

Efforts to continue their way of life as it had been before the army arrived were very important to many of the people of Niyiyobateri. They have tried their best to continue most of the family activities and the shared feasts that take place when hunters have good luck. And other shared interfamily recreational activities continue unchanged, in spite of observation and interference by the new residents.

The army people were told to encourage the people to keep the old ways, but many of the army personnel were reluctant to accept the idea that religious services were a real part of the culture. But the local leaders insisted that they were. Those meetings and discussions sponsored by the missionaries were one change that had been accepted long ago and was now considered a very important part of the lives of the majority of the people, especially the youth who had always considered this a part of their lives and their culture. because they had never known life without it.

Even with the new kinds of outside influence, and with the lack missionary assistance, Pedro, Samulito, and other leaders have done their best to keep keep these activities as a very important part of their lives.

Since Marg Jank was, for a while, allowed to return to Venezuela, though not to their area, the tribe's religious leaders have been very anxious to continue strong relationships with her, even though there is little or no likelihood that she can ever return to their village. They worked hard to do this through their e-mail, and by individual Indians occasionally being able to find some excuse to ride one of the army helicopters and get to Puerto Ayacucho, where they could visit her. But her activities have been very restricted.

All through the spring of 2008, Marg's stated purpose had to be leading a non-Indian Bible study group in Puerto Ayacucho. But most of her time was actually used trying to help the various people who came in from the outlying villages for medical help, or for getting their ID cards so they could work at odd jobs helping the government employees who have moved into their lives.

Most of those Indians who came to the city of Puerto Ayacucho had no knowledge of the Spanish language or of the money which was necessary to get a room. So much of the time, Marg's small 14th-floor apartment was crowded with people.

Pedro often found it difficult to encourage those who were ill to accept flights to the hospital in Puerto Ayacucho, which is the nearest city with a modern hospital. Some are still very hesitant. They have heard too much about the army helicopters that allow people to ride to the helicopter's destination, which is usually only part way to town and then having to wait a long time before another pilot will give them a ride the rest of the way.

Finally, during the last week of July 2008, after Marg and her Yanoamo helpers had spent fifty years translating the Bible into the Yanowamo language, the translation was completed, all 1090 pages of it. In August, a U.S. printing company signed an agreement to do the printing, and a campaign raised enough so they could proceed.

When they finally got word that Marg had received her first copies of these Bibles, all the Christian people of Niyiyobateri were very anxious to see them, but how could they get any copies?

One day, to everyone's surprise, two men arrived in Niyiyobateri in a private helicopter. For once, a pilot had actually made a direct flight all the way from Puerto Ayacucho in his own helicopter. This pilot said he could fly his own copter directly to his destination without all the stops that delayed the government helicopters. The passenger he brought planned to stay and visit the village for a week. The pilot would leave this passenger in Niyiyobateri when he went back to his home in Puerto Ayacucho, then he would return a week later to pick him up.

When asked, he gladly agreed to take someone else along, so that person would have a ride both ways.

348

This was exciting news! Some of the teachers and a couple of the Health Promoters talked with Pedro. They said they needed things from the city, and none of them could take the week off to go there. They were sure Pedro was the only Indian who'd had enough experience with the outside world to go to Puerto Ayacucho and do their shopping for them. Pedro had wanted to go, anyway. He needed to see a real eye doctor about problems with his eyes, and he wanted to see Marg. He also hoped to get some of the new Bibles they were hearing about.

During the week that he was in Puerto Ayacucho, the Health Promoters contacted him every day by radio, asking if he had been able to buy all the things they had given him the money for. And then teachers and others from the nearby villages who were on their cooperative e-mail system heard about what he was doing and e-mailed him at Marg's home asking if he could get some things for them, too. Everyone wanted to take advantage of the one time when there was a dependable friend in the city who would be on a direct flight all the way home without delays or weight restrictions, so they could count on their things actually getting to them.

At the end of the week, when Pedro was ready for the flight home, Marg gave him a stack of the new Bibles and also sent along a big box of books for the school children.

When Marg dropped Pedro off at the airport, the pilot laughed about the big stack of things Pedro was taking home, but gladly helped him load them all into the helicopter. Three other friends, who had gone to town earlier and had been unable to get a flight home, were there, and begging for a ride home. So the pilot gave them permission to go along.

Since the pilot was going back to Niyiyobateri to pick up the friend he had taken there, he did not expect to land anywhere on the way, but soon after they took off, he received a government radio message telling him that he could not fly beyond Tamatama without landing there and getting his flight plan officially approved.

When they landed, he was ordered to return to Puerto Ayacucho immediately and report to the authorities before he could make another flight to Niyiyobateri, or anywhere else!

As they unloaded all of Pedro's stack of supplies, the pilot promised that he would be back, probably in a day or two, to take him the rest of the way home, but he couldn't know for sure how soon that would be.

After a few days of waiting, Pedro and one of his friends decided to try to get home the hard way. They left most of the supplies he had gotten for people with the two other men, who would wait for the helicopter, then Pedro and his friend took as many of the supplies as they could cram into their backpacks, and made the two day trip to the Dawsons on the Padamo river by boat. They got another boat ride up the river to where they could begin a long four days' walk over the mountains and finally get home. The last two days were in a pouring rain.

In spite of being wrapped in plastic everything they brought home with them was soaked, including the eight Bibles.

Samuelito was really glad to see Pedro back and welcomed him with open arms. He was especially glad to finally see the new but damp Bibles. He and two others had spent most of their time for the last eleven years helping Marg with the translation. Now, at last, he could see the complete printed Bible, and have a copy of his own!

Everyone enjoyed sharing those new Bibles, but they had no way of finding the passages and stories they wanted to study. Pedro and Samulito tried developing a list of topics and related page numbers but found after they got a short list made, that it really was useless because all those page numbers mystified everyone. These two men had learned the numbers and their use from Marg, but in their own language, there still were only numbers one to four. With proper repetition they could actually get to sixteen. Anything beyond that had always just been "plenty too much." The page numbers these two put on their lists were meaningless to everyone else.

A month later, the other two friends who had been on the flight with Pedro, and the stack of supplies they had started home with, were still waiting in Tamatama.

69

CONFLICTS AND HOPES

The Indian people were often told that life in town was safer than in the jungles, but they soon learned the truth. Cacomi and his wife, Nekala, were planning to go to Puerto Ayacucho and help Marg, but the helicopter that would give them a ride was only going as far as Tamatama. Nekala decided that two days on a boat, going down the river below there, plus a long bus ride, was too much for her in her pregnant state, so Cacomi went alone. After he got off the bus, he took a taxi to Marg's home, but instead of taking him where he was going, the taxi driver took him far out of town, then stuck a knife in his ribs and robbed him of his baggage and all his money. Cacomi then had a four-hour walk back to town.

Enrique was also on his first trip to town. He was just outside a bank when it was held up and he was swept along with a group of people screaming and running for cover.

A woman and two men from Niyiyobateri were in a taxi near the edge of town when they passed a group who appeared to be arguing, but as they passed the whole group turned and tried to attack the taxi. The driver managed to get the windows up and the doors locked and maneuvered his way through all the people who were banging on the car and yelling for him to stop.

The next day, those three were going down the street when they heard a gunshot, then passed a spot where a crowd was gathering, along with the police and an ambulance. They didn't see the man who had been shot, but they saw his blood on the street.

They were glad to get into the seclusion of Marg's back room and were anxious to get on their way back to their own "civilized" territory.

Marg thought these frightening experiences would probably discourage others from coming to town, but hearing about them did not deter anyone else from flying in to help her when they had a chance.

Marg herself was very busy helping people from all the different Yanowamo settlements, who came to the city and knew nothing of city life, holding Bible discussion groups with them, and helping them adjust to the strange life of the city. She used her back room to accommodate a variety of friends who had no other place to stay when they were in town.

In celebration of the fact that the first bibles had finally arrived, the leaders of several of the Yanowamo villages decided that they should meet in Puerto Ayacucho and discuss ways that they, who were once all enemies, ready to kill anyone coming from any of the other villages, could now peaceably work together. They agreed on a time when they would meet in Puerto Ayacucho.

Four of those leaders from the Parima Mountain area were coming down the Orinoco River to join in that celebration when they came to the Rapids-of-Death above Puerto Ayacucho. They knew of no way to get land transportation to take them those last forty miles past the rapids. They hadn't talked to anyone who had been in those rapids and falls, probably because practically no one had tried it. They decided that it didn't look too bad and they should try going on down in their boat.

That boat was soon getting tossed to and fro, and they had to cling to the sides to keep from being thrown out. When the boat went over the many small falls, they were all crying and screaming in fear, sure it would turn over, but fortunately, it didn't. They were certain it was only God's will that saved them.

When, much later, Samulito told me about this experience, I clearly recalled and told him about the day, 47 years earlier, when the people in Puerto Ayacucho had told me that because of the Rapids-of-Death hardly anyone had tried to go up the river above there, but then Ramoncito Lujan, the Indian Commissioner, had taken me up the forty-mile trail past the Rapids-of- Death, and then took me up the river in his motorized canoe for my first contact with the Yanomami Indians. I told Samulio that ever since that day, I've been very thankful that the commissioner happened to be in Puerto Ayacucho at the same time as I was, or I probably would never have made contact with either the Yanowamo or Yanomami.

When I talked of that, Samulito was certain that, too, was God's will.

During the days that followed, Marg was kept extremely busy with the many responsibilities she had taken on, but she still was very disappointed by the fact that she couldn't be out in the wilderness areas helping with the teaching. That was the purpose for which she had come to South America fifty years ago.

Then one day Samulito came in and talked to her about her life. What he said to her was so important that she wrote it all out and sent the report by e-mail, to all her constituents, and I quote:

"Mother," he said, "I see what God is doing with you, and it is very good. We didn't want to let you leave, but it's like what I read in Exodus. Pharaoh said he wouldn't let the Israelites go; but that didn't stop God from leading them out of Egypt. Nobody can stop what God wants to do. I didn't know what you would do when you had to leave the jungle, but now I see all the Bible classes, and all the visiting with the Indians on the street and at the hospital, and I think: this is God's handiwork! And all the teaching that is going on! And all the people from other villages that I never thought would be interested at all! Now I hear what they say, and I see them asking you for the parts of the Bible you have printed out. It's like God did with Joseph, in Genesis. He told him to go where he didn't want to go, and it seemed like everything was going wrong. But it turned out good. God brought you here to help all the ones who were going to be coming here. This is very good."

70
AN INDEFINITE FUTURE

Although Venezuela has passed laws that prohibit missionaries from ever again visiting the Indians who live in the rain forest areas, the word finally came out that visitors who are in no way connected with the missions can get permission to visit the villages, that is, if they can show a reason for going there and are willing to put up with the completely unpredictable problems of arranging the necessary transportation.

I had been planning, ever since my first contact with the Yanowamo, 47 years ago, to write a book describing their culture and way of life. With that in mind, I had kept all the notes and recordings I had made on each of my visits with them. But I always felt pressured to get other writing done. This year, being ninety-two years of age, and not knowing what the possibilities would be for visiting them in the future, I felt this was the time I should finish that book.

I was ready to write Marg Jank and tell her I would stop in Puerto Ayacucho to visit her on my way to Niyiyobateri. Then I received an e-mail from her, saying that because of all the government's pressures and threats she had moved out of Venezuela and was now east of Niyiyobateri, in a Yanowamo village just across the border in Brazil. I wondered if that could be the village that Hekura had taken me to 47 years ago.

Then I got another e-mail saying that Marg's health would not permit her to continue her work, and she was leaving for Florida. Her son, Davy, and his wife, Marie, were going with her.

As I continued inquiring about the possibilities I finally learned that there was a pilot who would be willing to take me from Puerto Ayacucho to Niyiyobateri if I signed a statement that I was not doing missionary work and if, when I wrote my book, I would not include the name or other information about this pilot, or be definite about what parts of my book were fiction and what was fact.

When you do get on a flight to Niyiyobateri, and are coming in for a landing, it is a surprise to see that the airstrip, which used to have only two houses on one side and the shavano on the other, has now become Main Street.

Although there is still a shavano of sorts, there are buildings all along the air strip. In addition to the offices and residences of the Army Air Force and of two Health Promoters, there is a shop that sells clothes and conveniences, and a school in which there are full-time paid teachers instead of the shifting group of part-time volunteers. And there are homes of some Indians who have decided they like the comfort and convenience of the outsiders type of home.

Most of the people you meet on that street are wearing clothes. Even the men wear pants of some kind. But when they are off in the rain forest hunting tapirs and bushmaster snakes, wearing clothing would still be considered foolish.

As my plane landed I was surprised to see a group of men come running out, shouting, jumping in the air, and laughing, just as they had done on my first arrival there many years ago. But when I saw Pepito, Rosito, and Lujan in the lead, I knew these friends were anxious to make me feel welcome, and still a part of the tribe.

Dr. Cotabimi, the lady who had taken over Marg's home, was right there with them, pushing in to get to talk the the pilot. She begged him to take two people back to Puerto Ayacucho with him. One was a three-year-old girl who had to get to a hospital for an operation to save her life. The other was Davidio, the girl's father, who must go with her.

The pilot finally agreed, and a few minutes later the pilot, Davidio, and the little girl were in the air.

Pepito and Rosito really gave me an open arms welcome. But the one who really made me feel at home, and wanted to devote all his time to helping me was Lujan. He had been just an eight year old boy when I had helped to baptize him.

Pepito offered me a space to live in his kitchen, but Lujan said he had an extra hammock that he could hang in his home in the shavano. I preferred sleeping there because it would put me in contact with more of my old friends and made me feel more like I was again a Yanowamo.

Lujan was glad to discuss with me some of the information I had received from Marg the last two years and related some details so I felt more ready to write about it.

He told me that throughout the year of 2009, Pepito and several of his friends had been making visits to different villages whose only previous contact with outsiders had been one army team who surprised and alarmed them when they came in a helicopter. Pepito's group was trying to calm down the angry voices and discourage potential raids. But the reactions they got varied greatly. He said they do feel that with their promotion of friendly contacts, there is hope for continuing peace.

71

CAN WE SAY HIS NAME?

As I talked with some of the Yanowamo men about their present day lives, and the changes that had taken place, Marg Jank and her activities were frequently a part of the discussion, in spite of the fact that she had moved to Brazil. then back to the U.S. and had been told she could never again visit their village. She and the natives of Niyiyobateri were still frequently in contact by e-mail, and they counted on her to answer questions they had. They kept telling me the religious beliefs and other training they had received from the Janks were still having a great deal of effect on their lives. But I never, once, heard them mention the name of Marg's husband, Wally.

Marg had, of course, e-mailed me long ago to inform me of Wally's death, but she had told me nothing further, except that he died of a heart attack. I kept wondering about the Yanowamo people's reaction to his death, and their feelings about his absence.

Like me, they had always been amazed at Wally's bravery and his willingness to go into enemy territory where even the brave Yanowamo men would not dare to go go, except the one or two of them who had finally agreed to go with Wally and guide him on the trails. He had always told them he had no fear because God was always with him, and God would protect him. I wondered if, now that he had died, they might now doubt the validity of his teaching?

There were a lot of questions that I wanted to ask them, but how could I ask? Long ago, when we had first arrived here, we quickly learned that no one could ever speak the name of any adult because if an enemy heard a person's name, they could use it in their witchcraft and kill that person. But Wally had soon convinced them that the rule applied only to Yanowamo names, but his name, and the names he gave them were "Naba" names, not "real" names so the enemies could not use them for witchcraft, so they could be spoken freely.

However, another similar rule still applied. After the day of a person's death and the bone drinking ceremony no one could ever speak of that person, or refer to him in any way. It must be as if he had never lived.

This had seemed to us like a strange idea but we soon learned that it was rigidly enforced, and was never to be doubted or discussed.

Now, I realized that if I used Wally's name to ask about him, they would lose their respect for me, and it might also diminish their emphasis upon their feeling that I was considered one of them, a Yanowamo, not a foreigner, a Naba.

After thinking over other ways of asking, I finally said to Eladio, "Marg Jank is a great help to you and your people, and she can still teach you, and help you in many ways. Is it possible that if she had a male helper, more of your men would be interested in the things she teaches, and in learning more about the love of God?"

Eladio looked shocked for a minute, but then he said, "I'll have to think abut that!"

Late that evening Eladio walked into the house and after a few greetings he began telling me. "We have often spoken of the fact that we have a living God, who will always be a living God, and Marg need not hesitate to talk about him. It is important that we talk about and teach about him, and about his living son Jesus. It is only because of their living strength that we want to talk about them. I have been thinking today about those who have taught about them, who tell us that, when they are no longer here with us they will have gone to join God in his heaven, and we too, if we are loyal to God, will eventually go there and join them. Perhaps those who are actually living forever, with Jesus, can actually be remembered. Could we actually remember them, and talk about them?"

We both sat quietly, thinking, for several minutes before Eladio looked up at me and spoke again. "Once, not too long ago, three of us went to visit a village whose members had always been the deadly enemies of our parents. We, ourselves, had never dared to go into their territory, except once when we went there on a raid. We were certain one of our members had been killed by their witchcraft, and others could be.

"When we walked right into that enemy shavano the residents were shocked, so shocked that they actually listened as our leader told them that we no longer believed that we should be killing anyone, but that all people could and should be friends.

"After several days of listening to our leader, and seeing our confidence in him, they had become so interested in our teaching that they said that if we could assure them that they really could come to our village safely, several of them wanted to come to Niyiyobateri and learn more of our teaching. But they said we must come back here to our home first, so that we could assure everyone in both villages that they were coming as friends.

"The next night, on our way home, the three of us sat around the campfire talking, and our leader talked about the success of our journey. He assured the two of us that after this success my friend and I should now be confident enough to go to other villages farther north, and instruct them, and tell them of the power of the Loving God without thinking that we had to wait for him to go with us. We assured him that perhaps we would soon be ready to do that."

Eladio continued, "It was the next day that he was leading the way up a very steep mountain trail. Suddenly he turned with a pained look on his face and his arm clutched across his chest. He fell and tumbled over a couple times down the mountain side. We rushed to his side but he was not breathing, and I could detect no heartbeat. He had fallen, dead in his tracks.

"As we later discussed it, we realized that he was much older than either of us, or most of our friends, and we remembered that he had several times told us that he felt the Lord was waiting to welcome him to eternal life. He had assured us that, if we believed, God would welcome us too.

"We wonder if perhaps the Lord had been waiting for this one more success before he called our leader to his side. And perhaps, it was a sign of God's love that this could happen simply and quickly, and God chose this time and this way so our leader would not have to go through the long pain and misery that many others have to endure.

"We have since wondered, if he has reached eternal life, and is still living in Jesus home place, as he said he would be, perhaps it would actually be all right to speak his, and other believer's names, and talk of their lives, as I have done tonight."

Eladio didn't wait for my answer. He just got up and walked out without ever actually naming his friend.

72
STILL SHARING

I told Lujan that I would really like to go over to Hulacobateri while I was here. It would be great to visit any of my friends there who were still living, and to have one more chance to see a village that I hoped had been changed very little by the army or other outsiders.

When Lujan told his wife where we were going, she said, "Yesterday, Cotabimi was showing three of us women how she baked banana bread. When we got through, she gave some of it to each of us. That's a hard walk you will be making through those swamps so you will both be getting hungry. You better take two of these loaves of banana bread along so you don't have to take time out on the way to hunt berries to eat."

I said I appreciated it because although the Hulaco people had always been very willing to share. If a family we were visiting saw that we had nothing to eat they would insist on feeding us. With this year's drouth conditions, that might mean they themselves would go without food that evening. I gladly put those two small loaves in my little backpack.

After wading through swamps for two hours, balancing on a little log to get across the creek, and a lot more walking I was very glad to see the shavano ahead.

I lifted the poles out of the gate way to "open the gate" and although we weren't carrying any weapons, I led the way to the center and did the visitors pose so I could see if they would still do the welcome chant.

Even after all these years, several people recognized me and the chant was enthusiastic. In the Yanowamo way, my friends were laughing their heads off as they came out to greet me.

We wandered around the village, moving from one lean-to home to the next, greeting the adults I had met before, hugging their children, and looking at their many monkeys, parrots, and other pets. A lot of the people started following us. I wondered why, until someone mentioned that when I used to go there we had always wanted to talk to the group about the love of God, before we left.

I knew they were talking about the time when I had come there with Wally, but I couldn't say that because they were still following the policy of never mentioning a dead man's name. I told them I wasn't prepared to preach to them but a lot of them stayed with us anyway. When we were almost back to the entrance, a family asked us to come in and sit down. We stepped in under their lean-to roof, and saw the small bird they were roasting on the fire. It surely wasn't enough to even feed the four in their family, let alone Lujan, and me, and some of those who followed us. They brought out their five bananas and gave Lujan and me each one.

I was glad I had those two small loaves of banana bread in my pack. I got them out and gave them to the mother. Her eyes lit up as she got out her little sea shell knife and started to cut them into small squares.

As she did that, and we waited patiently four or five minutes for the little bird to finish roasting, the crowd that had been gathering, and had followed us, started drifting away. I was glad they were leaving because I wouldn't like to eat in front of people without sharing, and there wasn't enough bread to even give one bite to every person that had gathered.

But then everyone started coming back! I was shocked till one man set down a big gourd bowl full of berries. A woman swung her basket to the ground and brought out two baked fish. The small canoe that separated that home from the one on the left was soon filled with a variety of fruit and other foods.

The crowd was obviously ready to eat, but no one started eating. They all stood looking at me.

Lujan leaned over toward me and whispered. "They think that you won't want them to start eating till after you pray."

I was surprised that their memory of my visits with Wally and of his ways, was still so strong, but I bowed my head and started praying loudly, thanking God for such generous friends, for their willingness to help each other, and asking Him to help them retain their generosity, their concern for each other, their cheerfulness, and their humor, even as they became more and more influenced by other people.

After an hour of feasting, visiting, and laughing together, Lujan and I started home.

The next morning Enrique stepped into our lean-to and told me, "We usually have our church service in the school building but we think that today, with you here, there might be too many coming to fit into the classroom, and we want to have our service out on the hillside, like we often did when you were here before." I was glad to hear that.

When we got there I was surprised at how many people had gathered out on the hillside beside the airstrip. And men and women sat together!

I knew that in Niyiyobateri their Sunday church services have always been quite informal. Pedro, or one of the others who act as preachers, starts the discussion by reading a passage from the Bible, then talking a little about its application to their own lives. Following this there is usually a lot of discussion of other member's ideas.

This morning four or five of them started singing their translation of "I've Got a Home in Glory Land." Just like they had always done, each person who had come waited till he felt secure, then

began singing from the beginning of the song. When everyone had finished, Enrique brought out one of the big new bibles and asked Pedro to start reading the next chapter after what he had read last week. Pedro stepped out and read confidently.

I tried to translate back into English, for myself, as he read. "Jesus and his companions were on a boat to a lonely place but people had seen them going there and ran from all the villages and got there ahead of them. As he landed he saw a huge group, and he had compassion for them, and he began to teach them many things. When the time grew late his companions came to him and said, 'This is a lonely place and it is late. Send them away so they can go to the villages and buy something to eat.' But Jesus answered them, 'You give them something to eat.' And they said to him, 'Shall we go to the villages and try to buy enough food?' And he said, how many loafs have you?' 'Five, and two fish.' Then he told the people all to sit down on the grass in groups, and they sat down in several groups with many people in each group. And taking the five loafs and two fish he looked up to heaven, and blessed and broke the loafs, and gave them to his companions to divide between the people, and he divided the two fish among them all. And they all ate and were satisfied, and they picked up twelve baskets of broken pieces."

As soon as he stopped reading several of the people said, "How could he do that? How could he feed more people than our whole village with only five loafs and two fish? You can't do that!"

Before Enrique could try to explain his idea of it, Lujan spoke up. "Oh yes, you can. I saw it yesterday. We had two loafs and one little bird, and after Abufidoblau prayed, our host started to cut them up, and the whole village of Hulacobateri all filled their tummies and had lots of food left over."

I agreed. I said, "I've always wondered about that passage, myself. Now I understand. Maybe generosity was actually as important to the Hebrews as it is to the Yanowamo!"

73

TODAY

It was early in the morning of my last full day in Niyiyobateri, when Lujan told me that a group of my friends were going to their gardens to gather food, just as they had always done, and they thought I might like to go along. I told him I certainly would enjoy that. It would bring back so many good memories of the past, and help me take home more good memories of my life as a Yanowamo.

Counting me and Lujan there were six men and four women who headed for the gardens. It was a beautiful day, and I so enjoyed getting out on the trail through the forest just like we had done so many times long ago. Several times we stopped to pick berries. We pulled a sheet of caterpillars off the side of a tree, and the men shot one pigeon along the way. We even stopped to break open a termite nest and gather some termites which they packed into a folded banana leaf. It was so good to see the relaxed atmosphere, and hear the frequent laughter as we went down the trail, all of which made me feel at home again, and convinced me that life in the rain forest hadn't really lost the qualities I valued so much.

When we got to the garden they gathered the bananas they came after, and the women gathered a little fire wood, so they could build a fire and cook the bird, the termites,and the caterpillars for lunch.

Then Lujan's wife turned to me and asked, "Did you bring your matches?"

"No! I had no idea I might need them today. Don't some of you have some?"

She laughed, and said, "Good. Because you're here, we wanted to do things the old way today, so we brought our traditional fire building tools instead. She reached into her basket and brought out her fire starting tools. She handed them to me and said, "Maybe you'd like to start it."

I realized that in all my times with these people I had never actually started a fire with just the two pieces of wood, but I put some chips and grass on the end of the larger piece, put the end of the longer stalk in the hole in the larger piece, then putting a hand against each side of the long one, and moving my hands in opposite directions, I began to spin it around and around rapidly. When my arms were tired, and my hands felt like they would blister, I saw the red spark, then my tinder broke into flame and I piled more kindling on it.

Lujan was watching me. When the fire burst out he clapped his hands and yelled, "You did it!" then he turned to the other men and said, "I told you he's a sure enough Yanowamo! You all know that only the Yanowamo, and only the men can do that. Never the outsiders, and never the women!"

The men all agreed, and the two who I had not known well before seemed even more interested in getting better acquainted, and sharing their ideas with me.

As in the old times, we talked and laughed as we cooked and ate our traditional snack. Then, throughout the afternoon we wandered on through the forest, stopping frequently to dig roots or pick berries, or just to talk or answer each others questions.

Through the discussions that afternoon, along with all the others I had been having all week, I became convinced that most of the people feel that there have been few big changes in their daily lives. Some, however, admit that there has been some loss of the great sense of humor that had enabled nearly everyone to laugh off many of their problems. I thought there might be two reasons for that. The habit of laughing at problems instead of weeping or complaining had been promoted when all of them were living in the shavano and their neighbors were always within sight and hearing. A laughing, cheerful child got a lot of attention from the neighboring families because they all loved children. But when the child tried to get attention by crying, he had been ignored. The adults had walked away. So children had learned to laugh at trouble, and the habit of seeing humor in nearly any problem was promoted throughout their lives.

But now that many families are living in houses, some children are not developing that tremendous sense of humor that made them laugh more than any other people in the world. Also some of the adults had heard remarks from outsiders who thought laughing at injuries or serious problems was foolish. Some of the elders see that change and regret it.

The daily lives of those who work all day for army personnel or medical helpers are of course quite different from what they used to be, even outside their working hours. But even those workers still try to continue their interfamily picnics and get-togethers, and they still enjoy their opportunities to share with their friends when the hunting is good.

The Christian leaders are still trying to live by the Christian ways taught by the missionaries. And even without the missionaries their faith in God is giving them a more secure feeling and a more peaceful way of life.

But those leaders have been surprised that others even here in their own village have started talking as if they might resort to the old ways of making return raids if other villages make trouble. And the men talk of going back to their former ways of getting new wives by capturing them from other villages.

But the leaders say that talk of renewing these warlike ideas is much more popular in some of the other villages. The leaders here in Niyiyobateri realize that everyone can enjoy the natural environment more, and feel more free to work and play as they please because they can now get out and move about more freely since there is little possibility of their being attacked and killed by raiders.

They assured me that their strong cultural emphasis on generosity, sharing, and helping each other in many ways will never be lost.

As we entered the village several men walked over to meet us and asked if I had enjoyed my final day in Niyiyobateri. I started telling them how happy I was that they had hung on to so many of the cultural traits I admired. Then we saw Enrique coming out of the school building and hurrying toward us. He quickly informed us that they had just received two e-mails. A good one had come from Marg's son Davy, saying that he and his wife were leaving Florida and heading back to their home in the little Maco village east of us in Brazil. They would welcome any and all who could come there to visit them. Davy had also said that his mother, Marg, had recovered from her cancer to the extent that she was hoping to be able to follow them soon. That made us very happy because we had all been worrying, wondering if she was still alive.

The second e-mail said that even though all the New Tribes Missionaries had been kicked out of Venezuela, and would never be allowed to return, some Venezuelan residents had been given permission to become missionaries and go into the back country and work with the Indian people. Two of them had already gone to one of the tribes south of us and started learning the language, so they could start teaching them.

Lujan looked happily at him and said, maybe someday we will have missionaries with us again, even though Marg can't be one of them!

Then Enrique said, "But the other e-mail is not so good. It is very bad news from the hospital in Puerto Ayacucho. It was sent to inform us that Davidio, the man who had taken his three-year-old daughter there for an operation had suddenly become very ill. The doctor thought it must be from some disease he had caught in the hospital. Although he had only been ill for one day, he was already in such bad condition that the doctors thought there was only about one chance in ten that he would survive."

I said, "I never heard of a disease progressing that fast."

"It can't," the hekura (medicine man) standing beside me said. "We have been taught that the Naba diseases come from bacteria, tiny particles that have to grow inside your body before they effect you. They couldn't possibly grow in one day. Even Malaria germs take several days."

"Yes," another man said. "This has to be witchcraft. Some one has done witchcraft against him."

"But who could it be? We thought all our enemies had become friends!"

It was just after breakfast the next morning when my pilot arrived. I was walking toward the plane when Enrique caught up with me. "I thought you should know that a group of the men have been up all night talking about Davidio and his illness. They are all convinced that it has to be witchcraft and they are trying to figure out who would have done it. They have decided that it must be the village of Oponatheli. Five of them insist that if they get word that Davidio has died they will immediately go on a raid and attack Oponatheli. I tried to talk them out of it but they think that we should live by the old rules and that when I object I am acting like a coward."

All the way home I kept thinking of the cultural characteristics of my Yanowamo friends that I have prized and will miss so much: their desire to share and to and help each other, their willingness to forgive those within their own village who cause them trouble, their ability to laugh at many of the problems that would leave most of us angry or upset. l will greatly value those wonderful memories. I am so glad that the people of Niyiyobateri have been able to hang on to and live by many of those wonderful cultural habits. But I am sorry that this means that they may also abide by those with which we outsiders would never agree!

THE AUTHOR, HAP GILLILAND

While growing up on a ranch in Colorado, Hap Gilliland developed a great interest in nature and wildlife, and always took every opportunity to hike and backpack, and study the natural world. And because the Native American Indians lived closely with nature, and were a good source of information, he had a strong interest in their culture and way of life. Throughout high school and college he majored in biology and he enjoyed writing about the things he saw and learned.

During his ten years as a public school teacher, he used his summer vacations for hiking, mountain climbing, and advancing his education. After he completed his Doctorate and became a university Professor of Education, he conducted many teacher training workshops on Indian reservations throughout the West and was frequently invited to speak at national education conferences on adapting instruction to the cultures of the students. Leaders from other countries who heard him thought their teachers needed to hear his ideas and asked him to speak at their national conferences. Thus he became a world traveler.

When he travels on his own he prefers to arrange to stay in a family home and learn the culture by living it. He has done this in from two to eight different locations on each of the six continents and on some of the Pacific islands. He prefers going to the more remote areas where few tourists go; places such as Mongolia, Nepal, Northern Siberia, South Africa, the Andes, and the South American rain forest.

19 of the books he has written are children's books, mostly interpreting the true way of life of the Native American people. Half of his 22 adult books are college text books for use in training teachers. The rest are nature books, or are about his adventures and the cultures and way of life of the people with whom he has lived.